Tapping Potential

Tapping Potential

English and Language Arts
for the Black Learner

Edited by

Charlotte K. Brooks
with

Jerrie Cobb Scott

Miriam Chaplin

Delores Lipscomb

William W. Cook

Vivian Davis

Black Caucus of the National Council of Teachers of English
National Council of Teachers of English
1111 Kenyon Road, Urbana, Illinois 61801

To All Black Learners and to Their Teachers

Grateful acknowledgment is made for permission to reprint the following material. "Black English Dialect and the Classroom Teacher." Reprinted by permission of the International Reading Association. "'What Go Round Come Round': *King* in Perspective." From *Harvard Educational Review*, 1981:1, pp. 40–56. Copyright © 1981 by the President and Fellows of Harvard College. Reprinted by permission. "Yet Do I Marvel." From *On These I Stand: An Anthology of the Best Poems of Countee Cullen.* Copyright © 1925 by Harper & Row, Publishers, Inc. Renewed 1953 by Ida M. Cullen. Reprinted by permission of the publishers.

Book Design: Tom Kovacs for TGK Design

NCTE Stock Number 50101

© 1985 by the National Council of Teachers of English. All rights reserved. Printed in the United States of America. This material was previously published in another format by Brooks Associates of Washington, D.C.

Library of Congress Cataloging in Publication Data
Main entry under title:

Tapping potential.

Includes bibliographies.
    I. Afro-Americans—Education—Language arts—
Addresses, essays, lectures.   2. Afro-American children—
Language—Addresses, essays, lectures.   3. Black English—
Addresses, essays, lectures.   I. Brooks, Charlotte.
LC2778.L34T36   1985   428'.00896073   85-3905
ISBN 0-8141-5010-1

Contents

Acknowledgments

I thank the membership of the Black Caucus of the National Council of Teachers of English for its cooperation and continuing encouragement in the development and realization of this publication.

Special thanks are due from all of us—authors and editors alike—to Sandra Gibbs, Director of Minority Group Affairs and Special Projects of the National Council of Teachers of English. Dr. Gibbs efficiently and with grace and cheerfulness handled the essential communication needed for a publication whose authors and editors are scattered all over the continental United States and in the Virgin Islands. She assisted in editing, helped to plan the one or two yearly meetings the editors were able to manage at national conventions, and in countless other ways made our work possible.

The four editors assumed at a first request the difficult task of reading, editing and making suggestions for revision of the essays within their parts of the work. They are: Jerrie Cobb Scott, Language; Miriam Chaplin, Reading; Delores Lipscomb, Writing; and William W. Cook, Literature. These editors worked with the authors, with each other and with me in the finest professional way. I thank them.

Vivian Davis, our reader, read carefully and edited the entire manuscript with a critical and discerning eye. Her suggestions have been invaluable.

Charlotte K. Brooks

Foreword

Charlotte K. Brooks
Brooks Associates, Washington, D.C.

In recent years, newspapers have paid quite a lot of attention to black learners. In an October, 1982 issue of the *Washington Post*, under the headline, "Black SAT Scores 110 Points under Whites," a staff writer reported on the College Entrance Examination Board's *Profiles, College Bound Seniors, 1981*. In much smaller print a subhead stated, "Family Affluence a Factor." Under these words—which were all some people ever read—the writer said that blacks scored below whites, American Indians, Mexican-Americans, and Puerto Ricans. Even farther into the article, the writer reported analysts' findings that the wide disparities were caused by differences in family income, home environments, educational opportunities, and parental education. In the last paragraph the writer reported that SAT scores rose slightly this year, reversing an eighteen-year decline.

A second *Washington Post* article, later in the same month, bore this headline, "Minority Students' Gains Largely Responsible for SAT Score Rise." The same staff writer responsible for the earlier article now wrote that black scores rose by an average of nine points on the verbal part of the 1982 Scholastic Aptitude Test (SAT) while whites gained only four points. He quoted a director of evaluation at a midwestern university who said that the new figures might reflect the impact of financial aid programs over the last fifteen years. She felt that the trend is clearly upward for black learners.

Similar gratifying results appear in the most recent reports on reading and writing prepared by the National Assessment of Educational Programs (NAEP). Although black learners in the age categories assessed, nine-, thirteen-, and seventeen-year-olds, still received low reading and writing scores, they have made significant improvement —far more progress than others in many of the reading and writing tasks. Educators who have analyzed these figures have attributed the improvement to programs set in place in the 1960s and 1970s to assure better teaching and learning conditions for these students.

1

Both SAT and NAEP data substantiate what interested educators, historians, sociologists, psychologists, linguists, and others have said for many years about the education of blacks. Properly taught by persons who understand their strengths, varying backgrounds, and potential for learning and who take into account historical, socio-economic, psychological, and linguistic barriers, blacks not only can, but do learn like any other group.

In 1983 the many organization and task force reports on the current status of education pointed out again that a learning gap continues to exist—although it has lessened—between black and white learners. These reports make it clear, however, that minority learners can succeed with the help of well-prepared teachers, pro-grams tailored to their special needs, the right materials, and sup-portive families and communities.

Black learners are in trouble now since the programs carefully crafted over a twenty-year period are under attack. Just as the National Assessment of Educational Progress has shown consider-able gains in the reading and writing skills of black learners—gains attributable, at least in part to those very programs now being dismantled—the successful programs are being cut. Title I of the Elementary and Secondary Education Act, the Basic Skills Program, and even the Department of Education itself, are fighting for survival.

Purposes of This Book

One of the compelling reasons for the publication of this book is the need for information, based upon both research and experience, to help teachers of blacks at all levels to use approaches and methods known to be appropriate for blacks. Many of the same approaches and methods can be used for other minorities and for whites as well.

In this country's earliest years, most blacks were slaves and were forbidden by law to learn. Owned by ambivalent persons who sought for themselves liberty and knowledge, yet consistently denied them to others, only the more persistent blacks learned to read and write. Despite this, slaves demonstrated their potential for learning not only language and a new culture, but farming, trades, and any occu-pation they entered. Some, like Harriet Tubman, Nat Turner, Den-mark Vesey, and Gabriel Prosser, flouted and subverted slave laws and black codes. Others, among them Sojourner Truth and Frederick Douglass, became powerful users of the language, oral and written—just as Martin Luther King, Jr. did years later. Still others—Phyllis Wheatley, Jupiter Hammon, William Wells Brown, and David Walker, among them—easily and capably learned and used the written word, often poetically, in the style of their masters. Untold hundreds, unlettered, revealed in slave narratives their barely tapped potential for touching the heart with their tales of enslavement.

One of my English professors at Howard (Brawley 1921/1970) refers to the conflict during the early years of this century between Booker T. Washington, founder of Tuskegee Institute and a proponent of trade and business education for blacks, and W. E. Burghardt Du Bois of New England, a graduate of Fisk and Harvard, who believed in a thorough classical education, with attention paid to economics and science. In the dark days after Emancipation and Reconstruction, when the South was clamping the lid on black progress, through the use of repressive laws and the Ku Klux Klan, education for most blacks was either nonexistent or of poor quality.

In *Mis-Education of the American Negro* (Woodson 1933/1969) the historian writes: "the highly educated Negro often becomes sour. He becomes too pessimistic to be a constructive force and usually develops into a chronic fault-finder or a complainant at the bar of public opinion."

Another reason for this publication is the need to avoid the pessimism Dr. Woodson deplored. The contributors demonstrate that highly educated blacks are not pessimistic about their ability to make a difference. They refuse the role of fault-finders and complainants and have chosen to be a constructive force. They have spent more than two years gathering information, writing, and editing to provide the beginning of an effort to tap the potential of black learners. This work exhibits the concern of these black professionals in education—teachers, professors, researchers, and administrators—for black learners at all levels: preschool, elementary, secondary, and post-secondary.

In the same book (1933/1969) Dr. Woodson wrote about the concerns of teachers of English. What he said a half century ago still troubles those who teach blacks. "In the study of language in school, pupils were made to scoff at the Negro dialect as some peculiar possession of the Negro which they should despise . . . . [They were not] directed to study the background of this language . . . in short to understand their own linguistic history."

About the study of literature, he wrote: "From literature the African was excluded altogether. He was not supposed to have expressed any thought worth knowing. The philosophy in African proverbs and in the rich folklore of that continent was ignored to give preference to what developed on the distant shores of the Mediterranean." Although he said little specifically about the teaching of reading and writing, his interest in these important areas is evident throughout the text. In the era when Carter G. Woodson showed how badly many blacks were educated, schools in the South were segregated, but they had a relatively small cadre of excellent teachers, white as well as black, who worked hard at the difficult and poorly paid task of educating blacks. Taking a historical perspective in his book, Dr. Woodson cited the errors—sometimes intentional—taught in the segregated southern schools as well as in the ostensibly unsegregated northern, northeastern, and western ones. This miseducation extended from the days of slavery through the Civil War, Reconstruction, the First World War, and the Great Depression years.

Since that time, although enforced legal segregation is over, problems have remained. Massive (though sometimes passive) resistance to integration, opposition to busing, and the creation of tax-exempt, white academies have adversely affected black education. In spite of compensatory and remedial programs begun under President Franklin Delano Roosevelt and continued with special impetus after the civil rights decisions of the 1950s and 1960s and despite the renewed emphasis placed on such programs by President Lyndon B. Johnson's Great Society, Dr. Woodson would probably see today much evidence of the continued miseducation of blacks and other minorites, of the poor and the disadvantaged.

Unfortunately for the black learner, research in language, reading, writing, and literature has often gone unread or has been applied unwisely. Blacks and minorities are in programs designed for the mentally handicapped—a disastrous effect of well-intended legislation. Scores on standardized tests show blacks and some other minorities at the lowest levels, and in both urban and rural areas, blacks and other minorities are assigned to remedial programs. Their potential for learning has not been tapped, yet it is there.

Organization of This Book

Let us go now from the reasons for preparing this work to its organization. The language section of this publication is placed first because oral language—including listening and speaking—comes first in the life of the learner. This section begins with the language of the young child, progresses through essays on language and dialect in the classroom, and touches upon teacher attitudes. In her introduction to the section, Jerrie Cobb Scott refers specifically to the importance of language in the teaching-learning process.

From language we move to reading and writing. Because these are arts and skills assumed to be formally learned in school, not enough attention is paid by the general public to the informal kinds of reading and writing done by learners before they enter school.

In the reading section, the authors talk about the kinds of reading nourished and encouraged in the homes of successful learners. Articles in the reading section range from preschool through college, and address a number of important subjects. In her introduction to this part, Miriam Chaplin details specific areas of concern.

Writing, too, usually begins long before young learners enter school. It is another aspect of language, and most youngsters love to play with their own versions of the written tongue. Some recent research has even implied that young learners are, initially, more interested in writing than in reading. They want to create their own scribbled ways of communicating with others before they become interested in knowing what others want to say to them. Black youngsters have these interests, and profit from encouragement to express themselves in writing.

Delores Lipscomb, editor of the writing section, has selected essays representative of current writing studies and practical classroom practices. Her own brief introduction to the writing section leads the reader to the varied points of view expressed by authors in that section.

Literature has always been an extremely important part of the black experience. Folk stories, rhyming play, songs, and tall tales have come to the new world from Africa and have combined with other literatures to create a rich and useful heritage for those blacks who have had access to it. Unfortunately, because they have been denied literature or have been taught to dislike it, many black learners have been deprived of their heritage. Intellectually and emotionally, they have withered and died, their potential for learning their own literature, and thus about themselves, untapped and unused.

Again, Dr. Woodson writes: "After Negro students have mastered the fundamentals of English, the principles of composition, and the leading facts in the development of literature . . . they should direct their attention also to the folklore of the African, to the philosophy of his proverbs, to the development of the Negro in the use of modern language, and to the works of Negro writers" (1933/1969).

William Cook, who edited the literature section, speaks in his introduction about "the noise of reading." He gathers in and sums up varied themes when he touches upon the interrelatedness of language, reading, and writing as they affect black literature.

Dr. Woodson's views, concerns, and direction were fundamentally right. And, as we look back still further we can reconcile the positions of Dr. Washington and Dr. Du Bois in terms of the times in which they lived and in which they had to survive.

We have today a larger and more comprehensive view of language and literature and we would not confine the black learner to black perspectives alone. But we must begin where every successful learner in the world begins—with a clear, true, and informed view of his or her own language, literature, and culture. And we must go on from there, using the best of the past to inform the future, seeking useful research, and finding the finest pedagogical practices to ensure the very best education possible.

This book is intended primarily for teachers of English and language arts who work with black learners. It will be useful also for principals, supervisors, and other instructional leaders; it may be enlightening for parents and school board members. Some parts of the work, including the introductions to the language, reading, writing, and literature sections, provide overviews and philosophical stances, and some authors write about a broad spectrum of knowledge in their fields. Other authors are more specific in citing research and studies, providing exemplary curricula, and reporting what has worked well in their own classrooms.

The editor and contributors of these essays are black. Nearly all are active members of the Black Caucus of the National Council of Teachers of English, and most make it quite clear that their primary concern in this book is for the teaching of black learners by anyone— black or otherwise.

Although some of the writers do not once use the word *black* in their essays, the reader can assume that the theories and methods they cite are applicable to all learners, including blacks.

Sometimes black learners evince only the learning problems common to all others from the same geographical region or socio-economic class. Often, black learners are integrated into classes with other ethnic groups. Always, teachers—whether or not they teach black students— should be aware of and sensitive to what is said in this book.

References

Brawley, Benjamin Griffith. *A Social History of the American Negro*. New York: Macmillan, 1970.

Woodson, Carter G. *Mis-Education of the American Negro*. New York: AMS Press, 1933. Reprint. Washington, D.C.: Associated Publishers, 1969.

I Language

Introduction: Language and the Teaching-Learning Process

Jerrie Cobb Scott
University of Florida, Gainesville

Only two decades ago, the now familiar expression, "Black English is a systematic rule-governed language system," was quite controversial. The notion was perceived as nonsense by some, as unimportant by others, and as too obvious to be taken seriously by still others. Yet the last twenty years of debate, discussion, and research on language variation and its influence on the teaching-learning process have caused concerned educators to think seriously about if, or how, information about the black English language system could be used to tap the educational potential of more black students. The views of concerned educators presented in this section cover a large range of topics, but there are two central ideas that are found in many of the papers: (1) as educators, we must look to build on the strengths of black students rather than on their weaknesses; and (2) the more information we have about children, including their language and cultural patterns, the better able we are to understand and, therefore, to tap the strength of black children.

Viewing the language of the Afro-American speech community as systematic and rule-governed means viewing the acquisition of that language as natural, complex, and meaningful. This section begins with a discussion of the basic principles of language acquisition. Black children, like all other children, enter school with language competencies that are naturally acquired, nurtured, and nourished in the home and school environment. The first part of Karla Holloway's paper focuses on the naturalness of "errors" in learning. The second part links the natural processes of acquiring oral language to the teaching of reading. The author suggests that reading skills, like oral language skills, may develop more naturally if reading instructions were modified in accordance with natural language learning patterns. Implied in Holloway's discussion is the view that we can better tap the black child's learning potential by giving more attention to meaning—what the child means when speaking and what the language in reading textbooks means to the child. As teachers, then, we can be more effective if we have more information.

Much of what we know about the language of blacks comes from linguists. The whole notion of "systematic, rule-governed language behaviors" comes from linguistic and socio-linguistic descriptions of urban speech patterns. Clara Franklin Alexander provides information about the language of black Americans. Alexander provides a general description of the salient linguistic features most often associated with black English and samples of several linguistic patterns that may be used by black students. Many of the language patterns associated with black English are shared with other English dialects, but many other patterns seem to be unique to black speakers. Certainly it is the systematic differences between black English and other varieties of English that have caused concerned educators to ask: what kind of change in educational practice is needed to accommodate the language differences of black students? Alexander offers suggestions that can help teachers prevent problems that may occur in language-diverse educational settings. We can infer from both authors that often the learning potential of black students can be tapped by not turning them off to learning before they have discovered their own potential for growth.

Of the numerous issues raised regarding the school's responsibilities in language-diverse settings, none have attracted more attention than those raised in response to the *Students' Right to Their Own Language Resolution* (1974) and the King Court Case in Ann Arbor, Michigan (1979). The following two papers in this section discuss language and the teaching-learning process within the context of the above two events. Darwin Turner discusses the varied responses of educators to the *Students' Right Resolution* as well as responses to other issues having to do with educational accommodations for diverse language and cultural patterns. His discussion serves to remind the reader that everything is relative. That is, the *Students' Right Resolution* itself, along with other proposals for instructional programs for black students, should not be taken as an excuse *not* to consider black students as individual learners. It would be quite unfortunate if the new wave of objective linguistic descriptions and well-intentioned educational proposals became indistinguishable, in their effect, from the old waves that we seek here to break.

Smitherman's paper provides a much-needed clarification of the issues involved in the King Court Case, while Scott's discussion of the King Case suggests two key implications of the case for educators:

(1) that attitudes toward language are important to the learning environment and (2) that instructional materials targeted toward expanding language competencies, rather than remediating language differences, are essential. In the remaining papers of this section, the authors, Perry, Johnson, Edwards, and Finch, present practical suggestions for tapping the language potential of black students.

Again the view is presented that through wider dissemination of information about the language and cultural patterns of black Americans, it will be possible to reach more teachers, to teach more students, in short, to tap the potential of more black students. That this theme recurs in many of the papers is interesting. Perhaps it reflects the kind of keep-the-faith-in-teachers attitude that is so desperately needed among educators. All too often in discussion of language differences and educational changes, both teachers and students seem to be plotted against. Obviously, the most successful taps of learning potential are those where students and teachers work together in the teaching-learning process.

References

Anastasiow, N., and M. Hanes. *Language Patterns of Poverty Children*. Springfield, Ill.: Charles C. Thomas, 1976.

Dworkin, N., and Y. Dworkin. "The Legacy of Pygmalion in the Classroom." *Phi Delta Kappan* 60, (June 1979).

Morrison, T. "An Interview with Toni Morrison." *New Republic* (March 1981).

Seligman, C., G. Tucker, and W. Lambert. "The Effects of Speech, Style and Other Attributes on Teachers' Attitudes Toward Pupils." *Language in Society* (April 1972).

Scott, J. "Black Modes of Communication and Conflicts in the Schools." In *Cross-Cultural Communications in the Schools*, edited by C. Moody and K. Lind. Ann Arbor, Mich.: Program for Educational Opportunity, University of Michigan, 1978.

Smitherman, Geneva. *Talkin and Testifyin: The Language of Black America*. Boston: Houghton Mifflin, 1977.

Taylor, O. "Black Language and What to Do about It: Some Black Community Perspectives." In *Ebonics: The True Language of Black Folks*, edited by R. Williams. St. Louis: Institute of Black Studies, 1975.

Williams, F. "Psychological Correlates of Speech Characteristics." *Journal of Speech and Hearing* 13 (1970).

Williams, F., J. Whitehead, and L. Miller. "Attitudinal Correlates of Children's Speech Characteristics." Project #0-0336, U.S. Department of Health, Education, and Welfare, Washington, D.C.: Office of Education, 1971.

Learning to Talk—Learning to Read

Karla F. C. Holloway
Western Michigan University, Kalamazoo

"He just mumbles." "Most of their sentences are just two or three words long." "They don't understand basic concepts." "Most of their language is little more than grunts or groans."

Comments like these were made by a group of federally funded teachers who are committed to helping minority students prepare for elementary school. Their comments are not unlike many I have heard from elementary teachers who are compassionate toward their minority students, but woefully ignorant about their language capacity.

First, let's be honest. These mumbling, grunting, telegraphic classroom children are the same children who, outside the classroom, turn into linguistically gifted, verbose children. I had one teacher say to me that she couldn't understand why "they" were so quiet in the classroom and so loud on the bus. These children are not nonverbal. Their teachers are not verbally motivating.

The purposes of this paper are to explain the linguistic competencies of children whose surface features of language may be different from the standard, but whose deep structure competencies are the same as those of any school-age child. In addition, for teachers who have children in their classrooms who are culturally or linguistically different, and who may be concerned about the best ways to approach these differences, this paper will offer suggestions for pedagogy that are based on understanding the psycholinguistic processes that all children experience.

Language Acquisition

Language learning begins with an amazing sequence of activities. Recent language studies, and psychology/biology of language studies show how much language competence is an innate capacity (Clark

12

and Clark 1977; deVilliers and deVilliers 1979). We are born with linguistic ability. Lots of us like to think we teach babies and children everything they know, including how to talk. But if children learned language primarily by imitating the adults around them, a host of environmental and social factors (including how we talk to babies with "baby-talk") would make our children's first utterances so distinct and unique that language acquisition data would be hopelessly blurred. Instead, we have children's biological "mechanisms" working to insure a developmental pattern of language learning that sends each normal, healthy human infant through stages of cooing, babbling, single words, abbreviated language telegrams, and finally, somewhere between the ages of three and five, to something that closely approximates an adult model of speaking. Unless the children in our elementary classroom have some physiological deficiency preventing or hindering speech, then the teacher in her classroom needs to investigate why her children aren't *choosing* to talk.

Research is full of data on the child who grows up in an environment that encourages talk, communication, and experimentation with language (McNeill 1970; Brown 1973; Ferguson and Slobin 1973). Certainly this child will be eager to be verbal in many more situations than a child who may not have been encouraged as much. Recently, I had the opportunity to meet a youngster who had been in a number of foster homes since birth, the last one for almost a full year. He was three when we met, and entering what psycholinguists call a "critical period" for language development. Suddenly, I saw what some teachers had been telling me their children were like. He pointed when he wanted something, seldom said more than "uh-huh" and "uh-uh," and used one or two words for what could have been a sentence. But, within just *two* weeks after being placed in an adoptive home where his new family talked to him, requested and waited for answers to questions, explained and listened to him, this child's talking was nonstop. In fact, he'd show real pride when someone took the time to listen to him and when his parents requested that he explain, or tell them something. His three years of language competency was finally being heard. Unless we request the performance, the competence may remain untapped.

Language Acquisition and Language Models

We need to ask ourselves, "who is listening to our children?" If teachers who are listening expect failure, or have some antiquated notion that a child who does not use standard English is linguistically deficient (instead of linguistically different), then the self-fulfilling prophecy often results. If we expect that "these children" will talk and think poorly, then no matter what they say, we will hear mumbles and grunts.

One kindergarten teacher I know is especially successful in encouraging a rich linguistic environment in her inner-city classroom. Her students know she listens to them, because she makes their talking meaningful. For example, she might say to her class, "I forgot how to button my sweater; can you help me remember?" Her students know that they must proceed to guide her verbally through each step. Watching them learn that "Well, you just button it" is an inadequate direction, and learn instead to say something like "First, you take your fingers and hold the button on one side . . . ." is a real pleasure. What this teacher is doing is essentially taken from one of the most successful language acquisition strategies we know. She is giving her students a chance to broaden the universe of their language use.

I have said earlier that a child learns a great deal about language use because of a biological predisposition to do so. Even though this is true, there is one activity that seems to enhance this biological mechanism. Many parents, quite unintentionally, do a great deal of linguistic *expansion* with their children. A parent who does this may say something like "You want a cookie?" to their child who has said "Gimme cookie!" or "You hit the ball—good!" to a child who has said "I hit ball!" Expansion doesn't seem to be a bad response; at least the child has gotten the parent to respond. But actually, expansion does not help children learn any more about language than they already know. It does not give them any new language information or structures to understand.

McNeill cites and discusses studies on how a linguistic model helps a child's linguistic development. He defines an expansion as "an imitation in reverse. An adult, repeating a child's telegraphic sentence, typically adds the parts he judges to have been omitted" (1970, 108). Children do not learn language only by imitation. Modeling is commenting. McNeill explains it this way: "everything said by a child is commented upon rather than improved upon, as in an expansion" (1970, 109). Examples of modeled responses to the children's statements listed above are—"Oh, they're chocolate chip cookies, and I'll have one too." and "It went over the fence into our neighbor's yard." Models broaden the universe of linguistic information available to children and give those biological, innate devices more work to do. Apparently, the more information children receive, the more they are later able to utilize themselves.

Parents and teachers almost automatically expand in response to a child's statements. Interestingly enough, children almost never do this to other children, even those younger than themselves. In my current research project, I have observed how siblings have modeled conversations with each other while their parents are expanding what the child has said. We need to take a cue from our children.

Maybe if we knew what linguists know (that unless there is some physiological reason for what has been too quickly labeled the non-verbal child, we had better look to ourselves), then what we hear our children saying would not be mumbles. We would do a better job of giving children something to talk about. Language acquisition research provides evidence of the linguistic capacity of children. Talking meaningfully, responding with modeled language, having conversations (talking *with*, not *to* children), and learning to give instructions or directions are central to the classroom learning experience.

Language Acquisition and Reading

Comparing the conclusions of oral language acquisition research (Clark and Clark 1977) and the conclusions of reading-as-a-natural-language-process theorists (Smith 1979), suggests that the processes a child uses to acquire spoken language are similar to the processes a child naturally uses when learning to read. The child's innate ability functions in learning to read in the same way that it functions in learning to communicate orally. Of course, the child needs our motivation, support, and guidance, not only in acquiring oral language, but also in learning to read. Learning to read is learning what else the innate mechanism can do—if *we* as teachers allow it.

Again, the meaning and significance of the language activity are important. Children must be allowed the opportunity to make *sense* of the printed word, just as we allow them two or three years to make sense of the oral word. Reading happens when a child can make use of information about language, when the first things read made sense.

It's a shame, for example, that we spend so much time teaching the alphabet in sequence during the early stages of reading and teaching the child the "sounds" of letters. The child will not use the alphabetic sequence until he needs to alphabetize for dictionary work in the third grade. Teaching "letter sounds" is not teaching sense and meaning. How much more significant early reading could be if letters were parts of words and sentences from the very first day! A comprehensible unit like "Ayana's dress is blue" when Ayana has a blue dress is not only meaningful for that child but also easier to process than letters on an alphabet chart or "sounds" on a phonics flash card.

The truth is that we make the reading process more difficult than it need be by trying to simplify it. An adult's notion of simplicity is to break something down and take it out of context, while the child's natural tendencies are to view things holistically and to place them in a meaningful context. This contextual need is the language modelling principle all over again. Context provides a way to get to comprehension. Contextualization is basic to both the reading process and the language acquisition process. Children must comprehend before they can produce any language activity. This is a language acquisition basic (deVilliers and deVilliers 1978; Clark and Clark 1977; Smith 1975, 1979).

Another parallel between oral language acquisition and reading can be found in the developmental stages of child language acquisition. Children universally go through a stage of talking called "overgeneralizations" or "overextensions." We've all heard this. It's a child saying "He goed home" or "I doed it" or "She leaveded it at the park" before learning the irregular past tense forms. These are examples of children learning a rule (grammatical) and needing a period of applying the rule indiscriminately before they learn to discriminate its application appropriately. The same stage of making meaningful errors occurs in reading. These errors are called "miscues" to circumvent the pejorative content of "error." The miscue may not represent a rule that is misunderstood; some miscues stem from word substitutions—for example, the substitution of "woods" when the book says "forest." Still others stem from word omissions. Recently, I was listening to my daughter read a story to her younger brother. She read the sentences "The butterflies chase me," as "All those butterflies chase me." The page from which she read was covered with pictures of butterflies surrounding a little rabbit. She saw "all those butterflies" and made this observation a part of the printed text. Children who make these reading miscues are really interpreting rather than merely reproducing the text. They are learning that they can participate in the reading experience (as they have been participants in talking) by translating, substituting, or adding meaning.

In the early stages of reading, it is crucial that children not be discouraged from participating. If we are after word-perfect reading, we are looking for children who imitate, not who model. We are disregarding an important stage in the learning process: meaningful errors. Weaver (1980) reminds us that an *active* model of the reading process involves an exchange of information between the reader and the text. The reader is not simply a recipient but is contributing experiences and knowledge from a developing frame of reference. We must be careful, in "teaching" reading, to allow children to participate in the process of learning. We are, in effect, allowing their natural language acquisition mechanisms to function. Activities such as those suggested in a language experience program do this best. Activities suggested in skill based programs can be serious stumbling blocks for many children (Weaver 1980; Goodman and Burke 1972).

Psycholinguistic research explains how deleterious a phonics based skills approach is for any child learning to read (Smith 1973). But a program based on "sounds" or letters for a child whose own dialect may not recognize standard sound cues may be especially harmful. The harm is that this approach is confusing to the children who are required (to use the age-old example) to hear the difference between "pin" and "pen" when their dialect does not make a phonological distinction between the two.

Reading instruction that is not pseudo-simplified by dividing the content (again, that kind of simplification is an adult notion) into a sound component, a meaning component and a grammar component, but is instead a unified program of strategies is much more defensible from a language acquisition and use perspective. A strategy integrates. A strategy suggests that a child use all cue systems (sound, structure, and meaning) simultaneously to aid comprehension. It does not penalize the child by depriving him or her of a way to comprehension; instead, it paves the way.

From the psycholinguistic perspective of child language acquisition processes, some of the reading acquisition strategies that parallel natural language learning processes are as follows:

Oral Language Acquisition	Reading Acquisition
1. Comprehension comes before production (we can understand the language we hear as infants before we use it).	1. Children must be given opportunity to listen to reading before they "do" reading.
2. Oral language has stages of progression.	2. Reading ability develops gradually, through stages of awareness about language. Children must understand the concepts of reading before they read.
3. Children participate in language as speakers.	3. Children participate in language as readers.
4. Modeled language is active, it enriches. Expanded language is passive.	4. Early reading of sentences and ideas is more helpful than "decoding" isolated words and

meaningless sounds. Children must contribute and hear contributions to reading from their own experiences and language.

5. "Mistakes" are necessary to *practice* making sense and to reach adult competence.

5. "Miscues" are ways children learn what is in the text, ways they help themselves comprehend and become better readers.

6. Children learn to talk by having an entire and whole linguistic corpus to learn from—their hearing competent and complete oral language gives them their body of linguistic information to learn from.

6. Reading, if isolated into skills, destroys the whole and leaves confusing bits and pieces to be learned. Children learn best by having a whole and learning to understand it by using natural cognitive strategies.

Learning to talk can be the same as learning to read, if we believe enough in our children's natural learning abilities and provide them with a rich, supportive environment. In explaining the difficulties often experienced by minority children in our classrooms, we have no excuses that are language based. No matter what the dialect of our children, their language learning takes its impetus from a mechanism that functions because they are human. It boils down to this: if we think our children are mumbling, we need to give them things to shout about.

References

Brown, Roger William. *A First Language: The Early Stages.* Cambridge: Harvard University Press, 1973.

Clark, Herbert H., and Eve Clark. *Psychology and Language: An Introduction to Psycholinguistics.* New York: Harcourt Brace Jovanovich, 1977.

deVilliers, Jill G., and Peter A. deVilliers. *Language Acquisition.* Cambridge: Harvard University Press, 1978.

deVilliers, Peter A., and Jill G. deVilliers. *Early Language.* Cambridge: Harvard University Press, 1979.

Ferguson, Charles, and Dan Isaac Slobin. *Studies of Child Language Development.* New York: Holt, Rinehart & Winston, 1973.

Goodman, Yetta, and Carolyn Burke. *Reading Miscue Inventory: Manual-Procedure for Diagnosis and Evaluation.* New York: Macmillan, 1972.

McNeill, David. *The Acquisition of Language: The Study of Developmental Psycholinguistics.* New York: Harper & Row, 1970.

Smith, Frank. *Comprehension and Learning: A Conceptual Framework for Teachers.* New York: Holt, Rinehart & Winston, 1975.

_____, ed. *Psycholinguistics and Reading.* New York: Holt, Rinehart & Winston, 1973.

_____. *Reading without Nonsense.* New York: Teachers College Press, 1979.

Weaver, Constance. *Psycholinguistics and Reading: From Process to Practice.* Boston: Winthrop, 1980.

Black English Dialect and the Classroom Teacher

Clara Franklin Alexander
Medgar Evers College, Brooklyn, New York

This article offers some practical suggestions for the classroom teacher teaching students who speak a black dialect. In order that the reader know the context in which these classroom activities are proposed, a general discussion of black American dialect will precede them.

What is dialect? Johnson (1977) maintains it is "a variety of a particular language that differs from other varieties in terms of its lexicon, intonation, patterns, stress, grammar, and phonology."

All English-speaking persons speak some dialect of the language. Indeed, Smitherman (1977) contends that "pure" English is an "abstract." Some dialects, however, command more respect than others. For example, many Americans are favorably impressed by a person who speaks the British dialect of the educated and "upper" classes, while many Americans feel just the opposite about a person who speaks a black dialect.

History of Black Dialect

How did black English evolve? Simply, it evolved the same way that other dialects of English did—as a result of the culture, the environment, the needs of the group, and contact with other languages. The historical account below summarizes viewpoints of many linguists, though some points are subject to debate.

In the seventeenth century, the Portuguese, French, and Dutch roved the coasts of Africa. As a result, black Portuguese, French, and Dutch dialects were spoken by Africans who were in contact with these Europeans. Black English began in the same way. The ancestors of most of the black people in the Western hemisphere came from the west coast of Africa, where there were hundreds of languages with similar phonology and syntax. As the tendency in second language learning is to try to fit the new lexicon into the syntactical structure of one's native language, the English of Africans from different tribes was relatively similar because of similar native-language syntax and phonology. In the Western hemisphere, black English continued to develop as a result of contact with English-speaking overseers.

In the United States, black English may also include regional dialects. Thus, a black English speaker who lives in Massachusetts may also use some of the dialectal features of that geographical area. Similarly, we might hear two dialects from someone from the Midwest—black English dialect as well as the regional dialect. Most black Americans are bidialectal—that is, they have control of, or can use, two different dialects. In other words, they talk differently at different times, using a vernacular or casual form and a more "standard" form for more formal occasions. Each of these forms is a subdialect of the regional black dialect. Of course, many other black Americans also use a nonblack dialect called standard English. This dialect is sometimes called "media" English, implying that it has the respect of the educational, industrial, and military groups which have much of the power in the United States.

Myths about Black Dialect

1. Before being brought to the Western hemisphere, blacks spoke "savage gibberish" (Taylor 1971).
2. Increased contact with whites enabled blacks to speak in a more "civilized manner" (Taylor 1971).
3. Due to physical and cognitive deficiencies, blacks could not learn English properly.
4. Black dialect is part of the pathology of cultural deprivation.
5. Children's ability to learn is retarded because of the use of illegitimate linguistic systems such as black English.
6. Black English dialect is an inferior linguistic system.
7. Blacks are nonverbal.

Facts about Black Dialect

1. Black people who use a form of black dialect do not use all of the black dialect features at *all* times. Use of these features may vary from sentence to sentence.

2. The type of black English used is determined by sex, age, socio-economic status, geographical area in which one spent formative years, the speaker's purpose, setting, topic, and audience.

3. Black English dialect is a legitimate linguistic system with rules.

Let's examine the distinctive features of vernacular black English, since this is the dialect most teachers refer to as "black dialect." Also noted are some other dialect systems which share similar features.

Distinctive Features of Black Dialect

Phonology

Black dialect can be distinguished by the way it sounds. Consider, for example, the sound of the letter *t*. If *t* is the final letter of a consonant cluster, it is dropped. We therefore hear "sŏf" (soft), "ăk" (act), "adŏp" (adopt). This feature is also found in the British Cockney dialect.

The voiced *th* is often replaced by /d/ in black dialect. We therefore hear "dis" (this), "doz" (those). This feature is also found in Cockney; "daowz" (those).

For the sound of the letter *e* as in pen, /i/ is often substituted for /e/. For example, "Gimme dat pin." (Give me that pen.) This substitution can also be seen in the Cockney dialect—"stidi" (steady)—in the rural New England dialect—"bit" (bet), "yit" (yet)—and throughout the American South and southern Midwest.

Syntactic Features

Some of the syntactic features of the vernacular black English dialect are as follows.

The copula "to be." The invariant form "be" is used to denote habitual action or something ongoing. "We *be* playing after school." (We play every day after school.) "He be at work at 3 o'clock." (He is not available at 3 o'clock because he's at work at that hour.)

"To be" is deleted whenever one can use a contraction. It is deleted if it would be followed by a predicate, adjective, adverb, or noun in the present tense (Smitherman 1977). "He tired." "She at home." "This my mother."

The pronoun "it." "It" is used to denote presence, or to introduce statements. "It ain't nobody there." "It wasn't a store in sight." The use of "it is" to introduce statements is found in an Irish dialect. "It's sorry you will be." "It's sleepy I am" (Wright 1913).

Multiple negation. Multiple negatives are used in one sentence. "Don't nobody want no friends like that." In tracing the evolution of the English language one will find the use of *ne* in Middle English. *Ne* was used for emphasis. "He never hadde noping [nothing]" (Wright 1913).

Plural markers. The standard English dialect plural marker -*s* is omitted when there are other words in the sentence that indicate pluralization. "I got two book." "He have ten cent."

Possession. Possession is indicated by position and context, not by the possessive marker '*s*. "Carrie hair pretty." "That John cousin."

Subject stress. Subjects in a sentence are sometimes stressed by following a subject with a subject pronoun. "My father he be taking me out on Sundays." Scottish and other English dialects tend to use subject/noun-pronoun redundancy when emphasis is desired. This happens more frequently when the subject/noun is a proper name (Wright 1913). "Mr. Smith, he came to my house."

Lexical Features

The most well-known and widely used aspect of vernacular black English is the vocabulary, which is in a constant state of change and also influences other dialects. As the larger community adopts certain black vocabulary, shifts appear in the black lexicon so that the meanings of the words may vary in the two communities. Smitherman gives "rap" ("rap sessions") as an example. In standard English dialect it means serious talk. In vernacular black English dialect it now means romantic talk designed to win affection or sexual favors (1977).

Style. There are many distinctive features in the style used to project black dialect. For instance, a teacher who is not trusted or is disliked may be "bested." One initiates or responds to the teacher with the "ultimate" repartee, designed to deprecate or belittle the teacher in front of others. Everyone but the teacher will know that she or he has been "put down." Subtlety is paramount.

Loud talking challenges the teacher. This style element is intended to push the teacher into doing or saying something reckless. It's great fun seeing a teacher lose self-control.

"Playing the dozens" is a familiar style to most teachers. This involves insulting an opponent's family, preferably in rhyme. The participant who slings the most devastating or unanswerable insult is greatly admired and respected by the onlookers.

O'Donnell (1974) explains that to many blacks "language is not only a communicative device, but also a mechanism for control and power."

Two additional elements of style in users of black dialect are sharply angled body movements (Hurston 1934) and intonation. Black dialect uses a wide range in pitch from very low to high falsetto-type sounds. This stems from the African languages which (like most Chinese dialects) utilize various levels of tone to denote different meanings for the same word sound. To a lesser degree, standard English employs the same technique.

In the Classroom

What does all of this theory mean? What can classroom teachers do? The following points may provide some answers.

1. Not all black dialect speakers use black dialect all of the time.
2. Speakers of black dialect do understand the syntax of standard English.
3. Although helping students to become bidialectal is important, bidialectalism is not the first priority in the classroom. Teachers' priorities should be to:
   a. Develop an understanding of language and how it develops and changes.
   b. Become familiar with the dialect of students.
   c. Develop a respect for black dialect as a language system which reflects a culture.
   d. Transmit this respect to all students.
   e. Recognize that black dialect is a low-prestige dialect and that some students are very aware of this.
   f. Demonstrate to students your belief that they are capable of handling two or more dialects.
   g. Introduce them to other English dialects, such as those to which we are exposed when we travel in the United States.
   h. Help students to understand the role of lingua franca. At one time French was the international language. Today, English is a language which is spoken all over the world. Advise students that they may have no idea now of what paths they will take when they are older and that it is wise to be prepared and to learn this standard language now.

Dialects of ethnic subgroups offer examples of other English dialects to which students could be exposed. In *The Joys of Yiddish*, Rosten discusses the "priceless nuances of contempt that are achieved in Yiddish simply by shifting the stress in a sentence from one word to another" (1971, 72). "*Two* tickets for her concert I should buy?" (I'm having enough trouble deciding if it's worth one.) "Two tickets for *her* concert I should buy?" (Did she buy two tickets to my daughter's recital?)

The Pennsylvania Dutch dialect, which is a combination of Rhineland German, Swiss, and English, would be interesting to many students. Some charming examples may be found in *The Language of Man* (Littell 1971). "Don't eat yourself so full already—there's cake back yet—and Sally you chew your mouth empty before you say" (p. 85). "When I was in town today, I bought myself poor—buying new shoes for the kinner reaches me so in the pocketbook" (p. 86).

The students will enjoy hearing, saying and translating various dialects into their own or into standard English dialect while at the same time learning that there are many English dialects.

Does Dialect Affect Comprehension?

Some teachers feel that black dialect interferes with a student's ability to comprehend oral and written standard English dialect. Black dialect users do "acquire receptive control . . . though they may never change the way they speak (Goodman and Buck 1973, 11). Students from low socio-economic groups are avid TV watchers and are thus exposed to a variety of language styles. We may thus assume that many black dialect users are able to understand oral standard English dialect.

Teachers may ask about students' substitution of black dialect features when they read orally. Kenneth and Yetta Goodman have done much pioneering work in this area. They contend that if a child reads orally "They took pictures of they mother" (They took pictures of their mother), we should not conclude that there is a comprehension problem or error. If a child reads a passage silently and then retells the story in her or his own words, giving the salient points but using black English dialect, is there a "reading problem?" Most certainly not.

Dialect-involved errors (miscues) do not hinder comprehension (Goodman and Buck 1973). Bean (1978) in studying the Hawaiian Island dialect, agreed with Burke (1976) and Goodman (1968), Rigg (1975), and Sims (1972) that dialectal errors "did not interfere with meaning." If the deep structure of the students' interpretation is similar to the writer's deep structure (or actual meaning), surface structural variations should not be interpreted as evidence of poor or noncomprehension. In other words, students might express their interpretation of an oral or written message in nonstandard English, but if their meanings are the same as the speaker's or writer's, they must be given credit for understanding.

Black Dialect and Writing

Writing presents more of a problem. Teachers will find omission of markers such as the past tense -*ed*, possessive -'*s*, plural -*s* or -*es*, and lack of subject-verb agreement in the compositions of other students as well. According to Shaughnessey "What has not been noted as often, however, is the extent to which errors of this type also show up among nonblack students" (1977, 91). It is a good idea to get writing samples from students early in the school year and analyze them for the linguistic features which should be taught. Students cannot learn standard English dialect constructions unless they are taught.

Dialect and Testing

Some teachers are concerned about culturally-biased tests and the black English dialect speaker. Those who share this concern should find out about test construction and learn how to develop their own informal tests that will give them the information they want. For example, a teacher may wish to know whether his or her students can understand a particular passage or whether they can write a passage. If the teacher knows how to construct tests, she or he can evaluate a student's growth whenever desired.

The format of standardized tests can be examined by teachers and administered to students for five to ten minutes. Afterwards, the students' correct and incorrect answers can be discussed.

Classroom teachers must not avoid teaching students how to take tests. Employers must eliminate some job candidates, and one of the strategies used is to require candidates to take tests. Colleges require test scores before they will consider applicants, and many professions require the passing of tests before licenses are issued. Students should be prepared accordingly.

Allowances for Dialect

Finally, should "allowances" be made for speakers of black English dialect? Several facts must be remembered: (1) Speakers of black

English dialect are no more disadvantaged than speakers of any other dialect; (2) vernacular black English dialect reflects a culture; (3) as a group, users of vernacular black dialect are not "too slow" to learn standard English; and (4) vernacular black English dialect is a low-prestige dialect, but this is more a reflection of society's attitudes than of the speakers' ability to learn. If all of these facts are remembered, teachers will not feel it necessary to pamper black English dialect speakers or to feel sorry for them.

Suggested Classroom Activities

1. Have the students read some of the poems of black writers which offer opportunities for performance-response—perhaps the poetry of Gwendolyn Brooks and Langston Hughes.
2. Use student-developed stories (experience charts) which reflect their shared experiences. Allow students to read them orally.
3. Discuss the major dialect areas in the United States.
4. Discuss reasons for the different dialects and why dialectal differences should be respected.
5. Read aloud passages in other English dialects to help students to appreciate the variability of English and the legitimacy of their own dialect.
6. Discuss and role-play different situations in which vernacular black English dialect and standard English dialect would be used.
7. Teach the grammatical constructions of standard English dialect. Provide time for practice of these grammatical constructions.
8. Use pattern practice drills to help students develop an understanding of both black English dialect and standard English dialect. For example:
   a. I talked to Mary Ellen every day. I been talkin' to Mary Ellen.
   b. I talked to Mary Ellen a long time ago. I been done talked to Mary Ellen.
9. Have the students conduct a television survey and note which programs use noticeable dialects.
10. Assign students to watch a particular TV news program for one week. Have them observe the body language and speech of the commentators. Ask them to select one of the personalities, and in class set up a news panel in which they will mimic the newscaster's speech, style, and mannerisms.

11. Have groups of students write skits to role-play, employing both standard English dialect and black English dialect.

12. Play recordings of speeches of Dr. Martin Luther King, Jr., who was a master of bidialectal speech. See if students can hear in his speeches the call-response style of the international man.

13. Examine your own speech pattern and read to your students regularly (no matter how old they are). At times, they might read along silently while you read orally.

14. Teach conventional rules for punctuation and capitalization. Provide opportunities for practice.

15. Teach new vocabulary words every day. Provide opportunities for practice of these words.

16. Dictate passages which contain the language constructions to be reviewed. This activity provides students with practice in punctuation, capitalization, and spelling, while enlarging their vocabularies.

References

Bean, Thomas W. "Decoding Strategies of Hawaiian Islands Dialect Speakers in Grades 4, 5, 6." *Reading World* 17 (May 1978): 295–305.

Burke, Carolyn L. "Reading Miscue Research: A Theoretical Position." In *Findings of Research in Miscue Analysis: Classroom Implications*, edited by P. David Allen and Dorothy J. Watson. Urbana, Ill.: National Council of Teachers of English, 1976.

Herman, Lewis Helmar. *Foreign Dialects: A Manual for Actors, Directors and Writers*. 11th ed. New York: Theatre Arts Books, 1976.

Goodman, Kenneth S., and Catherine Buck. "Dialect Barriers to Reading Comprehension, Revisited." *Reading Teacher* 27 (October 1973): 6–12.

Goodman, Yetta M. "A Psycholinguistic Description of Observed Oral Reading Phenomena in Selected Young Beginning Readers." (Ph.D. diss., Wayne State University, 1967.) *Dissertation Abstracts International* 29 (1968): 60A.

Hurston, Zora N. "Characteristics of Negro Expression." In *Negro*, edited by Nancy Cunard. London: Wishart, 1934.

Johnson, Kenneth. "Summary of Ken Johnson's Speech and Recommendations." In *Strategies for Solving the Problems of Language Acquisition. A Blueprint for Action*, edited by Albert H. Berrion and Marianna Davis. New York: Harcourt Brace Jovanovich, 1977.

Littell, Joseph Fletcher, ed. *The Language of Man Vol. 5*. Evanston, Ill.: McDougal, Littell & Co., 1971.

O'Donnell, Holly. "Black Communicative Styles." *Elementary English* 51 (November/December 1974): 1091–95.

Rigg, P. S. "A Psycholinguistic Analysis of the Oral Reading Miscues Generated by Speakers of a Rural Black Dialect Compared to the Miscues of Speakers of an Urban Black Dialect." (Ph.D. diss., Wayne State University, 1974.) *Dissertation Abstracts International* 35 (1975): 7624A.

Rosten, Leo. "The Joys of Yiddish." In *The Language of Man*, edited by Joseph Fletcher Littell. Evanston, Ill.: McDougal, Littell & Co., 1971.

Shaughnessey, Mina P. *Errors and Expectations: A Guide for the Teacher of Basic Writing*. New York: Oxford University Press, 1977.

Sims, Rudine. "What We Know about Dialects and Reading." In *Findings of Research in Miscue Analysis: Classroom Implications*, edited by P. David Allen and Dorothy J. Watson. Urbana, Ill.: National Council of Teachers of English, 1976.

_____. "A Psycholinguistic Description of Miscues Generated by Selected Young Readers During the Oral Reading of Text Material in Black Dialect and Standard English." (Ph.D. diss., Wayne State University, 1972.) *Dissertation Abstracts International* 33 (1972): 2989A.

Smitherman, Geneva. *Talkin and Testifyin: The Language of Black America*. Boston: Houghton Mifflin, 1977.

Taylor, Orlando L. "Some Sociolinguistic Concepts of Black Language." *Today's Speech* 19 (Spring 1971): 19–26.

Wright, Elizabeth Mary, and Humphrey Milford. *Rustic Speech and Folk-lore*. London: Oxford University Press, 1913.

Black Students, Language, and Classroom Teachers

Darwin T. Turner
University of Iowa, Iowa City

Since the late 1960s, linguists and teachers have focused increased attention on a dialect which has been labeled "black English." During the middle 1970s, the Conference on College Composition and Communication (CCCC) and the National Council of Teachers of English (NCTE) passed resolutions affirming the right of students to use their own language without penalty in the classroom. In 1980–81, the document again received attention. Many teachers assume the cause-and-effect relationship of the first two statements to be greater than it is. Such teachers forget the many NCTE meetings during which a white, and sometimes isolated, linguist—James Sledd—berated those who would require a southern white child—or any child—to change a language pattern learned in the home. Many more teachers are confused by the issues and even more by the rhetoric with which the issues have been debated. I wish to discuss these matters briefly and anecdotally with minimal documentation.

Although I began by linking the resolution on the students' right to their own language with the topic of black English, I must separate them in order to summarize each clearly. For those of you who may have forgotten, the resolution reads:

> We affirm the students' right to their own patterns and varieties of language—the dialects of their nurture or whatever dialects in which they find their own identity and style. Language scholars long ago denied that the myth of a standard American dialect has any validity. The claim that any one dialect is unacceptable amounts to an attempt of one social group to exert its dominance over another. Such a claim leads to false advice for speakers and writers, and immoral advice for humans. A nation proud of its diverse heritage and its cultural and racial variety will preserve its heritage and dialects. We affirm strongly that teachers must have the experiences and training that will enable them to respect diversity and uphold the right of students to their own language (Committee on CCCC Language Statement 1974, 2–3).

Despite my own memories of Sledd's urgings, I must admit that I suspect that most English teachers who supported the resolution believed it applied only to Blacks, Chicanos, and Puerto Ricans. It is also true that black teachers endorsed the resolution. Essentially, I believe these teachers came from two groups. One group consisted of a number of blacks who, gaining self-esteem during the 1960s, sought to strengthen that identity by basing it on a language of black people, a language different from that of the Anglo-American oppressor While some blacks sought to learn African languages, other blacks, dismayed by the impossibility of determining which African tongue identified their ancestors, established their relationships with the Afro-American masses by affirming the language of the ghetto, the language of the masses—even before they had fully determined the characteristics of that language or dialect. The desire was laudable; a people should have a language, and Afro-Americans are the only American people who cannot point to a language, dialect, or brogue as that of their ancestors.

Convinced that racism permeates education and cynically convinced that most teachers have no interest in teaching, a second group contended that most English teachers do not improve the writing of students. They merely pass the students from grade to grade. If white students are treated so cavalierly, the argument continued, then why should black students be failed merely because their illiteracy is different from the illiteracy of white students who pass? Although I have not yet descended to this level of cynicism about English teachers (I am fairly far down but not quite there), I see again a validity in the argument. Certainly, every time Henry Kissinger mispronounces English words, I shudder to think how English teachers would evaluate the intelligence of a black student who mispronounced the language so badly.

Even though I joined these groups finally to vote for the resolution, I worried then, and worry now, whether it might not cause more harm than good for black students. I suspected that most teachers would not read or remember the generally thoughtul background statement on which the resolution was based.

The Forgotten Passages

Let me remind you of a few passages that I feared most teachers would never read.

American schools and colleges have, in the last decade, been forced to take a stand on a basic educational question: what should the schools do about the language habits of students who come from a wide variety of social, economic, and cultural backgrounds? The question is not new. Differences in language have always existed, and the schools have always wrestled with them, but the social upheavals of the 1960s, and the insistence of submerged minorities on a greater share in American society, have posed the question more insistently and have suggested the need for a shift in emphasis in providing answers. Should the schools try to uphold language variety, or to modify it, or to eradicate it?

.... The training of most English teachers has concentrated on the appreciation and analysis of literature, rather than on an understanding of the nature of language, and many teachers are, in consequence, forced to take a position on an aspect of their discipline about which they have little real information.

And if teachers are often uninformed, or misinformed, on the subject of language, the general public is even more ignorant. Lack of reliable information, however, seldom prevents people from discussing language questions with an air of absolute authority. Historians, mathematicians, and nurses all hold decided views on just what English teachers should be requiring. And through their representatives on Boards of Education and Boards of Regents, businessmen, politicians, parents, and the students themselves insist that the values taught by the schools must reflect the prejudices held by the public. The English profession, then, faces a dilemma: until public attitudes can be changed—and it is worth remembering that the past teaching in English classes has been largely responsible for those attitudes—shall we place our emphasis on what the vocal elements of the public think it wants or on what the actual available linguistic evidence indicates we should emphasize? Shall we blame the business world by saying, "Well, we realize that human beings use language in a wide variety of ways, but employers demand a single variety"?

.... We need to know whether "standard English" is or is not in some sense a myth. We have ignored, many of us, the distinction between speech and writing and have taught the language as though the *talk* in any region, even the talk of speakers with prestige and power, were identical to edited *written* English.

.... We need to ask ourselves whether our rejection of students who do not adopt the dialect most familiar to us is based on any real merit in our dialect or whether we are actually rejecting the students themselves, rejecting them because of their racial, social, and cultural origins.

.... An employer may have a southern drawl and pronounce "think" like "thank," but he will write *think*. He may say "y'all" and be considered charming for his quaint southernisms, but he will write *you*. He may even in a "down home" moment ask, "Now how come th' mail orda d'partment d'nt orda fo' cases steada five?" But he'll write the question in EAE [Edited American English]. Therefore it is necessary that we inform those students who are preparing themselves for occupations that demand formal writing that they will be expected to write EAE. But it is one thing to help a student achieve proficiency in a written dialect and another thing to punish him for using variant expressions of that dialect.

Students who want to write EAE will have to learn the forms identified with that dialect as additional options to the forms they already control (Committee on CCCC Language Statement 1974, 1–15).

I suspected that many teachers would use the resolution merely as an excuse for abdicating the responsibility of teaching black students anything about language. (Perhaps, like the second group of blacks, I am sufficiently cynical that I suspect that many white teachers do not care whether black students learn.)

Let me illustrate by quoting a white teacher. Disregard the content. Merely consider the vocabulary, construction, and such.

> My first quarrel with such a program is that it does not develop the ability of a person to use language which I would further define as performance capability in a variety of social contexts on a variety of subject matter. Instead, we utilize valuable time to set up drill exercises which are designed to get the individual to replace socially stigmatized forms with socially preferred ones. I cannot endorse as valid a program that sacrifices individual language growth in exchange for some nebulous and highly problematic "social security." The child comes to us with some ability to play the horn and no ability to play the piano. This type of program presumes that a mediocre ability to play the piano is to be preferred to a better than average ability to play the horn. I cannot accept this thesis.

The author expresses his disbelief that there is any value in teaching blacks to use standard English. But I strongly doubt that the author emerged from his mother's womb writing language on the level of the passage that I have quoted. Nor do I believe that he taught himself entirely. Someone taught him. If students are to be permitted to use their own language, teachers, as the NCTE resolution says, must have a knowledge of the students' dialect so that they can help students improve communication.

The idea that teachers should learn more than one dialect was regarded as heresy by some of the linguists in NCTE. They felt that teachers need to know only standard English. Obviously they had paid no attention to the young white teacher who, after a brief term of teaching black students, complained that she could not understand them: ". . . Their language was not so different from mine, but their inflections, intonations, expressions, and lack of what is referred to as standard English threw me."

The CCC background statement asserts, correctly or incorrectly,

> . . . when speakers of a dialect of American English claim not to understand speakers of another dialect of the same language, the impediments are likely to be attitudinal. What is really the hearer's resistance to any unfamiliar form may be interpreted as the speaker's fault. . . . When asked to respond to the content, they may be unable to do so and may accuse the speaker of being impossible to understand (Committee on CCCC Language Statement, 1974, 4).

Whether or not the teacher resisted for psychological reasons, the fact is that she did not understand the language being used by the children. Furthermore, she arrogantly assumed that they understood her dialect; she even believed, I suppose, that they would understand that, when she said "threw me," she meant "confused me."

I would suggest that such a teacher cannot help students improve in their own dialect. Without such knowledge, this teacher, if she adopts the resolution, will be merely ignoring the black students because she is persuaded that they cannot learn English, or she will be assuring herself that they—unlike most human beings—come to the first grade writing and speaking their English flawlessly. (Does it not impress anyone as strange that, while one group of Americans led by Shockley and Jensen still seeks to define blacks as intellectually inferior, another group unintentionally implies that they have a phenomenal mastery of their language?)

Since I contend that teachers who wish to adopt the CCCC/NCTE resolution must understand some basic facts about black English, let me focus the remainder of my discussion on a few facts and myths about that dialect.

For a description of "black English," I refer you cautiously to J. L. Dillard's *Black English* (1973), and even more cautiously to *Black Language Reader*, edited by Robert Bentley and Samuel Crawford (1973). Both books suffer from weaknesses. The essays in the second book range from insight to asininity. Nevertheless, both provide a description of such deviations from edited American English as eliding medial consonants in pronunciation ("tied" for "tired"), omitting the present tense verb from sentences ("He heah now"), using the verb "be" to indicate a continuing state ("He be workin' on his lessons for four years"), omitting the verbal affixes *s*, *ed*, and so on.

In brief digression, let me say that I strongly doubt that many black Americans exhibit *all* of the variations identified with black English. Hence, the teacher looking for a perfect example of the black-English user may be disillusioned or may create one. There is, however, a more serious problem in identifying users of black English.

I started to begin this part of the discussion in the following manner: "I glad I here, but I be real confuse bout this subjick—black English—dat evuhbody be talkin bout." By delivering a few words in what I hope is an approximation of the so-called black English, I hope that I have shown that I am not trying to evade my racial identify, pretend to be middle-class, or whatever it is that black people are supposed to be doing when they do not speak black English. Now that I have affirmed my identity as a black, please excuse me if I continue the remainder of this discussion in that language which I learned first from my mother who, a college graduate, was black inside as well as outside; that language which I learned also from two black adults who sometimes tended me during the day. Although they were rural and southern-born, they did not speak "black" English— probably because they did not know that they were expected to.

I would have begun in this somewhat bizarre manner because I am well aware that some people are so convinced that black English is the native voice of all blacks that they often hurl four allegations into the faces of blacks who protest against that assumption: The first allegation is that, as even Dillard states, eighty percent of the black people in the country use black English. (I do not know how he arrived at this figure, since I strongly doubt that even pollsters have interviewed eighty percent of black America.) The second allegation is that, since four-fifths of black Americans speak black English, any who do not have educated themselves away from their black heritage in an effort to become middle-class Americans. The third is that, since the first two allegations are true, any black American who denies them must be defensively trying to guard blacks against the assumption that their intellectual inferiority is evidenced by their language. The fourth is that, if the unconvinced black is sincere, he or she is a middle-class black who is separated from other blacks, or she or he lacks the linguists' facility for listening to speech.

I warned you that I would be anecdotal; I must also be personal. Most of these allegations, which have been printed in professional journals and books, are made by white scholars and teachers who know so little about blacks that these scholars and teachers make sense only to other equally unknowledgeable people.

Let us consider the four allegations in terms of my own experience as a black person who has lived in this country almost one-half century and who can talk about personal relationships with other blacks who date back another half-century: I have already questioned the first allegation—that four-fifths of black Americans speak and must write black English. I have never taught in high school, but I have taught more than a quarter of a century in black colleges in

Georgia, Florida, North Carolina, and Maryland; and have taught black college students reared in many different states. Of the four characteristics I have echoed as distinctive of black language, the only one which I have found significant in teaching composition is the failure to affix *s* and *ed*. (Most of the sentence fragments that I have seen in students' writing do not result from the omission of a verb but from another cause.)

The second allegation—that blacks who do not speak black English are trying to be middle-class or to evade their racial identity—undoubtedly characterizes some blacks. Almost any statement about human beings characterizes some blacks. In my own life, however, I recall that in college I tried to be more colloquial and imprecise in English so that I would not embarrass my white classmates who did not use English as effectively. (Incidentally, until I entered the ninth grade, all of my teachers and classmates were black.)

The third allegation is that blacks who are conservative about black English are being defensive. Maybe some are. Most are not. The fourth is that, if sincere, they do not know other blacks. Can you imagine how absurd this allegation is when it comes from a white who has probably had minimal contact with blacks and who fails to comprehend how America's apartheid forces all classes of blacks into a single setting. Again, let me use myself as an example. I cannot, would not, deny that I was born into a middle-class family. But I attended school—grades one to six—in an all-black school in the heart of the inner-city ghetto: even in such a "northern" city as Cincinnati, segregation was practiced in schools as it is in Boston, Detroit, Chicago, and other cities today. My classmates were not middle-class. For grades seven and eight, I attended another all-black school, which graduated some of its students into reformatories. After four years of high school, college, and graduate education in predominantly white institutions, I taught in Georgia at a private college, where many of the black students fell short of rural southern standards of the middle-class. If they had been more "middle-class," their parents might have chosen to enroll them in a college more expensive than the one at which I taught. In Maryland, while teaching in a college, I was forced for economic reasons to live in a settlement of soldiers and factory workers. (There were three college instructors in the complex of more than three hundred homes.) While working on a doctorate, I supported myself by working among blacks in a steel mill, by clerking in a drugstore in Chicago's south side, and by waiting tables. My experiences are not unique among middle-class black males.

Yet teachers who publish articles in professional journals would inform me that the black middle class is too isolated from black common people to know how they speak. How arrogant can the ignorant be?

The point of this tirade is simple. Teachers who wish to practice the policy of the resolution on the students' right to language must not assume that a brown or black face means that the teacher has no need to educate that child in language. The teacher must determine who the child is and what language the child speaks.

An Allegation Worth Considering

A different allegation, which is true, is that many black people who insist that black children must learn to read and write "standard" English (EAE or edited American English) are concerned that blacks have opportunity in the job market. Two strong forces oppose this view: nationalistic blacks and idealists (call them liberals if you will). The nationalistic blacks argue that employers should be compelled to respect black dialect; the liberals, echoing that idea, point to the whites who have gained position without effective command of standard English and to the blacks who are restricted despite their language proficiency.

Both the nationalists and the liberals see America with idealistic eyes. In time, America *may* become color blind. At present it is not. Although use of language may not matter in menial jobs, it does matter for the better paying jobs (and for entrance to the professional schools), where employers sometimes are seeking documentable reasons for rejecting blacks. Once, when I expressed this idea, a white acquaintance cited former Mayor Daley of Chicago as an example of the fact that failure to command standard English does not prevent a person from attaining high position. But I asked him and I ask you, outside the artificial worlds of entertainment and athletics, how many blacks without a command of English have whites appointed or elected to significant positions?

Remember, in addition, that the CCCC Background Statement does not say that students need not learn to write standard English. The statement reads, "It is necessary that we inform those students who are preparing themselves for occupations that demand formal writing that they will be expected to write edited American English" (1974, 15). It would be tragic if that statement were to be forgotten.

I do not deny that many blacks who write English effectively will not necessarily prosper in a white racist society: standard English will not necessarily earn jobs for them. But I am raising the alternative question, How restricted is the opportunity for blacks who do not command such language skills? Are idealists (black or white) imprisoning blacks in menial jobs with a naive hope that a white-oriented society will respond favorably to black differences tomorrow after a three-century record of continuing effort to prove the intellectual inferiority of blacks? Blacks can learn to write standard English. As the CCCC background paper states, If speakers of a great variety of American dialects do master EAE—from Senator Sam Ervin to Senator Edward Kennedy, from Ernest Hemingway to William Faulkner—there is no reason to assume that dialects such as urban Black and Chicano impede the child's ability to learn to write EAE while countless others do not (1974, 8).

There are at least three other myths which must be ignored by the teacher who wishes to teach language effectively to black children.

One, promulgated in professional journals, is that black English and other dialects lack the vocabulary for precise thinking and precise expression. Unfortunately, this nonsensical idea, disseminated often by university professors who are seeking self-esteem, is widespread. I have heard it in faculty meetings where the university professors spoke the imprecise jargon all too characteristic of such meetings. I have heard it expressed by a frequently quoted linguist, who stated that young black children could not think. (When challenged, he admitted, for that moment, that he meant that teachers speaking a different dialect could not follow or understand the thought processes of some black children.) Such attitudes are arrogantly ignorant. The mode of language has little to do with precision of thought. When particular snobbisms are eliminated, the mode of expression has little to do with clarity. For example, when my older son was a child, he often spoke (and still writes) a variation of black English. But, long before he reached his teens, I had learned to admire his capacity for effective reasoning and clear expression. Even while we teachers encourage students to avoid using localisms, we must not delude ourselves that they cannot match our capability for thinking or that they cannot communicate. (If I were cynical, I might say that, having little else respected by a capitalistic society, we academics delude ourselves that we have the power of precise communication when, in fact, we may be failing to communicate with anyone outside our circle. Who are the demented—those inside, or those outside?)

A second myth arises among those teachers who have recently learned that blacks give such names as "shucking" and "dozens" to their word games. With the pomposity of anthropologists serenely confident that none are alive to dispute their discoveries, some teachers explain such word play in a way to distinguish it from communication by any other group. For example, I read, in a professional journal, an essay in which a young white scholar tried to explain how black students' rhetoric affects their written compositions. In addition to confusing the meanings of "the dozens" and "signifying," peer-group games which relatively knowledgeable black students would rarely use in English composition classes, the anthropological teacher explained "shucking" to his fellow whites in such a way that he implied that blacks are the only ones who have ever lied to extricate themselves from difficult situations. (I read some of these professional essays with fascination. If I were not black, I might be impressed; because I am, I do not know whether to laugh or cry. I now sympathize with those emerging nations that have restricted the entrance of anthropologists because they are tired of being studied.)

At another extreme is a third myth which would distinguish blacks from other Americans. One college instructor has shared with other teachers her presumption that black students hear in black English. (Notice the generalization about all blacks.) Therefore, she says, they spell in black English. Let us apply that reasoning to whites: Bostonians hear in Bostonian; therefore they spell *Boston* "Baston." Southerners hear southern; therefore, they spell *honor* "honah." Furthermore, that teacher, who tells other teachers to follow her practice of requiring students to spell words as she pronounces them, ignores the probability that she has some kind of dialect. Finally, I would be pleased to learn how her word drills help students distinguish the spellings of "proceed," "precede," "supersede," and other such familiar examples of the refusal of American English to be a language which can be spelled accordingly to sound.

In this brief comment, perhaps I have told you little. Perhaps I have entertained some of you or annoyed others. I certainly have done little to provide you with a methodology for instructing all black children. I have not even taken a firm stand on the question of whether to adopt the resolution or whether to teach standard English or whether to urge bidialectalism. But, if I have persuaded you that no single methodology is suitable for teaching all black children, I have attained one goal. Educationists talk about the need to teach children as individuals. I ask you to remember that black children are children too. Look at them as individuals. And before you abandon them in their own language because of your humanitarian motives, ask yourself whether you have learned what language they are using and whether there is anything you can do to help them improve in language. Finally, I ask you to test cautiously whatever you hear about blacks and our language: Anthropologists and linguists sometimes err. As you think about my remarks, please remember, as I stated earlier, I am a black using the words and grammar—the language—of my black mother and father and the language—as far as I know—of their parents. Should not this be considered "black English"?

References

Bentley, Robert H., and Samuel D. Crawford. *Black Language Reader*. Glenview, Ill.: Scott, Foresman & Co., 1973.

Committee on Conference on College Composition and Communication Language Statement. "Students' Right to Their Own Language." *College Composition and Communication* 25 (Fall 1974).

Dillard, J. L. *Black English: Its History and Usage*. New York: Vintage, 1973.

"What Go Round Come Round": *King* in Perspective

Geneva Smitherman
Wayne State University, Detroit, Michigan

That teacher, he too mean. He be hollin at us and stuff.
Browny, he real little, he six, and he smart cause he know how
to read.

Two of the plaintiff children in King

The children are the future and the hope of black America. Therefore, it is fitting and proper to begin with the words of those children
who brought the federal lawsuit in the nationally prominent but
widely misunderstood case of *Martin Luther King Junior Elementary School
Children v. Ann Arbor School District Board*. Although this case has come
to be known as the "Black English Case," it was as much a case about
black children as about black English. As Judge Charles W. Joiner
himself said, "It is a straightforward effort to require the court to
intervene on the children's behalf to require the defendant School
District Board to take appropriate action to teach them to read in the
standard English of the school, the commercial world, the arts, science
and professions. This action is a cry for judicial help in opening the
doors to the establishment. . . . It is an action to keep another generation from becoming functionally illiterate" (473 F. Supp. 1371, E.D.
Mich. 1979).

The precedent established by the *King* decision represents the first
test of the applicability of 1703(f), the language provision of the 1974
Equal Educational Opportunity Act, to black English speakers. The
case suggests new possibilities for educational and social policies in
our struggle to save children and develop future leadership. As the
plaintiff children's chief consultant and expert witness during the two
years of litigation, I shall provide an analysis of *King* and its implications for public policy and black community development in light of
the stark reality of white racism and class contradictions among
blacks in the United States.

Background

Briefly, the background facts of the case are as follows. On July 28, 1977, Attorneys Gabe Kaimowitz and Kenneth Lewis of Michigan Legal Services filed suit in eastern District Court located in Detroit, Michigan on behalf of fifteen black, economically deprived children residing in a low-income housing project on Green Road in Ann Arbor, Michigan. By the time the case came to trial in the summer of 1979, one family with four children had moved out of the school district, leaving eleven plaintiff children to litigate the case.

Initially, the plaintiffs' action was directed against the State of Michigan, the Ann Arbor School District, and officials at Martin Luther King Junior Elementary School, where black children comprised 13 percent of the school population of predominantly white, upper-class children. The allegation was that the defendants had failed to properly educate the children, who were thus in danger of becoming functionally illiterate. Specifically, plaintiffs charged that school officials had improperly placed the children in learning disability and speech pathology classes; that they had suspended, disciplined, and repeatedly retained the children at grade level without taking into account their social, economic, and cultural differences; and that they had failed to overcome language barriers preventing the children from learning standard English and learning to read. Actions taken by school officials, such as labeling the children "handicapped" and providing them with museum trips and other types of "cultural exposure," had failed to solve the academic problems of the children. The attitude of school officials was that the school had done its job, and that perhaps the children were uneducable. Yet close scrutiny of the academic records and psychological and speech-language evaluations failed to uncover any inherent limitation in the children's cognitive or language capacities. Further, the children's mothers were not persuaded that the academic and behavioral problems were due to slowness or mental retardation. The mothers' intuition was corroborated by professional judgment: their children were normal, intelligent kids who could learn if properly taught.

The Trial

During the pretrial stages of *King*, Judge Joiner tried to settle the case out of court, perhaps wary of the precedent that would be set. The "Friends of *King*," as we, the children's advocates, came to call ourselves, prepared a reading program which the officials rejected.[1] The

Complaint was revised and amended several times to comply with Joiner's orders. For the course of future litigation in this area, the most critical revision was that all claims relative to economic, social, and cultural factors were dismissed. Joiner contended that there is no constitutional provision guaranteeing the right to educational services to overcome unsatisfactory academic performance based on cultural, social, or economic background. To put it more pointedly, the U.S. Constitution can provide protection on the basis of being black, but not on the basis of being poor.

In Judge Joiner's reasoning, it was necessary to focus the issues in *King* on a decidedly narrow set of arguments. He dismissed all of the plaintiffs' claims except one which forced the lawsuit to be tried solely on 1703(f), which reads in part: "No state shall deny equal educational opportunity to an individual on account of his or her race, color, sex, or national origin, by . . . the failure to overcome language barriers that impede equal participation by its students in its instructional programs." Restricting the case to the issue of language barriers, Joiner instructed plaintiffs to specify the nature of the barriers, the lack of appropriate action to overcome them, and the resulting denial of educational opportunity based on race. What began as much more than a "Black English Case" would now focus narrowly on language issues, and its outcome would depend on the interpretation of a single sentence. For the plaintiffs and their "friends of *King*," it was clear that the trial would depend on expert testimony. During the four-week trial, a biracial team[2] of expert witnesses in the fields of psychology, education, linguistics, and reading testified on behalf of the plaintiff children. The members of this team advised the court of the extensive research in their respective fields, the relationship of this knowledge to language barriers, and the obligation of schools to overcome these barriers.

Significantly, the defendant school board called no expert witnesses. Its attorney simply relied on cross-examination of the plaintiffs' experts—a strategy consistent with the community's self-righteous posture. Ann Arbor prides itself on being a liberal community, and ranks among the country's top six public school systems in academic achievement. It is also the home of the prestigious University of Michigan and a multi-million dollar research program that has included the study of race, language, teaching, and learning. Indicative of its presumed enlightenment, Ann Arbor had decided to promote racial and economic integration by opting in the 1960s for scattered-site, low-income housing; poor blacks live in the same neighborhood and attend the same school as affluent whites and blacks. The Ann

Arbor defendants, reflecting a blame-the-victim methodology, contended that their school district could not possibly have failed to practice equal educational opportunity. Although apparently confident about being vindicated, the school district nevertheless employed the expensive Detroit law firm that had successfully defended Detroit's suburbs before the U.S. Supreme Court in the *Bradley v. Milliken* school desegregation case.[3]

The trial proceedings established that the school district had failed to recognize the existence and legitimacy of the children's language, black English. This failure of the teachers to recognize the language as legitimate and the corresponding negative attitudes toward the children's language led to negative expectations of the children which turned into self-fulfilling prophecies. One critical consequence was that the children were not being taught to read. On July 12, 1979, Judge Charles W. Joiner, a resident of Ann Arbor himself, issued what he later described as a "rather conservative" ruling: on the basis of failing to overcome language barriers, the Ann Arbor School District had violated the children's right to equal educational opportunity. *Though black English was not found to be a barrier per se, the institutional response to it was a barrier.* In short, this ruling affirmed the obligation of school districts to educate black children and served to establish, within a legal framework, what has been well documented in academic scholarship: black English is a systematic, rule-governed language system developed by black Americans as they struggled to combine the cultures of Africa and the United States. The district was given thirty days to devise a remedy.

The intent of the Equal Educational Opportunity Act (EEOA) is fairly clear. Initiated by President Nixon and passed by Congress at the height of the antibusing crusades, the EEOA shifted the policy emphasis from desegregation to quality education, and thus, in classic U.S. fashion, attempted to reconcile the two contradictory forces of white racism and black aspirations. Therefore, much of the impetus behind the new legislation was related to racial issues. Because bilingual legislation had already been in existence for four years, however, the inclusion of 1703(f) within the EEOA raises the question of whom this obscure language provision was originally designed to protect. In fact, once Joiner had ruled this a language case, the Ann Arbor School District immediately filed a motion to dismiss on the grounds that 1703(f) did not apply to black English speakers but only to those with foreign language backgrounds. Had this reasoning prevailed, of course, there would have been no case, since this was the only remaining claim of the plaintiffs that Joiner had allowed to stand.

Emphasizing former HEW Secretary Elliott Richardson's interpretation that the statute protected the "legal right of any child [with] a language handicap" (118 Congressional Record 8928, 1972), Joiner denied Ann Arbor's motion and issued the following ruling that represented our first victory in the case:

> The President's [Nixon's] list of persons covered by his proposal is only merely illustrative but could well include students whose "language barrier" results from the use of some type of nonstandard English. . . . The statutory language places no limitations on the character or source of the language barrier except that it must be serious enough to impede equal participation by . . . students in . . . instructional programs. Barring any more legislative guidance to the contrary, 1703(f) applies to language barriers encountered by students who speak German (451 F. Supp. 1332, E.D. Mich. 1978).

The court's ruling in this regard meant that the case would not have to be based on the theoretical problem of differentiating a language from a dialect, nor consequently, on specifically determining whether black English is a language or a dialect. Yet it was an issue that really was not—and, in fact, cannot be—dismissed, for the lack of theoretical clarity and intellectual consensus on the question presented serious difficulties formulating our legal arguments and pedagogical remedies. Further, this confusion serves to account, in part, for the broad misinterpretations of *King* and the continuing ambivalence about black English in the lay community.

Language or Dialect

In categorizing linguistic phenomena, a commonly applied test is that of mutual intelligibility. If speech data from Community A can be understood by Community B, and vice versa, with relative ease, requiring only slight adjustment on the part of each group of speakers, we can generally conclude that the two sets of speech data derive from the same source, that is, they are variations of the same language. Since there is an overlap between Africanized (black) English and Euro-American (white) English, mutual comprehension exists between blacks and whites, suggesting that black English is a dialect. There are also areas of significant linguistic differentiation between the two speech communities, however, which can lead to a lack of understanding and confusion, and can contribute to the conceptualization of black English as a language. (See Dillard 1972; Fasold and Shuy 1970; Labov 1971; Smitherman 1977, 1980; Valdman 1977.)

A few examples will serve to more fully illuminate the nature of the language-dialect controversy. An often-cited characteristic of black English, strikingly distinguishing it from standard white English, is the use of *be* as a full verb form, as in the opening quotation "He be hollin at us and stuff." This use of the verb "to be" derives from an aspectual verb system that is also found in African Pidgin English, and in the Gullah Creole spoken by blacks living on the Sea Islands along the southeastern seaboard of the United States. Its use conveys the speaker's meaning with reference to the qualitative character and distribution of an action over time. In the case of "He be hollin at us," the speaker indicates habitual action. The standard English verb system of past, present, and future tenses cannot accommodate this type of construction, while the black English usage has captured all three tenses simultaneously. The closest standard English equivalent would be: he is always (or constantly) hollering at us; he frequently (or often) hollers at us; or, he sometimes (or occasionally) hollers at us. Other examples of aspectual *be* collected from taped interviews with the plaintiff children are: *When school is out dis time, uhma be going to summer school; They be hitting on peoples;* and *I like the way he be psyching people out.* Black English also allows for sentences without any form of the copula, as in *He real little; He six; My momma name Annie; She my teacher;* and *They always fighting.*

In black English, possession does not require the inflectional *z* (written as *s* preceded or followed by an apostrophe), but rather, is indicated by juxtaposition, as in these examples from the children: *She took him to his grandmother house; Popeye girlfriend;* and *My daddy name John.* Consider the potential for linguistic confusion to the nonblack English speaker that can result from the co-occurrence of two or more features of black English within a single statement, as in the following item from the "Black Language Test" (Smitherman 1975): *"She the girl momma."* Does this mean that she is the mother of the girl in question; that she is a very young girl who is the mother of a child; or, that she is a girl being pointed out to somebody's mother?

It is not only in phonology (sound) and morpho-syntax (grammar and structure) that critical differences between the black and white speech communities occur. Intelligibility can be affected by the lack of familiarity with the rhetorical and semantic strategies of black English. For example, Muhammad Ali, hero and rapper par excellence to virtually the entire black English-speaking community, nearly caused an international diplomatic disaster by using the rules of "talkin black" when he said: "There are two bad white men in the world, the Russian white man and the American white man. They are the two baddest men in the history of the world." Although the Tanzanians, to whom Ali was speaking at the time, apparently understood his meaning perfectly well, the standard white English-speaking world did not. He was castigated for using a term interpreted in the Websterian tradition as evil, wicked, negative, or not good. In the semantics of inversion used by the descendants of African slaves, however, "bad" can mean powerful, omnipotent, spiritually or physically tough, outstanding, wonderful, and with emphasis, very good. For this feature of language use in black English, Dalby (1969; 1972) cites linguistic parallels in Mandingo and several other African languages. His work remains the most rigorous treatment of the lexico-semantic system of black language from a diachronic perspective. (See also Dillard 1977; and Major 1970.)

I have deliberately chosen the example of Muhammad Ali because the contrasting black and white American interpretations of his verbal showmanship place the language-dialect controversy in bold relief. Although Ali's language appears to be English—and fairly standard English at that—the correct interpretation of his meaning requires the listener to have access to sociocultural data outside the realm of standard English. Ali represents the bad man of words in the black oral tradition. Through boastful talk, pungent rhymes, verbal repartee, and clever "signifyin" (indirect language used to tease, admonish, or disparage), the rapper establishes himself or herself (but more generally himself) as a cultural hero solely on the basis of oral performance. Preachers, politicians, and other black leaders reflect this tradition. A clever rapper can talk himself out of a jam, and in sessions of ritual insult such as "playing the dozens" (talking about somebody's momma or other kinfolk), tension is relieved and fights often avoided. Those who are verbally adept at the art of "selling woof (wolf] tickets" (boasting) often do not have to prove anything by action. It is believed that the African concept of *Nommo*, word power, can indeed "psych your opponent out." Thus, when Ali engages in the art of black braggadocio, the louder and badder he talks, the more blacks applaud him, but the more whites, lacking cultural experience in this tradition, censure him. Ali symbolizes a cultural value manifested in black language behavior, suggesting that we are dealing with more than surface dialect differences.

The black English language-dialect controversy reflects a fundamental contradiction within linguistics itself as to how language is to be defined, conceptualized, and studied. The classic dichotomy between *langue* and *parole* (loosely, speech and language) is evident in the differences between Chomskyian theoretical linguistics and Hymesian "socially constituted" linguistics. Chomsky (1966, 1972) abstracts language from social context and focuses on its structure—sound patterns, grammatical structure, and vocabulary. Hymes (1974) more broadly conceptualizes language within the framework of culture and society, and focuses on the use and users of language: their history, culture, values, world views, and social structure are considered basic to understanding a given language. The former is the more popular view of language and that taken by Judge Joiner when he demanded that we identify language barriers without reference to the children's cultural characteristics, which he deemed "irrelevant to a cause of action under the language barrier statute" (463 F. Supp. 1027 at 1030, E.D. Mich. 1978).

Elsewhere (Smitherman 1979), I detail the relationship of this general controversy in linguistics to study and research on black English. The point is that the semantics within which one formulates a general theory of language can determine whether one views the issue as black language or as black dialect. If one considers only words, grammar, and sounds as the essence of language, then black speech data might tend to look more like a dialect of English. If one also considers the history and social rules that govern the use, production, and interpretation of the words, grammar, and sounds, then black speech data more nearly resemble a different language. Applying this to *King*, if black English is a dialect, then the language barriers are mere surface differences that do not impede communication between teacher and student, nor between student and material written in standard English. If the barriers are not in language per se, we must look elsewhere for impediments to the children's access to equal educational opportunity. In this case they were found in attitudes of teachers and other school personnel toward language. On the other hand, if we are dealing with a language, then the barriers reside not only in attitudes, but also in actual linguistic interferences that hamper communication. Since linguistics cannot offer the definitive word on language-dialect differentiation, it ultimately comes down to who has the power to define; or as Max Weinreich once put it, the difference between a language and a dialect is who's got the army (1931).

With the *King* case clearly, if narrowly, focused on the language issue, Joiner outlined four areas to be covered in our final amended complaint. We were to identify the language barriers confronting the plaintiff children, specify how these barriers had impeded the equal participation of the children in the instructional program of King School, set forth the appropriate action that defendants had allegedly failed to take, and identify the connection between the defendants' failure to take appropriate action and the race of the plaintiff children.

The several versions of the complaint had consistently highlighted structural and nonstructural interference phenomena as constituting the basis of the language barriers confronting the plaintiff children at King School. These, we argued, represented essentially a languages-in-contact interaction (Weinreich 1963). Structural interferences derive from the structural differences between two languages—a mismatch of linguistic structures on the levels of phonology, lexico-semantics, and/or morpho-syntax. Nonstructural interference phenomena refer to differing attitudes and conflicting values about the two speech systems and the individuals who use them. The analysis of Muhammad Ali's speaking style illustrates both structural and nonstructural interference phenomena in operation. These phenomena are actually inextricable, though they are often expressed as a dichotomy to create an analytically convenient, if artificial, schema that readily lends itself to empiricism.

Because the language-dialect conflict remains unresolved, there is no consensus among language scholars as to whether there are both structural and nonstructural interferences between black and standard/white English ("What go round come round"). Some black psychologists (Simpkins 1976; Simpkins, Holt, and Simpkins 1976; Williams 1972; Williams, Rivers, and Brantley 1975; Wilson 1971) contend that the points of mismatch between standard and black English constitute cognitive barriers to meaning for black English-speaking children; that is, they have to translate standard English input data. Such mismatches seem to occur on the larger level of rhetorical patterning and discourse rather than being simple points of interference, as suggested in the contrast between "He look for me last night" and "He looked for me last night." This is not the cognitive-linguistic deficit argument espoused by Deutsch (1963), Bereiter and Engelmann (1966), and others, but a postulation that the two different speech communities employ differing thought patterns and conceptions of reality and that these differences are reflected in different styles of discourse. Cooper (1980), for example, suggests that standard English speakers employ a more impersonal style with greater distance from the material of their discourse.

Although the evidence is not definitive, the best available data and expert judgment, particularly from black psychologists, seem to suggest that black English speakers have language-based problems, and only those who master code-switching make it through the educational system successfully. With inconclusive research data at this point, coupled with the inadequacy of current language models to account for differences in discourse structure, the "friends of *King*" were 'unsuccessful in persuading the court that structural linguistic barriers existed. Although Joiner conceded that "there was initially a type of language difference," he reasoned that "it did not pose a communication obstruction" in teacher-student interaction (473 F. Supp. 1371, E.D. Mich. 1979).

Attitudes about Language

Research on sociolinguistics in the education process has been most fruitful and convincing in uncovering underlying attitudes about language. Specifying the nature of these nonstructural barriers proved to be our most powerful legal strategy. In the educational context, negative linguistic attitudes are reflected in the institutional policies and practices that become educationally dysfunctional for black English-speaking children. Research on language attitudes consistently indicates that teachers believe black English-speaking youngsters are nonverbal and possess limited vocabularies. They are perceived to be slow learners or uneducable; their speech is unsystematic and needs constant correction and improvement (Esselman 1978; Shuy and Fasold 1973; Williams 1972; Williams, Whitehead, and Miller 1971). These beliefs, though linguistically untenable, are essentially those held about black English speakers.

Myths and misconceptions about language and negative attitudes toward language diversity are fostered in the school and perpetuated in the general populace of the public school experience (Pooley 1974). Schools and teachers are seen as guardians of the national tongue. Condemned as immoral, ignorant, and inferior are all those who depart from the idealized norm of standard English which, as Pooley's research (1969) so powerfully demonstrates, teachers themselves preach but do not practice. It was this type of mental set that led King School teachers to correct constantly, to the point of verbal badgering, some of the plaintiff children's speech, thereby causing them to become truly nonverbal; to exclude them from regular classes in order to take speech remediation for a nonexistent pathology; to give them remedial work since "that's the best they can do"; and to suspend them from class for trivial and inconsequential acts of so-called misbehavior.

The use, or rather misuse, of standardized tests is a prime example of institutional policy detrimental to the educational success of black

English-speaking children. Intelligence tests and other diagnostic and assessment tools used in the schools have been normed on white, middle-class, standard English speakers and are obviously linguistically and culturally biased against poor black children. For example, standard speech articulation and language assessment tests measure forms and distinctions that do not exist in black language. One set calls for the distinction between "Ruth" and "roof," which in black English are pronounced the same. Examples of this feature of black English in the speech data from the King School children include: "maf" ("math") work; "birfday" ("birthday"); "bof" ("both"). Another set of test items calls for the singular/plural distinction to be made by changing the verb form, as in the task requiring children to match pictures with the examiner's spoken sentences: "The cat is playing" vs. "The cats are playing." In black English, each sentence would be expressed without the verb and without the morphemic indication of plural. Plurality is generally realized by context in black English. Examples from the plaintiff children include "Two captain," "a few cartoon," and "two year." In sum, what we were able to show is that these linguistically biased instruments of educational institutions cannot possibly validate the problems nor the promise of a black English-speaking student (Bliss and Allen 1978; Green 1975; Taylor 1971; Williams 1972; Williams, Rivers, and Brantley 1975).

This impressive array of social science research on attitudinal language barriers led the court to conclude that "if a barrier exists because of language used by the children in this case, it exists . . . because in the process of attempting to teach the students how to speak standard English the students are made somehow to feel inferior and are thereby turned off from the learning process" (473 F. Supp. 1371, E.D. Mich, 1979).

Since black English is viewed negatively by standard English-speaking teachers, it is not difficult to reconstruct the process whereby this language barrier impeded the educational success of the plaintiff children. King School teachers denied that the plaintiff children even spoke black English, contending that "they talk like everybody else." In contradiction, however, were their own formal commentaries on the children's school records indicating the use of black English forms, test data showing low verbal ability in standard English, and the taped samples of the children's speech, excerpts of which were cited in the final amended complaint and detailed during the trial. Because teachers did not even acknowledge the existence, much less the legitimacy, of the plaintiff children's language, they obviously failed to "take it into account" in teaching standard English. It is not, then, black language in and of itself that constitutes the barrier, but negative institutional policies and classroom practices relative to black English that were, and are, key causes of black children's reading problems. Since reading is crucial to academic achievement in all school subjects, the inability to read at grade level prevents equal participation in the educational programs of the school.

The Decision

What, then, was the appropriate action the defendant school board had failed to take? It had not instituted policies to assist King School teachers and personnel to handle the linguistic and educational needs of the plaintiff children. As Joiner indicated: "The court cannot find that the defendant School Board has taken steps (1) to help the teachers understand the problem; (2) to help provide them with knowledge about the children's use of a 'black English' language system; and (3) to suggest ways and means of using that knowledge in teaching the students to read" (473 F. Supp. 1371, E.D. Mich. 1979).

In his opinion, Joiner refers to the crucial data from social science research on effective schools for poor black children (Brookover and Beady 1978; Edmonds 1979; Weber 1971; Edmonds and Fredericksen 1978). This research has established that appropriate action by schools can result in educational achievement despite pupil characteristics. Educational climate is the critical variable, not the race or class of the children.

Finally, the relationship between the district's lack of appropriate action and race lies in the manner in which black English has developed and is maintained as a unique speech system. The speech patterns of black Americans developed from an African linguistic and cultural base which was transformed by their experience in the United States, and reinforced and sustained by racial oppression and segregation, on the one hand, and by the response to racism, in the form of ethnic solidarity, on the other. The institutionalization of racism in America, through both *de facto* and *de jure* mechanisms, has meant exclusion of blacks from participation in the dominant culture, and has resulted in the continuance of two separate societies and two distinct, if not entirely separate, languages.

Blacks, however, have been differentially affected by white racism, and that has created class distinctions within the black community. Differing degrees of competence in standard English is one way these distinctions are manifest. Not all black children suffer from language barriers. Indeed, at King, the only black children having great difficulty were those from the Green Road Housing Project, who were both black and poor. The other black children attending King were from middle-class, professional families. Though these middle-class children spoke black English, they were also competent in standard English: they were skilled at code-switching and, hence, "bilingual." This is precisely the case among those blacks who have successfully negotiated the educational system and become middle class. Thus, it may be said that a black speaker's ability to code-switch is a behavioral manifestation of the interaction of race and class. Not being adequate code-switchers, the economically deprived plaintiff children experienced language-based problems in school. The language barriers for the Green Road children were thereby directly related to racial, as well as economic discrimination, but Joiner had ruled out the latter as a consideration.

Put more succinctly, negative language attitudes are directed toward the "blackness" of black English; the attitudes and the language itself are the consequences of the historical operations of racism in the United States. To the extent that the district failed to take appropriate action, such failure was connected to the race of the plaintiff children by virtue of their speaking black English, and the barriers created are therefore directly related to race. This, in turn, obligates the district to take appropriate action under the Equal Educational Opportunity Act of 1974 to eliminate the discrimination. Such action would consist of an educational plan designed to help teachers identify black-English speakers to help these children learn to read standard English.

The educational plan approved by Joiner, however, falls far short of the mark. As Attorney Kenneth Lewis noted, the plan "amounts to no more than yet another shot in the arm of teacher inservice programs [which] only travels halfway to a full solution to overcome language barriers impeding learning" (Lewis 1980). Clearly, a teacher inservice program is desirable and needed to alter teacher attitudes toward black English. Programs of this nature are not uncommon, particularly among school districts undergoing desegregation. Yet such programs are pitifully inadequate as a remedy to eliminate barriers to equal educational opportunity. Inservice training should simply be a component of a more comprehensive education remediation plan that would have as its central theme the teaching of reading and other communication skills. In sum, with no assessment of teacher behavior and actual classroom practice, the Ann Arbor approach is premised on the theory that benefits will accrue to the children after teachers are properly trained and thereby develop new attitudes. This remedy is too slow and too limited for the immediate educational crisis facing poor black youth in schools in the United States.

Based on the procedural strategy and the outcome of *King*, there are several additional approaches to the formulation of public policy that would address this crisis. First, judicial processes are critical in shaping educational policy and practice. Joiner was reluctant to tread these waters, and partly for that reason. Ann Arbor's education plan is woefully inadequate. Despite the lament that the courts are too involved in the management of social institutions, the judiciary can promote the just and humane administration of large social bureaucracies that seem incapable of righting themselves. As the custodian and protector of values, the judiciary should be more involved, not less, in social management. The public school, more so than any other institution, directly involves and affects every citizen of the United States. Education is everybody's business—including the judge's.

Second, we need a school effectiveness policy monitored and enforced by the courts and by appropriate citizens' bodies. Accountability must be demanded and delivered. Race and class cannot be used to justify miseducation. There is now an overwhelming body of data to demonstrate that, as Edmonds put it, "some schools work, and more can" (1979). Further, schools must be willing to adopt policies to overcome cultural and economic handicaps. This is a basis for future litigation since this claim was dismissed early on in *King*. An argument could be made that culture and class are handicaps just as are physical infirmities. As Kaimowitz (1981) later put it, "Economic, social, and cultural factors, as well as the racial factors . . . and the language factor, must be taken into account."

Third, there should be a national moratorium on tests—standardized, employment, and other such assessment instruments. All evidence points to the cultural and linguistic biases of such tests. *King*, along with *Larry P. v. Riles* No. C-712270 RFP (N.C. Cal. October 1979), attests to the inadequacy of tests for evaluating and diagnosing black children. These rulings reinforce the call for such a moratorium, already issued by a number of professional and concerned citizens' groups.

Fourth, one outcome of Joiner's ruling was clearly to give legalistic legitimacy to a speech form spoken at times by 80–90 percent of the black community in the United States (Dillard 1972; Smitherman 1977). As a corollary to *King* and coincident with the goals of the Bilingual Education Act, we need a national public policy on language that asserts the legitimacy of languages and dialects other than standard English. As recommended by the Task Force on Language

Policy and National Development (in press), a parallel tactic might be the development of awareness campaigns on black English conducted in communities throughout the country.

Fifth, just as *King* reaffirms the viability and appropriateness of black English, it also demands that students gain competence in standard English. As sociolinguists have maintained, effective speakers, writers, and readers have a highly developed level of communicative competence, that is, using language forms in socially appropriate contexts. Such competence allows one to manipulate a variety of speech forms, adapted to various audiences, media of communication, intention, and other social variables. There is not simply one form of standard English, but varieties of standard English—formal, informal, and colloquial. Similarly, there are varieties of black English conducive to communicating in various social situations; black church language, proverbs, and street raps are examples. The recognition of black English alongside standard English reinforces the call for a curriculum policy that would mandate and facilitate teaching of communicative competence.

Sixth, because of the distortions of *King* perpetrated by the media, a potential weapon for black child advocacy has been grossly misunderstood. There were over three hundred newspaper and magazine articles and editorials (Bailey 1981) along with numerous television and radio broadcasts. Yet media sensationalism prevented the issues from being clearly and fully delineated. There was a persistent attempt to discredit the plaintiffs' mothers and to exonerate the school district, and survey results indicate that many people received negative views of black English from media coverage of *King* (Wilks 1981). Black and other nonmainstream communities have traditionally been the victims of biased media coverage. Communities must rally to force the media to adhere to a standard of ethics and to establish media clearinghouses to counter the dissemination of inaccurate and distorted information (Task Force on Media and Information Dissemination 1981).

Seventh, in some circles it has become fashionable to disavow the need for and utility of academic research. *King*, however, reaffirms the need for more, not less, research, of the kind that is responsive to the needs of black and other similarly dispossessed communities. Joiner also commented in his ruling on the value of research in informing the court (473 F. Supp. 1371, E.D. Mich. 1979).

He noted the efficacy of the personal appearance and involvement of experts as advocates for the children. Research efforts of this kind should be encouraged, and blacks should be involved from the beginning. Creative ways must be found to encourage the allocation of funds for research on black children and youth. At the very least, blacks should vigorously monitor all such research to insure that only projects with policy implications for improving the education of black children and youth receive top priority.

To complete our analysis of *King*, I shall briefly examine the issues of black double-consciousness and class contradictions which were raised during the legal proceedings. "Double-consciousness" was first described by Du Bois when he said:

> After the Egyptian and Indian, the Greek and Roman, the Teuton and Mongolian, the Negro is a sort of seventh son, born with a veil, and gifted with second-sight in this American world—a world which yields him no true self-consciousness, but only lets him see himself through the revelation of the other world. It is a peculiar sensation, this double-consciousness, this sense of always looking at one's self through the eyes of others. . . . One ever feels his twoness—an American, a Negro: two souls, two warring ideals in one dark body. . . . The history of the American Negro is the history of the strife—this longing to attain self-conscious manhood, to merge his double self into a better and truer self. In this merging, he wishes neither of the older selves to be lost (Du Bois 1903/1961, 44).

With respect to black speech, I describe the manifestation of double-consciousness in language as "linguistic push-pull": the push toward Americanization of black English counterbalanced by the pull of its Africanization (Smitherman 1977). Both linguistic forms have been necessary for black survival in white America—standard English in attempts to gain access to the social and economic mainstream, black English for community solidarity, deception, and "puttin on ole massa." In "If Black English Isn't a Language, Then Tell Me What Is?," (*New York Times* July 29, 1979) written shortly after the *King* trial, Baldwin spoke eloquently of the role of black English in the black experience: "There was a moment, in time, and in this place, when my brother, or my mother, or my father, or my sister, had to convey to me, for example, the danger in which I was standing from the white man standing just behind me, and to convey this with a speed, and in a language, that the white man could not possibly understand, and that, indeed, he cannot understand, until today."

With the beginnings of education for blacks in the late nineteenth century, linguistic push-pull became more pervasive in the Afro-American community. As Woodson (1936/1969) tells us, that education has always been away from—not toward—black culture, language, and community. Relating his critique specifically to language, Woodson (1933/1969) noted that: "In the study of language in school,

pupils were made to scoff at the Negro dialect as some peculiar possession of the Negro which they should despise rather than directed
to study the background of this language as a broken down African
tongue—in short to understand their own linguistic history, which is
certainly more important for them than the study of French Phonetics,
or Historical Spanish Grammar" (1933/1969, 19).

This ambivalence about a dimension of blackness so close to personal identity explains the mixed reactions of blacks to *King*. Despite
the decidedly forward advancement in black pride during the 1960s,
there continues to be a lingering self-consciousness about the value
of black culture and black language, even among those who speak
it most frequently and who, in their more culturally chauvinistic
moments, decry "nigguhs who talk all proper and white."

This linguistic push-pull also serves to account, in part, for the
paucity of research on black speech by contemporary black scholars.
Seeing the value and distinctive African character of black English,
white researchers have produced a sizable body of data attesting to
the systematicity, use, and functions of black English. Not all of this
research has been to our betterment. In particular, blacks have decried
treatments such as Folb's *Runnin' Down Some Lines* (1980) and Jackson's
Get Your Ass in the Water and Swim Like Me (1974) because they focus on
the sensational words and phrases in black speech. Black language is,
after all, more than "jive-ass" lingo of ghetto teenagers or the "pussy-
coppin" raps of prisoners. The "more than" awaits the treatment
of black scholars who can continue in the black intellectual tradition
of Frederick Douglass, W. E. B. Du Bois, Carter G. Woodson, and
Lorenzo Turner. All wrote positively about—and in Turner's case,
thoroughly analyzed—black English long before post-1960 white
scholars. In fact, Turner's *Africanisms in the Gullah Dialect* (1949)
was quoted, while still in manuscript form, by white anthropologist
Herskovits in *Myth of the Negro Past* (1941), surely one of the rare
instances in which a white scholar acknowledges an intellectual debt
to a black scholar.

Black teachers and educators are often more negative toward black
English-speaking children than are white educators. This reaction of
educators and other black leaders to *King* serves to remind the black
community that our class contradictions were never resolved in the
1960s era of black progress ("What go round come round"). Briefly,
their fear is that black speech will prevent blacks from getting a share
of the rapidly shrinking pie—a threat, as Baldwin indicated in his
keynote speech to the National Invitational Symposium on Black
English and the Education of Black Children and Youth, that is no
longer in the power of the United States to give, as the Third World

continues to cut off America's historically free and ready access to resources (Baldwin 1981). Several editorials by noted black columnist Rowan (*Detroit News*, July 11, 1979) are representative of the disturbing reaction of many members of the black middle class. Stating that *King* was one of the "silliest and potentially most destructive" cases to affect the education of black children, he argued that this approach would "consign millions of ghetto children to a linguistic separation [as if it doesn't already exist!] which would guarantee that they will never make it in the larger U.S. society." Note that it is not high unemployment, or the shifting balance in world economic power, or the crises caused by a highly advanced, technological capitalist society in the United States but "linguistic separation," mind you, that will keep black children and youth from making it in the United States.

The language, education, and other public policies typically proposed by black middle-class leadership will not serve the needs of the black underclass. Their programs only ensure that a few blacks slide past the gatekeepers. Limited by an analysis based solely on race, without considering issues of class, they are unable to propose solutions that address the broader structural crises that affect all groups in United States society, but affect poor blacks with disproportionate severity. While *King* reminds us that standard English is a *sine qua non* of survival in our complex society, the harsh reality is that if all blacks commanded the language of textbooks and technocracy, the system, as it is presently constructed, could not accommodate all of us. Further, if our society could solve the problem of black unemployment—and that's a big if—it would only shift the burden to some other group. It would do nothing to address the fundamental cause of unemployment.

There are no spoils to the victors in *King*. Though the ruling set a legal precedent establishing that black English falls within the parameters of the statutory language of 1703(f), it is an acknowledged reformist strategy. But it is a tool now available to other communities for manipulating the legal system to obtain a measure of redress from our continuing oppression.

The fate of black children as victims of miseducation continues to be the bottom line in the "Black English Case." *King* gives us yet another weapon in our struggle to save the children and develop future leadership. The case began with a claim of institutional mismanagement of education for children from the Green Road Housing Project. It ended with a claim of institutional mismanagement of the children's language. For those who know that language is identity, the issue is the same: *the children's language is them is they mommas and kinfolk and community and black culture and the black experience made manifest in verbal form.*

Notes

1. Since their children's low reading level was among the parents' chief concerns, one of Joiner's early attempts at mediation was to suggest that we draft a program targeted at reading. Philosophically, the program stressed inservice training, schoolwide involvement, community input, youth-training-youth, and the integration of multicultural material in all school subjects, at all grade levels, and for *all* children at King School. Pedagogically, emphasis was on a multidisciplinary approach to their teaching of reading, on the use of language experience and black cultural approach, and on oral and written activities aimed at developing communicative competence. The defendants objected, contending that the program was too broad in scope, that it did not address the specific, individual cases of the fifteen plaintiff children, and finally, that they had already been using some of the suggested approaches and materials with the plaintiff children, but nothing seemed to work.

2. In addition to myself, the biracial team of experts included: Richard Bailey, University of Michigan; J. L. Dillard, Northern Louisiana State University; Ronald Edmonds, Harvard Graduate School of Education; Daniel N. Fader, University of Michigan; Kenneth Haskins, Roxbury Community College; Milford Jeremiah, Morgan State University; William Labov, University of Pennsylvania; Jerrie Scott, University of Florida; and Gary Simpkins, Watts Health Foundation.

3. In 1970, the NAACP, acting on behalf of one white parent and several black parents, filed a federal suit against the Detroit School District and the State of Michigan (Milliken was governor). The claim was that black children had been deliberately segregated and were receiving an inferior education. In his historic 1971 decision, Judge Stephen Roth ruled that Detroit schools had been intentionally segregated, and he ordered cross-district busing between Detroit and its predominantly white suburbs. At that time, Detroit's schools were 65 percent black. In his decision, Roth indicated that following the 1967 "civil disturbance," Detroit had suffered the most rapid exodus of whites of any northern city school system. In 1974 the Supreme Court overturned the Roth decision on cross-district busing and thus sounded the death knell for integrating Detroit's schools, which today are 86 percent black.

References

Bailey, R. "Press Coverage of the Black English Case." In *Black English and the Education of Black Children and Youth: Proceedings of the National Invitational Symposium on the King Decision*, edited by Geneva Smitherman. Detroit: Center for Black Studies, Wayne State University, 1981.

Baldwin, J. "Black English: A Dishonest Argument." In *Black English and the Education of Black Children and Youth: Proceedings of the National Invitational Symposium on the King Decision*, edited by Geneva Smitherman. Detroit: Center for Black Studies, Wayne State University, 1981.

Bereiter, C., and S. Engelmann. *Teaching Disadvantaged Children in the Preschool.* Englewood Cliffs, N.J.: Prentice-Hall, 1966.

Bliss, L., and D. Allen. Language Screening and Assessment Test for Preschool Children of Diverse Backgrounds. (Interim report to National Institute of Health. Research Project NIH-NINCDS-76-03) Detroit: Wayne State University, 1978.

Brookover, W. B., and C. Beady. *School Social Climate and Student Achievement.* New York: Praeger, 1978.

Chomsky, Noam. *Cartesian Linguistics.* New York: Harper & Row, 1966.

——. *Language and Mind.* New York: Harcourt Brace Jovanovich, 1972.

Cooper, G. "Black Language and Holistic Cognitive Style." Paper presented at the Association for the Study of Afro-American Life and History Conference, New Orleans, October 1980.

Dalby, David. *Black through White: Patterns of Communication in Africa and the New World.* Bloomington, Ind.: Indiana University Press, 1969.

——. "The African Element in American English." In *Rappin' and Stylin' out: Communication in Urban Black America,* edited by T. Cochman. Urbana, Ill.: University of Illinois Press, 1972.

Deutsch, M. "The Disadvantaged Child and the Learning Process." In *Education in Depressed Areas,* edited by A. Passow. New York: Columbia University Press, 1963.

Dillard, J. L. *Black English: Its History and Usage.* New York: Random House, 1972.

——. *Lexicon of Black English.* New York: Seabury, 1977.

Du Bois, W. E. B. *The Souls of Black Folk.* Chicago: A. C. McClurg, 1903. Reprint. New York: Fawcett, 1961.

Edmonds, Ronald, and J. R. Fredericksen. "Search for Effective Schools: The Identification and Analysis of City Schools That Are Instructionally Effective for Poor Children." Cambridge, Mass.: Center for Urban Studies, Harvard University, 1978. Photocopy.

Edmonds, R. "Educational Policy and the Urban Poor: Search for Effective Schools." In *Black English and the Education of Black Children and Youth: Proceedings of the National Invitational Symposium on the King Decision,* edited by Geneva Smitherman. Detroit: Center for Black Studies, Wayne State University, 1981.

——. "Some Schools Work and More Can." *Social Policy* 9 (1979): 28–32.

Esselman, B. "An Investigation of Third and Fourth Grade Reading Teachers' Perceptions as Related to Those Who Speak Black Dialect in the School District of the City of Highland Park, Michigan." (Ph.D. diss., Wayne State University, 1977). *Dissertation Abstracts International* 39 (1978): 1320A.

Fasold, Ralph W., and Roger Shuy, eds. *Teaching Standard English in the Inner City.* Washington, D.C.: Center for Applied Linguistics, 1970.

Folb, Edith A. *Runnin' Down Some Lines.* Cambridge: Harvard University Press, 1980.

Green, R. L. "Tips on Educational Testing: What Teachers and Parents Should Know." *Phi Delta Kappan* (October 1975): 89–93.

Herskovits, M. *Myth of the Negro Past.* Boston: Beacon Press, 1941.

Hymes, D. *Foundations in Sociolinguistics.* Philadelphia: University of Pennsylvania Press, 1974.

Jackson, B. *Get Your Ass in the Water and Swim Like Me.* Cambridge: Harvard University Press, 1974.

Kaimowitz, G. "Commentary on the *King* Case." In *Black English and the Education of Black Children and Youth: Proceedings of the National Invitational Symposium on the King Decision,* edited by Geneva Smitherman. Detroit: Center for Black Studies, Wayne State University, 1981.

Labov, W. "The Notion of Systems." In *Pidginization and Creolization of Languages,* edited by D. Hymes. New York: Cambridge University Press, 1971.

Lewis, Kenneth. "Analysis of the *King* Case." Detroit, 1980. Photocopy.

Major, Clarence. *Dictionary of Afro-American Slang.* New York: International Publishers, 1970.

Pooley, Robert C. "The Oral Usage of English Teachers." In *Language and Teaching: Essays in Honor of W. Wilbur Hatfield,* edited by V. McDavid. Chicago: Chicago State College, 1969.

_____. *The Teaching of English Usage.* Urbana, Ill.: National Council of Teachers of English, 1974.

Shuy, Roger, and Ralph W. Fasold. *Language Attitudes: Current Trends and Prospects.* Washington, D.C.: Georgetown University Press, 1973.

Simpkins, G. "Cross-Cultural Approach to Reading." (Ph.D. diss., University of Massachusetts–Amherst, 1976.) *Dissertation Abstracts International* 37 (1976): 5669A.

Simpkins, Gary, G. Holt, and C. Simpkins. *Bridge: A Cross-Culture Reading Program.* Boston: Houghton Mifflin, 1976.

Smitherman, Geneva. "Black Language Test." Detroit: Center for Black Studies, Wayne State University, 1975. Photocopy.

_____. *Talkin and Testifyin: The Language of Black America.* Boston: Houghton Mifflin, 1977.

_____. "White English in Blackface, or Who Do I Be?" In *The State of the Language,* edited by L. Michaels and C. Ricks. Berkeley and Los Angeles: University of California Press, 1980.

_____. *Black English and the Education of Black Children and Youth: Proceedings of the National Invitational Symposium on the King Decision,* Detroit: Center for Black Studies, Wayne State University, 1981.

Taylor, O. "Recent Developments in Sociolinguistics: Some Implications for ASHA." *American Speech and Hearing Association Journal* 13 (1971): 340–47.
Task Force on Language Policy and National Development. In *Black English and the Education of Black Children and Youth: Proceedings of the National Invitational Symposium on the King Decision,* edited by Geneva Smitherman. Detroit: Center for Black Studies, Wayne State University, 1981.

Turner, Lorenzo Dow. *Africanisms in the Gullah Dialect.* Chicago: University of Chicago Press, 1949.

Valdman, A. *Creole and Pidgin Linguistics.* Bloomington, Ind.: University of Indiana Press, 1977.

Weber, G. *Inner-City Children Can be Taught to Read: Four Successful Schools.* Washington, D.C.: Council for Basic Education, 1971.

Weinreich, M. "Tsveyshprakhikayt: Mutershpracht un tsveyte shprakh." *Yivo-Bleter* 1 (1931): 301–16.

Weinrich, U. *Languages in Contact.* The Hague: Mouton, 1963.

Wilks, M. "Black English and the Media." In *Black English and the Education of Black Children and Youth: Proceedings of the National Invitational Symposium on the King Decision,* edited by Geneva Smitherman. Detroit: Center for Black Studies, Wayne State University, 1981.

Williams, F., J. Whitehead, and L. Miller. *Attitudinal Correlates of Children's Speech Characteristics.* Austin: Center for Communication Research, University of Texas, 1971.

Williams, R. L. *The BITCH 100: A Culture-Specific Test.* St. Louis: Washington University, 1972.

Williams, R. L., L. W. Rivers, and M. Brantley. "The Effects of Language on the Test Performance of Black Children; Developing Cultural Specific Assessment Devices: An Empirical Rationale; Disentangling the Confusion Surrounding Slang, Nonstandard English, Black English and Ebonics." In *Ebonics: The True Language of Black Folks,* edited by R. Williams. St. Louis: Institute of Black Studies, 1975.

Wilson, R. "A Comparison of Learning Styles in African Tribal Groups with Afro-American Learning Situations and the Channels of Cultural Connection: An Analysis of Documentary Material." Ph.D. diss., Wayne State University, 1971. *Dissertation Abstracts International,* 1971, 32/5A, p. 2497.

Woodson, Carter G. *The Mis-Education of the American Negro.* New York: AMS Press, 1933. Reprint. Washington, D.C.: Associated Publishers, 1969.

———. "The Education of the American Negro." In *The African Background Outlined or Handbook for the Study of the Negro,* edited by Carter G. Woodson. Washington, D.C.: Negro Universities Press, 1936. Reprint. New York: New American Library, 1969.

The King Case:
Implications for Educators

Jerrie Cobb Scott
University of Florida, Gainesville

In 1978, the parents of eleven black children charged school officials with denying their children equal educational opportunities by failing to help the children overcome a language barrier. The court found it appropriate to: require the defendant Board to take steps to help its teachers to recognize the home language of the students and to use that knowledge in their attempts to teach reading skills in standard English (Court Memorandum and Opinion 1978: 41). This case, *Martin Luther King Junior Elementary School Children v. Ann Arbor School District Board*, has attracted the attention of people from virtually the whole spectrum of American society. Naturally, the responses to the decision varied, but by and large, the case brought to the attention of educators two important points about black English. First, the decision recognizes the existence of a language system that elicits negative attitudes when used in the school environment. Negative attitudes are transformed into low expectations; low expectations are transmitted to and fulfilled by students. This cycle, described as either the Pygmalion effect or the pattern of self-fulfilling prophecies, has been shown to be a major factor in the academic failure of black students, though other factors contribute as well. Second, the decision legitimizes the use of information about the language of Afro-Americans for planning educational programs, especially reading programs.

Before discussing the two major points of this paper, it is useful to review some of the key points about the case. First, note the statute under which this case was tried:

> No state shall deny equal educational opportunity to an individual on account of his or her race, color, sex, or national origin, by . . . the failure by an educational agency to take appropriate action to overcome language barriers that impede equal participation by its students in its instructional programs (U.S.C. 1703).

Contrary to popular opinion, the case was not directed toward settling the language vs. dialect controversy which had been debated in academic settings over the last decade; rather, it was directed toward determining whether or not the language system used by the eleven black children constituted a barrier in the educational process and whether or not the schools might have taken more appropriate action to help youngsters overcome these barriers. The language barrier, it was argued by the plaintiffs, was not based on students' inability to understand English. The language is a barrier in the educational process because of the stigma attached to it, the lack of respect given to it, and the lack of knowledge about it. All of the above factors have been shown to lead to damaged self-concepts of students, low expectations regarding the educability of students, ineffective instructional methods, and sometimes to inappropriate placement of students, e.g. classes for the learning disabled, the mentally handicapped, and the speech impaired.

A variety of views on the implications of the decision for educators can be found. At one extreme, there are those who interpret the decision as an explicit mandate not to teach standard English but to teach black English only. At the other extreme is the view that large scale language programs will be implemented for the purpose of teaching standard English to speakers of black English. There is also the interpretation that the ruling implies that no changes need take place at all in that some school programs have been acting in accordance with the ruling all along. The interpretation of the Ann Arbor School District Board was that the mandate required the Board to provide inservice training that would give school personnel wider exposure to the language and language learning patterns of black students. Finally, the response that best reflects the view of the lawyers and the expert witnesses in this case is that *King* implies the need for educators to reexamine the academic progress of blacks and other speakers of low prestige dialects in desegregated or language diverse educational settings. Educators might ask, then, what it means to recognize the existence of a language system other than the idealized standard English language system and what it means to legitimize the use of information about a variety of linguistic systems in planning educational programs.

The Recognition of a Language System

To recognize that a language system exists is to admit that black children engage in highly complex language learning processes, as do children from any other ethnic group. Many of the readiness experiences thought to be important in developing communication skills are provided within the Afro-American speech community. For example, at a very early age black children learn to construct rhyming patterns; they are given numerous opportunities to use contextual cues for making distinctions between words that sound alike but have different meanings—homophones. Black students are quite apt at expressing a single idea in a variety of ways—paraphrasing. And they enjoy, even at kindergarten age, rearranging words to create new ideas or novel expressions, e.g. Ronald MacDonald to MacDonald Ronald. One could go on with numerous other features of language that are learned by children prior to entering school, features that might also be associated with readiness for school related language tasks. However, the point here is that the recognition of a language system would suggest the need for different attitudes about what black children learn, i.e., systematic rule-governed language patterns, and about how they acquire these language patterns, i.e., through natural yet complex language learning processes.

Attitudes are important. In his discussion of impediments to learning, Judge Joiner refers specifically to nonacceptance attitudes in the Court Memorandum of *King*:

> The research evidence supports the theory that the learning of reading can be hurt by teachers who reject students because of the "mistakes" or "errors" made in oral speech by black English speaking children who are learning standard English. This comes about because "black English" is commonly thought of as an inferior method of speech and those who use this system may be thought of as "dumb" or "inferior" (1978:18).

By implication, attitudes toward the language and the users of the language can influence the teaching-learning process. However simple it might sound, the task of changing attitudes is deceptively complex. Research findings reported by such people as Williams (1970), Williams, Whitehead, and Miller (1971), Taylor (1975) and Seligman, Tucker, and Lambert (1972) have shown that negative associations between speech patterns and other characteristics of a speaker, including educability of students, are made in seemingly unjustifiable ways. But more important, the negative associations seem to shape some of the expectations that teachers have about the language, personality traits, motivational levels, and academic potential of students who either speak a low-prestige dialect or who happen to be members of an ethnic group whose language patterns are stigmatized (Williams, Whitehead, and Miller 1971). Another important point about these research findings is that they suggest that attitudes about language are often formed unconsciously. Certainly it is difficult to change feelings that we are unconscious of. It is also difficult to change behaviors that communicate unconsciously formed attitudes, as is indicated by research on teacher behaviors that communicate low expectations.

That negative attitudes lead to negative results is not by any means new information, but we have just begun to investigate how negative attitudes are communicated in the classroom. Research by Dworkin and Dworkin (1979) has led to the identification of teacher behaviors that communicate low expectations to students, perhaps unintentionally. Some examples are limited opportunities for responses, emphasis on weaknesses rather than on strengths, absence of challenging questions, and the failure to ask probing questions when a response seems to be partially correct (Kernan 1979). So, in addition to the already complex problem of changing attitudes which are formed unconsciously, we have another complex problem—changing behaviors that communicate low expectations to students.

Changing Attitudes

When we speak of changing attitudes toward language, we are forced to deal with the fact that we are talking about changing feelings that people may not be consciously aware of and changing behaviors that people may not consciously control. These two factors suggest that attitudinal changes must be approached in a systematic way. Following is a brief description of three important steps in approaching attitudinal changes in a systematic way.

The First Step

First in the sequence is the recognition of the need for attitudinal changes. Information such as that presented in workshops and in the growing body of literature on the topic of language variation and related educational problems offer convincing evidence that many of the negative attitudes toward both low-prestige dialects and their speakers interfere with important educational goals. After being exposed to more objective descriptions of language and to empirically based findings on the negative influence of negative attitudes toward language and learning, educators tend to agree that attitudes should be changed. For example, workshop consultants have indicated that participants are more tolerant of language differences after they have received more information about different varieties of English. Acceptance on this level does not guarantee that the more positive attitudes will be communicated to students in the classroom. Thus, a second step is needed.

The Second Step

The next step involves the careful monitoring of behaviors that communicate low expectations. In addition to those teacher behaviors identified by researchers, we might add still another—insensitive patterns of correction. (For a fuller discussion of student anxieties which are created through insensitive patterns of correcting students, see Scott's discussion of cross-cultural communication conflicts in the classroom, 1978.) Each of these behaviors, i.e. providing response opportunities, positive feedback, challenging questions, sensitive corrections, can be observed, evaluated and controlled; they lend themselves well to monitoring.

It seems that the implementation of monitoring plans works best when conducted with other colleagues. That is, small groups or teams might meet periodically to discuss their observations, evaluations, and progress with monitoring behaviors that communicate low expectations. Interesting discoveries can be made. For example, one teacher reported that he discovered that he engaged in nonacceptance behaviors, not because of his negative attitudes toward students or their language, but because he was quite sensitive to the embarrassment caused by asking students challenging and probing questions when he knew full well that they could not answer the questions. When a team member asked. "What can the students do well? What are their strengths?," he admitted that he wasn't quite sure. This kind of response points to the need for a third step in our systematic approach to attitudinal changes: observing for positive attributes of students.

The Third Step

The third step involves careful observation of students' language learning behaviors and communication patterns and monitoring of evaluative statements about students, particularly students who have been unsuccessful in performing school-related tasks. In the same way that we accumulate data on students' weaknesses, we can accumulate data on their strengths. In other words, we can design a 'balanced data bank' on students' performance. I am suggesting that a list of positive evaluations to match the list of negative evaluations of students' performance and behaviors would provide a more accurate profile of a student. From my experience with teacher workshops on this topic, I have found that school personnel tend to respond to this last suggestion enthusiastically, noting that the balanced data bank technique is practical and easy to implement. Some teachers have used the technique with students and with parents. Unsuccessful students have a difficult time finding enough positive attributes of themselves to balance the negative attributes. Their responses are quite similar to that of the teacher mentioned above—they're not quite sure what the strengths are. Armed with the information provided from the balanced data bank technique, the teacher can avoid the problem mentioned in step two, i.e., changing one set of behaviors only to take on another set that might be no more effective than the first. And ideally, the three steps mentioned here would complement each other, thereby fulfilling my criteria for a systematic approach to attitudinal changes.

Admittedly though, I have not been successful with selling the entire approach to any single group, though many have shown strong preferences for the balanced data bank technique. What seems more important than the total acceptance of my model is the acceptance of the basic principle of the model: attitudinal changes are dependent upon systematic approaches. The approach offered here involves the dissemination of information, observation and self-monitoring of teacher behaviors, observation and evaluation of students' strengths and weaknesses.

This discussion of attitudes has more to do with the learning environment than with the instructional materials. The focus on attitudes and learning environment is, however, in keeping with the ruling in *King*. A careful reading of the court order will reveal that the language barrier is often referred to in connection with nonsupportive learning environments that are created from negative attitudes toward the home language of some students. If the language is no longer perceived as illogical, unprincipled bundles of mistakes, then those attitudes shown to interfere with the educational process can no longer be supported.

The Use of the Language System for Planning Instruction

To legitimize the use of the black English language system for planning instructional programs is to admit that information is available that can and should be used to better accommodate the learning needs of black English speakers. Usually when we think of accommodating the needs of minority students, we think of remedial programs. It should be noted that the plaintiffs in *King* did not request special programs for the eleven children. Parents were already concerned about the amount of time their children spent out of the regular classroom, most often in remedial programs. One objection to remedial programs is that they are generally based on deficit models. With language this means that language differences are, in effect, treated as language deficiencies. In addition, when dialect variation is addressed in regular programs, language differences are seldom given respectable treatment. Considering the notion that we are dealing with a language system, and that information about the system can be incorporated into instructional programs, the implications are that special programs need not be remedial and that regular programs need not always present information about dialect variation in a negative way. The problem of changing instructional materials is, in many ways, similar to that of changing attitudes. People tend to be willing to acknowledge the existence of different linguistic systems or sub-systems but unwilling to behave as though the differences are anything but deficiencies. Resistances to change are found in both special and regular instructional programs.

To illustrate my point, I will consider one of the proposals offered for accommodating students in language diverse classrooms. The basic design features for a special instructional program are offered by Anastasiow and Hanes in their book *Language Patterns of Poverty Children*. The authors maintain that "poverty children" (rural whites, blacks, and Puerto Ricans) speak a "structured and rule-governed language, . . . are equal to their middle class peers in language development, . . . and are capable of achieving in school" (1976, 101). But they also note that "until poverty children have ample experience in matching their own language with that of the school, formal reading instructions should be replaced with an intensive oral language program" (1976, 104). As late as 1976 we find the advocacy of pedagogy that was rendered as unacceptable nearly a decade before. That is, most investigations of dialect and reading problems agreed that it was impractical and unnecessary to delay teaching reading until after students have learned to speak standard English. It is equally important that such a proposal comes after the acknowledgment that linguistic differences do not reflect linguistic deficiencies. From the perspective of language pedagogy, the notion advanced by these authors is that instead of remediating deficits, we should be remediating differences. Put more dramatically, students must give up, "the right to be" for "the right to read." The language that students bring to school, different though it may be, is an intimate part of their being.

In legitimizing the use of information about the black English language system for educational planning, one would expect for goals of special instructional programs to be targeted towards expanding language competencies rather than towards remediating language differences.

Seldom do we find references to changes in regular classroom material with regard to accommodating diverse language and cultural background of ethnic minorities. In regular instructional programs, language samples associated with dialect variation usually serve as examples of incorrect, unacceptable, uneducated, or inappropriate language patterns. It is possible, however, to include information about the language and cultural patterns of ethnic minorities in a more positive light.

For example, spelling textbooks often contain sections on word-etymologies. African and Afro-American derived words could be included in such sections. In literature textbooks, analyses of literary froms could include samples of metaphors, alliteration, etc., from speech samples representing the Afro-American speech community. In reading textbooks, exercises for developing inferential skills might contain samples of proverbs frequently used in Afro-American speech communities. Excellent examples of each are provided by Smitherman (1977) in her book *Talkin and Testifyin.*

Whether one takes *King* or the current literature as a point of reference, the recognition of black English as a language system implies the need for attitudinal changes, and the legitimacy given to using information about the black English language system suggests that we must find more positive ways to treat dialect variation in the classroom. Indeed one might take as a point of reference the observations of the well-known author Toni Morrison. In response to the questions "What do you think is distinctive about your fiction? What makes it good?" She replied:

> The language, only the language. It is the thing that black people love so much—the saying of the words, holding them on the tongue, experimenting with them, playing with them. It's a love, a passion. . . . The worst of all possible things that could happen would be to lose that language. There are certain things I cannot say without recourse to my language. It's terrible to think that a child with five different present tenses comes to school to be faced with those books that are less than his own language, which is him, that are sometimes permanently damaging. He

may never know the etymology of Africanisms in his language, not even know that "hip" is a real word or that "the dozens" meant something. This is a really cruel fallout of racism. I know the standard English. I want to use it to help restore the other language, the lingua franca (1981, 27).

References

Anastasiow, N., and M. Hanes. *Language Patterns of Poverty Children.* Springfield, Ill.: Charles C. Thomas, 1976.

Dworkin, N., and Y. Dworkin. "The Legacy of Pygmalion in the Classroom." *Phi Delta Kappan* 60 (June 1979).

Kernan, S. "Teacher Expectations and Student Achievement." *Phi Delta Kappan* (June 1979): 716–18.

Morrison, T. "An Interview with Toni Morrison." *New Republic* (March 1981).

Seligman, D., G. Tucker, and W. Lambert. "The Effects of Speech, Style and Other Attributes on Teachers' Attitudes toward Pupils." *Language in Society* (April 1972).

Scott, J. "Black Modes of Communication and Conflicts in the Schools." In *Cross-Cultural Communications in the Schools*, edited by C. Moody and K. Lind. Ann Arbor, Mich.: Program for Educational Opportunity, University of Michigan, 1978.

Smitherman, Geneva. *Talkin and Testifyin: The Language of Black America.* Boston: Houghton Mifflin, 1977.

Taylor, O. "Black Language and What to Do about It: Some Black Community Perspectives. In *Ebonics: The True Language of Black Folks*, edited by R. Williams. St Louis: Institute of Black Studies, 1975.

Williams, F. "Psychological Correlates of Speech Characteristics." *Journal of Speech and Hearing* 13 (1970).

Williams, F., J. Whitehead, and L. Miller. "Attitudinal Correlates of Children's Speech Characteristics." Project #0-0336, U.S. Department of Health, Education and Welfare, Washington, D.C.: Office of Education, 1971.

Language Tips: The Black Ebonics Speaker and the Reading Process

Jesse Perry
San Diego City Schools, California

Because language arts education involves two receiving processes—reading and listening—and two production processes—speaking and writing, the major achievement goals of an English language arts program should be to enable students

> to speak effectively in a variety of situations and to a variety of audiences,
>
> to listen carefully in a variety of situations,
>
> to write with clarity in a number of situations,
>
> to read with understanding and assurance, and
>
> to think logically and creatively.

A functional language arts program would include additional aspects such as providing for real language experiences—conversation, dramatization, improvisation, letter writing, and reports. These language arts experiences should develop a broader sequence of language capabilities. Speaking and listening are the first experiences of the child. Therefore, oral communication is the most widely used method of expression. Vocabulary building, grammar, usage, and creative expression are also necessary components of a functional language arts program of which reading is an integral part.

Often, when the question of social class dialects is raised, the dialects as spoken by black Americans readily come to mind. No single dialect is spoken by black Americans. The dialects of many persons in this group are very similar to the dialects of white Americans living in the same geographic region. The attitude of teachers reflected in their reactions to a student with a dialect different from their own may be a significant factor in the development of the student's self-image and consequent success in language arts and reading.

Students who speak a dialect should be *motivated* to use standard English at the earliest time possible. On the other hand, the elementary student dialect speaker should not be forced to change language patterns too early; if this is done, the student-school relationship may be destroyed. Students come to school with language patterns developed over several years; therefore, it is not possible to change those students' dialect overnight, even if that were a desirable goal. A gradual presentation of new speech patterns is more effective than a forced presentation at the beginning of the school experience. It is important for children to feel they are bringing something from home to the school. To deny the student's language is to deny the student, for language is a major part of one's total self.

What can the teacher do?

Provide opportunities to listen to folktales or riddles written in dialect and in standard English.

Enhance student awareness of alternative dialects through the use of films, records, tape recordings, and filmstrips of outstanding black persons, especially recorded speech of these persons.

Use pattern practice activities with students as a method of teaching an alternate dialect.

Johnson (1968) advises the use of certain sequential second-language techniques in teaching of standard English.

1. Select one sound or grammatical item to teach.
2. Help the pupils to *hear* the sound or *recognize* the grammatical structure.
3. Have the pupils *reproduce* the standard item.
4. Help the pupils to *hear* or *recognize* the difference between the standard item and the equivalent nonstandard item.
5. Have the pupils discriminate between the standard and nonstandard item.
6. Encourage the pupils to use the standard item in their speech.

In conclusion, then, three things are needed. First, institutions at all levels must be willing to change. Second, teachers who are knowledgeable about language and language learning must evaluate such learning. And finally, students must be willing to consider—based upon language experience—some alternate ways of communicating to a wider audience now and for the rest of their lives.

References

Bentley, Robert H., and Samuel D. Crawford. *Black Language Reader.* Glenview, Ill.: Scott, Foresman & Co., 1972.

Johnson, Kenneth R. *Teaching Culturally Disadvantaged Pupils.* Chicago: Science Research Associates, 1968.

Jones, C. Dalton. "Ebonics and Reading." *Journal of Black Studies* 9 (June 1979).

Lin, San-su C. *Pattern Practice in the Teaching of English to Students with a Non-Standard Dialect.* New York: Bureau of Publications, Teachers College, Columbia University, 1965.

Woodford, Jean. "Ebonics: A Legitimate System of Oral Communication." *Journal of Black Studies* 9 (June 1979).

Tips for Language Teaching: Teacher Attitude and Ghetto Language

Helen H. Johnson
McMichael Junior High School, Detroit, Michigan

Differences in previous school experience and training, in emotional maturity, in social activities, and in environmental background present real challenges in all classrooms. When these differences are manifest in a classroom of thirty or more disadvantaged students with a different dialect, the real challenge becomes a horrendous nightmare for teachers, especially for some English teachers. They agonizingly escape to a "new teaching experience," an early retirement or a "different job which offers greater challenges for a person with special talents."

Researchers studying motivation of children for school work have found that disadvantaged black children are impressed early with the idea that their futures are limited. In the presumed absence of long-range opportunities, the children naturally are more inclined to think in terms of satisfying their immediate desires than they are inclined to prepare in school for eventual success. Ghetto dialect, while substantially different from standard English, works at home and in the neighborhood. In the homes and neighborhoods where poor black children grow up, education does not seem to make much difference in how people live. Quite often, students' reactions to school are miniatures of the feelings their parents have about the bigger world of work—it can not or will not work for them.

The effects show first in language, the most vital tool. The students are lost because they cannot communicate their feelings nor can they evoke the feelings of others. They need the vital tool which will make it possible for them to "let out" and "bring in" information. Teach them, then, how to express their ideas and how to get ideas from others in order to help them develop as individuals. This development of and exposure to ideas will give the individual hope, which is basic for anyone who is going to do anything useful in life. Teachers help tremendously when they allow a child to appreciate his or her own language competence and capabilities, and at the same time rid themselves of the misconceptions that a disadvantaged child does not have ideas or does not have a well-developed language.

Teachers might encourage changes sooner and faster by providing alternatives which enrich and expand those language competencies and capabilities which exist. Lessons geared to effect dialect changes should not be the initiating lessons for the disadvantaged. Whoever teaches those lessons, if and when they are taught, must know how to anticipate the problems of the class. Such comprehension is possible only if the teacher is familiar with the structure of both the language he or she uses and that which the students use. When the teacher understands what the student's dialect is and what it represents to the child, what the second dialect is and what *it* represents to the child, then the second dialect (in this case, standard English) can be introduced as an alternative. In this final phase of language study, the teacher might only need to say to the class, "This is strange, but it's human and worth knowing."

The following short list suggests some of the attitudes and competencies needed by the ghetto teacher.

1. Respect the culture within the community.

2. Respect differences in people.

3. Do not limit the ghetto child to standard English.

4. Do not sell standard dialect as the sole selector of the winners or the losers.

5. Talk about the variety of American culture, put the student into a context in which he must use another dialect. Discover how easily he learns to speak the "language of affairs."

6. Involve children, especially black children, in the study of the varieties of language.

7. Develop and use materials which stress *informal* uses of language, the conversational style of American language.

8. See that materials, if written in dialect, include the varieties of that dialect so that they are more realistic or relevant. Much more is involved than omission of "s" on the third person singular.

9. Give the task of "tidying-up" speech to those trained in the area. They know more about what speech is and what it is not. English teachers have little or no training in language and cannot make necessary distinctions. They are stopped, generally, be-

cause too many accept only *that language* which is *their language.* All language exercises, all literature, and all compositions reflect *their choices.*

10. If the decision is made to teach standard English as a second dialect, consider the following observations seriously:
    a. No teacher should announce the acquisition of standard English as an aim—that is part of the problem.
    b. So many black and poor children have been and are being harmed by insidious attitudes of some teachers that they now expect injuries when someone shows up with a corrective package.
    c. Teachers should stop talking about respecting language differences and begin acting as if they indeed do. Standard English cannot be sold as a panacea for economic discrimination because the child knows better.
    d. Perhaps the most difficult decision of all is to determine who is to decide on what *is* to be changed.

References

Francis, W. Nelson. *The Structure of American English.* New York: Ronald, 1958.
Goodlad, John. "Schools for Individuals." Lecture given at Wayne State University, Detroit, Michigan, July 8, 1966.

Inner-City English

Walter F. Edwards
Wayne State University, Detroit, Michigan

Ideally, the teacher should strive to make the inner-city English (ICE) speaker bidialectal. The standard dialect should be taught for its functional value, but the native dialect should be tolerated if not actively promoted. It is, of course, nonsense to think that it is impossible to learn the standard dialect without first cleansing the tongue of the vernacular.

I see no benefit in a program aimed at teaching inner-city English in schools. The domains of inner-city English are in the homes, the streets, the clubs, the poetry, and song lyrics of black people. Inner-city English will thrive, as all living languages will thrive, as long as the social dynamics which brought them into being are active. In the school, the major emphasis should be on written standard English, and the black child should be encouraged to learn to use this variety as effectively as possible.

Many sympathetic teachers of English in inner-city areas are genuinely puzzled as to what use should be made of inner-city English in the classroom. I feel that its linguistic properties should be acknowledged, and children who natively speak it should be given the special attention they need: not special attention as dunces and linguistically impoverished nuisances, but as children from a different linguistic background than their white or middle-class black peers. This means that speakers of inner-city English deserve the same sympathetic attention and social status in class similar to that normally accorded to, for instance, a Spanish-speaking child in a Portuguese language class.

What I am saying here should not be taken as being a rejection of what Dr. Geneva Smitherman said in an interview reported in *Teacher's Voice* (1978). Dr. Smitherman was essentially inveighing against speech tests and other interview procedures which use the speech of black people as a means of denying them employment and other forms of social and economic advancement. I agree with Dr. Smitherman's statement that, "in terms of written language which is for the purposes of conveying information you need a kind of uniformity" (1978, 8). I'm suggesting that standard English be that uniform system.

Clearly, those who advocate teaching inner-city English in schools are not without scientific support. Simpkins, Simpkins, and Holt's (1977) successful experiment in teaching black children to read material in black English made that point persuasively. Nonetheless, I feel that it is possible, and desirable in terms of the ultimate goals of the American education system, to teach children to write and read standard English in schools. There is, however, very little chance of success if the grammatical and phonological (including the prosodic) features of inner-city English are not taken into central consideration in English teaching programs in inner-city areas. Applied linguists are challenged to provide teachers with solid material to do the job properly in Detroit and other cities with large black working-class populations.

Finally, I suggest the following game-plan for teachers of English in schools where black children speak inner-city English predominantly.

1. Learn the linguistic rules of inner-city English. This knowledge is obtainable from the relatively large number of books already published on the subject (e.g., Labov 1966, 1972a, 1972b; Dillard 1972; Fasold 1972). Several colleges and universities offer courses in the subject.

2. Use the linguistic information to predict where such speakers will have pronunciation, prosodic, and grammatical difficulties in speaking and writing standard English as that dialect is spoken and written in the region.

3. Prepare teaching materials which address the specific difficulties which you anticipate your students will have or which they already have.

4. Integrate these tactics with your regular methods and programs for teaching written and spoken standard English.

5. Above all, do not approach the teaching of English to inner-city English speakers in a manner which can cause them to feel that their natural speech habits are diseased.

References

Bailey, C. J. *Variation and Linguistic Theory*. Washington, D.C.: Center for Applied Linguistics, 1973.

Dillard, J. L. *Black English: Its History and Usage*. New York: Random House, 1972.

———. *Lexicon of Black English*. New York: Seabury, 1977.

Edwards, Walter. "Sociolinguistic Behavior in Rural and Urban Circumstances in Guyana." Ph.D. diss., University of York, England, 1975.

———. "Linguistic, Cultural, and Social Considerations in the Preparation of ELT Programmes in Guyana." Paper read at AILA Congress, Montreal, 1978.

Fasold, Ralph. *Tense Marking in Black English*. Washington, D.C.: Center for Applied Linguistics, 1972.

Kurath, Hans, and R. McDavid. *The Pronunciation of English in the Atlantic States*. Ann Arbor, Mich.: University of Michigan Press, 1972.

Labov, William. *Social Stratification of English in New York*. Washington, D.C.: Center for Applied Linguistics, 1966.

———. *Language in the Inner City*. Philadelphia: University of Pennsylvania Press, 1972a.

———. *Sociolinguistic Patterns*. Philadelphia: University of Pennsylvania Press, 1972b.

Rickford, John. "The Insights of the Mesolect." In *Pidgins and Creoles: Current Trends and Prospects*, edited by D. DeCamp and I. Hancock. Washington, D.C.: Georgetown University Press, 1975.

———. "Carrying the New Wave into Syntax—The Case of BE BIN." In *Analyzing Variations in Language*, edited by Ralph Fasold and Roger Shuy. Washington, D.C.: Georgetown University Press, 1975.

Simpkins, Gary, C. Simpkins, and G. Holt. *Bridge: A Cross-Cultural Reading Program*. Boston: Houghton Mifflin, 1977.

Smitherman, Geneva. "An Interview." *Teacher's Voice* (November 1978): 8–9.

Wolfram, Walter. *A Sociolinguistic Description of Detroit Negro Speech*. Washington, D.C.: Center for Applied Linguistics, 1969.

———. "The Relationship of White Southern Speech to Vernacular Black English." *Language* 1 (1974): 498–525.

Tips: Deciphering Dialect

Jacqueline Brice Finch
College of the Virgin Islands, Christiansted, St. Croix

How perplexing it was to discover that I did not understand the "English" of some of my black students when in 1971 I began teaching in a high school on St. Croix, the largest of the United States Virgin Islands. As a third-generation black Washingtonian, I considered myself able to cope with almost any form of black English. However, my background did not prepare me for the multiplicity of dialects which abound on this Caribbean island. First, Crucian, the dialect spoken by natives of St. Croix, did not exactly duplicate the dialect spoken on St. Thomas, only forty miles away. Next, the students from the British islands, such as Barbados, Jamaica and Antigua, often spoke with a British accent. Imagine hearing "white British English" emanating from a definitely chocolate soul! That phenomenon alone interfered with my comprehension. Add a dribble of "continentals," students and a teacher who had been raised in the United States, with their attendant dialects, and the panoply was complete.

Although many educators have addressed the issue of dialect and the teaching of English, I have learned to use the following procedure to foster communication not only between student and teacher but also among students with the optimum goal of achiving proficiency in the use of standard American English in the classroom:

1. During orientation, discuss dialect as a valuable and useful means of communicating under certain conditions (e.g., strengthening ethnic, cultural, and peer group bonds); encourage students to contribute examples.

2. Be frank about your ignorance of particular dialect words, expressions, etc.

3. Be patient with students, allowing them to articulate their messages without interruption.

4. Be courteous in asking them to repeat words unintelligible, perhaps only to you.

5. Never ridicule or allow other students to ridicule the speech of a student.

6. Be supportive of the students, encouraging them to practice standard English.

7. Encourage students to teach you their dialect, explain the nuances, to better enable you to teach them standard English.

8. Once the class is comfortable with language differences, allow students to share in the query response to "what do you mean?"

Having taught on the high school and college level for nine years, I am still on par, not above, my students in deciphering dialect. We are all learning each other's English to utilize the standard better.

II Reading

Introduction: Reading

Miriam T. Chaplin
Rutgers University, Camden, New Jersey

At every level of education, there are large numbers of minority students who experience difficulty in reading tasks. For many years, researchers, educators, parents, and legislators with varying degrees of sincerity have sought to solve the "reading problem," but their efforts have not been completely successful. Test scores reveal that more minority students are learning to read today then ever before, but there are still many students who exhibit severe deficiencies. Moreover, it appears that as students move up through the grades, they become less able to meet institutional demands in reading. Therefore, the "right to read" publicly acknowledged by the Commissioner of Education more than a decade ago has become another of the basic freedoms that eludes minority students.

Frank Smith (1974, 237), has said that "reading involves the mixture or interreaction of information that the reader receives through his visual system and information that he already has available in his head, behind his eyeballs." James Moffett (1968, 15) identifies reading as a "shallow mechanical activity and a deep operation of mind and spirit." Both of these definitions imply that reading is far more than a visual decoding process; it is an experience which demands the students' participation on a linguistic, cognitive, and emotional level. In order to guide students' development in reading, instruction must encompass more than an emphasis on the printed symbols. It must give an equal amount of consideration to the students who are called upon to process the symbols and synthesize them with prior learning. In many reading lessons, however, particularly those designated as remedial instruction, teachers spend an inordinate amount of time teaching children to "break the code" without focusing attention on the interpretation that lies beyond the symbols. For too many minority students enrolled in these classes, reading becomes an external thing to be learned rather than a dynamic verbal transaction between the reader and writer. Those students who are adept at code breaking are considered good readers. They are successful at completing correctly the steady stream of duplicated lessons and workbook exercises as well as the isolated skill items on standardized tests. As a result, they are rubber stamped "average" and little attention is given to "what's behind their eyeballs" or to their "mind and spirits." On the other hand, there are those students who require a more personalized holistic approach and as a result do not relate to the mechanical aspect of reading. Their inability to attain the levels expected of them leads to failure, and they find themselves labeled "remedial." Since this metaphoric malady is rarely ever cured, these students bear this stigma through all of their school years.

Minority students can be found in either of these groups, and it is apparent that their needs are not being met adequately. More importantly, their capacities for achievement are not challenged. These students are the subjects of the articles that follow. Written by authors who are themselves minorities, the articles contain philosophies and techniques that emanate from the experiences of these authors as teachers and researchers. Hence, there is a comfortable balance between theory and practice. While no effort has been made to seek consensus, the articles represent a collective belief that the potential of minority students is yet to be tapped and every educator has a responsibility to tap it.

Dorothy Strickland's article, "Giving Them a Better Start in Language and Reading" provides a comprehensive framework for beginning reading instruction. She examines the role of parents in the educative process, the effects of community pressures on the school, evaluation and teacher preparation. In addition, she offers practical suggestions that can be used to foster language development which she identifies as an important aspect of reading instruction.

"Using a Black Learning Style" is the title of an article by Dr. George Cureton, who uses the black learning style as the basis of an innovative approach to reading instruction in the elementary school. The target population for this method is the inner city child, but it can be used in other situations as well.

The attitude of the classroom teacher is the focal point of the article written by Constance and Beauford Batty. These authors identify techniques that are applicable to any elementary classroom situation but are especially helpful to persons working with minority students.

Minority students in the secondary schools often complain of the generation gap between their parents and teachers, and themselves.

Ire Adams Page presents a strategy for "Closing the Generation Gap and Turning Students on to Reading." Using poetry and prose written by black authors, Page shows how she motivated a group of Upward Bound students to read.

For a multiplicity of reasons, minority students have never fared well on standardized tests. Much effort has been expended to identify the reasons for this difficulty, and some of the observations appear to be accurate. In spite of this, students are still faced with tests. Indeed, the testing concept is so entrenched in education that it is unlikely that it will disappear in the near future. The wisest course of action is to prepare minority students to compete with others in the testing situation. This is the rationale behind the article by Dr. Irwin McPhail, "Why Teach Test Wiseness?".

My own article, "Implications in Personal Construct Theory for Reading Instruction," is a brief analysis of George Kelly's theory and the impact it can have on reading instruction for minority students. The dichotomy between the power of the human personality and the historical powerlessness experienced by minorities is viewed as a primary factor in the reading difficulties encountered by students.

Finally, Dolores Straker reviews "Reading Materials Printed in Black English." Based on a conviction that there is a mismatch between black children's oral language and printed materials in standard English, Straker's article identifies dialect readers, programs in oral language development, and programs which emphasize teacher awareness of black English as three approaches which could have a positive effect on the reading performance of black children.

The key to effective instruction and successful readers lies in the teacher's ability to foster a link between students' internal perceptions and external realities. When this occurs, motivation is imminent and the stimulated student will make progress. Growth moves outward from the student. In Moffett's words: "The teacher's art is to move with this movement, a subtle act possible only if he shifts his gaze from the subject to the learner, for the subject is in the learner" (1968, 59).

References

Moffett, James. *Teaching the Universe of Discourse.* Boston: Houghton Mifflin, 1968.

Smith, Frank. "Reading." In *Language and Language Arts,* edited by Johanna DeStefano and Sharon Fox. Boston: Little, Brown & Co., 1974.

Early Childhood Development and Reading Instruction

Dorothy Strickland
Columbia University, Teachers College, New York, New York

The Way Young Children Learn and the Implications for Reading Instruction

Probably the single most important idea for teachers to keep in mind as they plan for young children is that each is an individual worthy of dignity and respect for his or her uniqueness. This suggests that the reading program at any level should be flexible enough to accommodate a variety of cognitive styles and learning rates. Materials and activities must broaden the range of possibilities rather than reduce them to a lockstep, narrowly defined skill system.

A respect for individuality will encourage the reading teacher to provide instructional materials and learning experiences that offer a wide range of opportunities for success. For example, to extend the enjoyment of a story read aloud, one child may enjoy quietly browsing through the book on her own. Another child may enjoy painting or drawing a picture related to the story and perhaps dictating a caption to go along with his picture. Still others may wish to dramatize a scene from the story. This will take planning with a brief discussion of characterization, setting, and plot. Still other children may enjoy dictating a brief response to the story or listening to a teacher-prepared, tape-recorded version of it. All of these children would be engaged in profitable language experiences that are reading related, yet each may choose one or more of the activities to engage in.

Children learn best when they are active participants in the instruction. Even very young children can be a part of the decision-making process determining what and how they learn. Young children should be given an opportunity to suggest content for experience stories and to select materials for reading aloud. Children can help share in planning projects and in developing interest centers. They should be encouraged to bring in their books, pictures, and objects, and to present their ideas for discussion. Teachers should be aware of the child's ability to contribute to the daily environment in order to foster active involvement in the learning process.

Children learn to communicate in a variety of ways. They communicate by listening, talking, by making body gestures, movements, and facial expressions, and by writing and reading. The reading program should reflect the idea that reading is but one facet of a broader communications process. It is an extremely important facet to be sure, but nevertheless, it is but one part of a total communications network. Research tells us that children who excel in one area of communication generally do well in all the others. Teachers should look critically at each aspect of the language arts so that when activities are planned, they will take advantage of every opportunity to extend and integrate the kinds of language experiences being offered.

Young children learn best through firsthand interactions with people, materials, and ideas in their environments. The reading program should foster the child's concept development in relation to direct experiences. Story charts and child-written books and poems can grow out of the natural hands-on activities in which children are engaged. Recipes, for example, should be prominently displayed and read before children begin to cook. By so doing, children will learn something about the usefulness of reading and the importance of following directions.

A trip to the grocery store should be preceded by the creation of a list of things to buy. The list should be written with the children watching and the items checked off as they are purchased. Every opportunity to relate reading to the children's real world will help build interest in reading as something necessary just as listening and talking are necessary and useful for their needs.

Children learn and express themselves both through what they know and what they feel. They need opportunities to communicate their feelings and to share in what others are feeling. The reading program should foster the affective and cognitive development of young children simultaneously. For example, a discussion and listing of words that tell how they feel when they are happy or sad or a discussion of how they might have reacted if they had been a certain storybook character will help them to value language as an effective means of communicating emotions.

Young children also need opportunities to experiment with language. Their most productive experimentation is included in their play. They need to play with ideas, test them out, make mistakes, and try "new" ways of doing things. Just as we allow children to manipulate blocks, paints, and clay, we must also allow them to experiment with words and letters and with the sounds that letters represent. Children who have numerous opportunities to create individual and group story charts, and who are read aloud to frequently, very naturally become curious about the words and letters that represent the ideas expressed. Teachers should use this natural curiosity to develop the reading concepts children need to acquire.

For example, occasionally making a second story chart that is identical to one the children have already enjoyed allows pupils to compare sentence strips cut from the second chart with those on the original. Sentence strips may then be cut into individual words and reconstructed into sentences using the original chart as a guide. Individual words and letters may be matched with those on the original story chart. An array of games and activities may be developed in which children are having fun manipulating language and developing important concepts about reading at the same time.

Language Development and the Implications for Reading Instruction

In addition to knowing something about how children learn, the teacher of young children should know something about the nature of language and language development. Teachers often have misconceptions about the language-learning process. They will often remark that a particular child or group of children has no language. In reality, by the time a child enters first grade, he or she knows all the phonemes (sounds) that are used in his or her dialect and the major structural or grammatical patterns as well.

Another common misconception is that children must be taught the meanings of the first words they learn to read. Actually, these words should be in the children's listening and speaking vocabularies. What the child must learn to do is to associate sets or configurations of written symbols that represent the words he knows. After children learn to read, of course, many new words will be acquired through both reading and writing activities.

Teachers should remember that speech comes before written language. Writing is code for speech. Children must learn to break that code. Since children learn to speak long before they learn to read and write, they already know their language. Their need is to learn to decode its written representation. It makes sense to begin with a representation that is real language for the children being taught.

Reading programs that make use of the child's own natural language as a foundation for word recognition skills would seem to be more akin to the natural language learning patterns of children.

The Reading Process and the Implications for Reading Instruction

The "reading process" describes what people do as they read. Teachers of young children would profit from acquainting themselves with theoretical models describing the reading process so that their instruction may be more related to language development and to what we know about how children learn. Models have been developed of what is thought to be happening from the initial perception of written symbols to the point where a meaningful message is understood by the reader. These models are necessarily theoretical in nature, since few of the behaviors of reading can be observed. A useful source of information about theoretical models is that of Singer and Ruddell (1976).

Models of the reading process generally include prediction by the reader, a search for data to confirm guesses, and an understanding of the message. The child's own general knowledge, language ability, and familiarity with the material help to build a store of expectations that allows him or her to predict what words might make sense in a given passage. These expectations may be tested by the child using various understandings about language and knowledge of the content. As we consider these components of the reading process, it becomes obvious that they are very much like those processes used by the child as he acquires oral language. Using this as a theoretical base, the teacher can develop strategies for reading that are natural and which make sense to the child (Pflaum 1974, 114).

For example, printed forms of words should always be presented in meaningful context, already a part of the speaking vocabulary of the child. Children should expect to get meaning from printed material and should have opportunities to have their own oral language transformed into print and read aloud. To the beginning reader, reading may well be regarded as listening to talk which has been written down.

In summary, children need to develop a sense of what a word actually is and to develop consistent expectations of meaningfulness in reading from the very beginning. As instruction proceeds, they know about language and the written materials they encounter. Children will add and maintain words within their sight vocabularies when they begin to perceive sound-symbol correspondences. Thus, they should be encouraged to use context and decoding clues in combination as a means to test new words.

Emerging Issues

During the 1960s, educators in the United States took a close look at preventive approaches to reading failure. A large amount of federal funding for research studies and innovative projects at the pre-first-grade level led to the exploration of ways to improve the learning capability of children termed "disadvantaged." The results of these efforts had far-reaching implications for all children and, to a great extent, served as the basis for the current issues outlined below.

Continuity between Preelementary- and Elementary-School Programs

For many years a demarcation existed between what were considered appropriate instruction practices for preelementary-school children and the instructional objectives and practices of the elementary school. The lack of articulation which continues to exist between these two levels of education places an unnecessary burden of discontinuity on the child's education.

Preelementary and elementary schools in the same community should cooperate by at least sharing information related to curriculum goals and practices. In some cases they might even develop a cooperative curriculum which would reflect the developmental growth patterns of the children they serve. This effort works best if parents and community agencies are included in the planning.

Establishing and Articulating Theory and Practice

Opinions differ on what kind of early childhood education is desirable. In terms of reading and language arts instruction, these differences are both wide and varied. As adults, we make the decisions about what is desirable for the education of young children. We set goals, develop specific objectives and plan educational procedures accordingly.

A major issue in preelementary education today is the proliferation of packaged reading and language arts programs. Such programs are all too often purchased as a response to public pressure for an earlier start in reading rather than the natural outgrowth of thoughtfully conceived instructional goals and objectives. Thus, the packaged programs tend to dictate the goals and objectives of the instructional program rather than respond to them.

One critical task for early childhood educators is the examination of what they believe about how children learn and what the content and method of the learning should be. They must provide themselves with a theoretical framework or point of reference from which to operate. Although this point of reference may range anywhere from a preacademic/behavioristic model to a discovery approach, it should reflect what both the administrators and the teachers of a given program believe.

Once the theoretical framework has been established, program goals should follow. From these, the content and methodology will naturally flow. In all cases, the program's goals, content, and methodology should relate to the theoretical framework that has been established. For example, if the theoretical framework includes a model of learning that stresses motivation by external reinforcement and product-oriented goals, the instructional objectives would develop through carefully structured sequences from simple to complex. Immediate feedback and reinforcement for each set of behavioral objectives would be important. The classroom environment and schedule of activities would be highly structured with a minimum of distractions.

If the theoretical framework includes a model of learning that stresses active learner participation and goals that focus on the process rather than the product, the instructional objectives would develop through a planned orderly schedule; however, there would be considerable flexibility and children would be motivated to inquire and extend their understandings. Affective and cognitive goals would be balanced. The classroom environment would include interest and learning centers. Activities would be integrated in content and by direct and indirect instruction. (Nurss 1976.)

Therefore, when materials are made or purchased and when activities are planned for child learning, they should reflect the philosophy of education in operation. This philosophy or theoretical framework should be developed by administrators and teachers in cooperation with parents and should be articulated both in what the educational staff says and does.

The Role of Parents in Reading Instruction

Parents should understand that they are the child's first and most important teachers of reading. It is virtually impossible to overestimate the importance of home influence on the child's acquisition of reading skills.

In most cases, parents still have almost the sole responsibility for the child's development during the critical years of language learning. We know that reading is a language process. Therefore, the kind of start the child gets during these important language learning years will have lasting effects.

Parents have always had a profound influence upon the education of their own children. As parent involvement becomes increasingly prevalent, however, the effects of parents upon the general quality of instruction in the schools is strengthened. The decisions that parents make—both as the heads of individual families and as members of the school community—have far-reaching implications. In order to serve children well, these decisions must come from responsibility and knowledge rather than as reactions to frustration and confusion.

Thus, when parents ask about the reading program, their questions should be answered with clarity and forthrightness. But whether they ask or not, there are several facts they should know.

They need to know the importance of their own role as teachers of reading.

They need to know how reading is related to speaking, listening, and writing. They should understand how the broad array of communications activities helps to enhance reading readiness and indeed are an integral part of the reading program.

They should be aware that there are many approaches to the teaching of reading at any level. They should be informed of the instructional goals of the program in which their child is enrolled and given examples of the types of activities that foster those goals.

Parents should know that just as there are many different approaches to reading instruction, there are also many different ways in which children approach the task of learning to read. Parents seem to accept the fact that their children differ in size, weight, coloring, and temperament. They must be helped to understand that individual differences are equally prevalent and perhaps even more significant when they are applied to learning.

Teachers need to share, with parents, their knowledge about the literature that is available for children, and they need to help parents clarify the home's responsibilities during the reading-learning years. These responsibilities would include reading aloud to children, helping children select books, serving as a reading model, playing language games with children and taking care of hearing, vision, and speech problems promptly.

The Challenge of Community Pressure for an Earlier Start in Reading

Community pressure for earlier starts in reading seems to be increasingly prevalent throughout the United States. A good reading program within a school will provide opportunities for reading at all levels. However, it will never demand from an individual child more than he is maturationally equipped to handle.

Following this premise, no school would force all children into a single regimented system of instruction. Instead opportunities for reading—signs, labels, and child- and teacher-authored books and story charts—would be possible for the very young. Children would have many opportunities to expand language orally and to increase their listening comprehension as a foundation for more and more complex skills in reading and writing. Children would acquire language skills in as natural a manner as possible, so that reading almost seems to happen as a matter of course.

School personnel should not and need not box themselves into a position of being for or against reading instruction at the preelementary level. What they need to do is to articulate the child-centered, language arts-oriented language development program as *the reading program.*

Alternatives for Evaluation

For many years, educators have been concerned with the dangers of standardized testing, particularly the overreliance on and the misuse of standardized test scores. Such tests are becoming more common at the preelementary level where children are often administered a reading readiness test. In some cases, a test of general mental abilities or concept development may also be given. Often, the tests are neither administered nor scored by the classroom teacher, with the results being returned in the form of a list of overall scores or categories in which children have been placed.

At best, such evaluation is severely limited in its usefulness. When used as the primary source of measuring progress, however, it may lead to erroneous conclusions, since it may not accurately reflect the educational goals and objectives of the program of the children being evaluated.

Observation checklists and recordkeeping are two valuable evaluative methods that may supplement or substitute for standardized testing. The use of checklists has already been mentioned as a useful diagnostic tool. Checklists should be used as guides that help furnish a sense of what the child has accomplished and where help is needed. They serve to remind teachers of the concepts that may be missing in a child's repertoire. For example, a language arts checklist at the preelementary level might include the following examples:

Oral language—children express themselves in telling about their art work, can retell a story in sequence, and listen when other children are talking.

Visual skills—children recognize their own names in print and discriminate shapes, letters, and words.

Interest—children ask the meaning of words and signs, show an interest in books and listening to stories read aloud.

Recordkeeping is another important evaluative tool. Records must be kept systematically and on a long-term basis if they are to reveal useful information. In addition to anecdotal information related to the child's social, emotional, and cogntive development, assorted samples of the child's work should also be included. Teacher's records, assessments of the child's work, and reports to parents should also be added. Recordkeeping provides useful information about individual children, and offers invaluable information for program evaluation.

Screening Children for Learning Problems

One rapidly growing trend in the United States is the practice of screening very young children for possible learning disabilities. A series of tests or informal diagnostic procedures may be given, often upon entrance to kindergarten. These procedures may include a wide range of skills including general knowledge, language, and motor skills.

While the underlying purpose (the prevention of failure in learning) is a noble one, such procedures can be limiting or even damaging to children. Tests performed on children at this age are much less reliable than those performed on older children. Young children do not always do their best when they are confronted with entirely new situations. New materials, procedures, and new people with whom they must interact are likely to intimidate young children. Moreover, when such tests are given prior to school entrance, they do not take into account the valuable information that a teacher's observation and experience can add.

Screening for learning problems should be an ongoing process at every level. Systematic observation by a trained professional, the class-room teacher, and referrals to appropriate specialists when required may be the method that is not only most accurate but most fair to the child. There are numerous developmental checklists available to help guide teachers in their observations of children. Such checklists are often accompanied by suggested activities to help teachers make judgments and to provide practice in particular skills. In some cases, school systems have developed their own observation guides with suggestions for appropriate activities to assist in long-term screening and follow-up.

In summary, hasty judgments made in the press of time and under stress-filled circumstances for the child may result in incorrect labeling and misguided or needless referrals. The skilled classroom teacher, trained in observational techniques and in child growth and development should be at the heart of any diagnostic and prescriptive program in the schools.

Teacher Preparation

Traditionally, the goals of preelementary and elementary education have been vastly different. We have already seen that it has been relatively recent that the goals have begun to overlap. Because of this early division of roles, preelementary teachers were often trained very differently from those who were planning to teach at the elementary levels.

Since reading is taught at the preelementary level, preelementary teachers need to view reading in its broadest sense—all the language related activities that involve putting speech into print and print into speech. Such teachers need a firm foundation in language development and language arts instruction. They also need to know the appropriate procedure for fostering language growth at various stages of development.

Preelementary-school teachers need to be acquainted with instructional procedures normally used with older children, as well. Teachers need to understand how the skills students are developing now will be reinforced later on. They should be able to help the child who is already reading by providing activities that are appropriate to that child's stage of development.

Elementary and preelementary teachers need the same training in reading and language arts instruction. Many of the basic procedures are viable for instruction at any grade level, and the compelling need at the preelementary level to constantly link instructional practices to principles of child growth and development would be useful for teachers of older children.

More importantly, teacher-training institutions, agencies, and professional organizations must provide the kind of preparation described at both the preservice and inservice levels.

Balancing the Program: Affective and Cognitive Goals

Many educators are concerned that introducing print before first grade will lead to neglecting important socio-emotional and affective learnings. Indeed, this can happen where rigid, time-consuming programs are initiated.

A reading program that has at its base materials developed from the child's own experiential background will automatically produce a balanced program of affective and cognitive goals. This kind of teaching encourages personalized instruction whereby the teacher and the child share important ideas, experiences, and observations. Cognitive and affective learnings are integrated and ongoing throughout the day. Children and teachers are encouraged to be creative in the learning process.

Preelementary Programs As an Integral Part of the Educational Structure

Preelementary education has increasingly become recognized as an integral part of the total education offerings of the community. The significance of lifelong education has been extended from the cradle to the grave. While in many instances the education of the very young child may include or be restricted to educational programs designed to help parents fulfill their roles more effectively, it has also become increasingly common for children to be enrolled in some type of schooling from infancy.

Where preelementary programs exist, they are often viewed not only as educational opportunities but as a means for providing health and social services. They thus become an important socializing agency of the community. The quality of preelementary schooling and caregiving may have critical effects upon the present and future development of children as human beings. Public and private schools and agencies must work together to coordinate efforts on behalf of the child, the family, and the community.

The Need to Provide a Wide Range of Individual Differences

Much has been written about respect for the individual's rate and style of learning, especially as it relates to the acquisition of reading skills. Indeed, this point has been discussed as one of the most significant factors related to how children learn. However, understanding how children's learning styles operate involves focusing on more than modalities, e.g., whether the child prefers an auditory, visual, or tactile mode. In terms of learning styles, teachers must also be concerned with whether or not the child is an effective, independent learner or a youngster who needs a great deal of step-by-step direction or whether the child learns best in a small group or in a one-to-one setting.

In order to observe these differences, it is necessary to provide for them. A sound reading program at any level would be flexible enough to provide opportunities for those children who appear to have a preferred modality to learn that way. It will also provide opportunities for support in other modes of learning. Thus, in attempting to help four-year-olds to recognize their names, the teacher may print the names on cards to be posted on each child's locker or on some other prominent place. The children may draw, cut, and paste a small picture on their name cards as an additional clue. The teacher may also take a child's finger and trace the letters as the teacher and the child say the name or the name may be traced in sand or salt.

At the preelementary level, one of the best ways to move in the direction of individualized learning is to begin with some large group activity and then extend the learning with small group work and one-to-one instruction. An experience chart, for example, based on some whole group activity would be a record of the children's dictated response to that experience. It could be read to them and discussed by the group extensively. Many small group and individual extensions of that activity may naturally follow. Some children may reread the entire chart or the lines they have contributed; others may wish to create additional sentences. Some may draw pictures that relate to the content of the chart and dictate their own personal stories to accompany them.

A class word bank, consisting of words written on cards by the teacher may be created to which children add words they select from each new chart. An individual or group of children may use the words in the word bank to reconstruct sentences from the chart or to form new sentences.

Most important, the activities must be so varied that all children can participate at their own level and be successful.

Integrating the Language Arts

We have already discussed the importance of the integration of the language arts as it relates to what we know about how children learn. It remains a critical issue in the teaching of reading today, although research clearly points to its value.

Research has indicated repeatedly that children who are successful in one facet of the language arts are much more likely to be successful in others. Certainly our own experience and observation tell us that young children who acquire good listening skills and who demonstrate strong oral language development are likely to have very little difficulty in acquiring the skills necessary to be successful readers. And, much more often than not, it is the good readers who are the better writers of both personal and practical composition. Instruction in one area, then, would seem to increase facility in the others, which suggests that reading skills are not acquired in isolation and should not be taught as if they were. Every attempt must be made by parents and teachers to relate and coordinate reading with listening, speaking, and writing activities.

References

Allen, R. Van. *Language Experiences in Communication.* Boston: Houghton Mifflin, 1976.

Auleta, Michael S., ed. *Foundations of Early Childhood Education.* New York: Random House, 1969.

Ausubel, David P. "Viewpoints from Related Disciplines: Human Growth and Development." *Teachers College Record* 60 (February 1959): 245–54.

Beyer, Evelyn. *The Language of Children.* Washington, D.C.: Childhood Resource, 1972. Audiotape.

Bruner, Jerome Seymour. *The Process of Education.* Cambridge: Harvard University Press, 1960.

Cazden, Courtney Borden. *Child Language and Education.* New York: Holt, Rinehart & Winston, 1972.

Cohen, Dorothy H. *The Learning Child.* New York: Vintage Books, 1972.

Coody, Betty. *Using Literature with Young Children.* Dubuque, Iowa: W. C. Brown, 1973.

Durkin, Dolores. *Teaching Young Children to Read.* Boston: Allyn & Bacon, 1972.
————. *Teaching Young Children to Read.* 2d ed. Boston: Allyn & Bacon, 1974.

Foundations of Reading and Writing. 16mm. 1974. Distributed by Campus Films, New York.

Gesell, A. L. *The First Five Years of Life.* New York: Harper & Row, 1940.

Hunt, J. McVicker. *Intelligence and Experience.* New York: Ronald, 1961.

Larrick, Nancy. *A Parent's Guide to Children's Reading.* 4th ed. New York: Doubleday, 1975.

Leeper, Sarah H., Ruth Dales, Dora Skipper, and Ralph Witherspoon. *Good Schools for Young Children.* New York: Macmillan, 1974.

Lindberg, Lucile, and Rita Swedlow. *Early Childhood Education: A Guide for Observation and Participation.* Boston: Allyn & Bacon, 1976.

Nurss, Joanne. "Readiness Revisited, Diagnostic and Instructional Implications." Speech presented at Queens College/Psychological Corporation Conference, New York, October 1976.

Parker, R. K., ed. *The Preschool in Action: Exploring Early Childhood Programs.* Boston: Allyn & Bacon, 1972.

Pflaum, Susanna W. *The Development of Language and Reading in the Young Child.* Columbus, Ohio: Charles E. Merrill, 1974.

Singer, Harry, and Robert B. Ruddell. *Theoretical Models and Processes of Reading.* 2d ed. Newark, Del.: International Reading Association, 1976.

Smith, E. B., K. S. Goodman, and R. Meredith. *Language and Thinking in the Elementary School.* New York: Holt, Rinehart & Winston, 1970.

Stauffer, Russell G. *The Language Experience Approach to the Teaching of Reading.* New York: Harper & Row, 1970.

Strickland, Dorothy S. *What Every Parent Should Know about Early Childhood and Reading Development.* Tapes J169 and J170. Fairlawn, N.J.: Jab Press, 1976.

Using a Black Learning Style

George O. Cureton
Medgar Evers College, Brooklyn, New York

Many educators argue for and against the existence of a black learning style—a distinct style of learning for black children, who for complex historical, social, and economic reasons experience difficulty with academic work, especially reading.

Those who oppose the idea of a distinct "black learning style" believe that to suggest a difference in learning style between blacks and others is to reinforce the insidious myth that inner-city children are inferior. Instead, these opponents tell us that these children suffer from a lack of motivation and do not have the same motivation as middle-class children.

Motivation is important, and in fact necessary, but it will have little effect until the inner-city child's learning style has been established. Moreover, the type of motivation differs from that of the middle-class child, who usually comes to school already motivated to a considerable degree. Jackie, our inner-city child, often does not. So it is important that we understand the type of motivation that turns him or her off to learning, and that we know how to utilize his or her strengths so that motivation leads to learning. As Reissman (1976) says,

> In everybody's style there are certain strengths. And everybody has an Achilles' heel. In developing a significant change in learning, one must control the Achilles' heel and utilize the strengths. This is the central problem of the strategy of style, especially in its application to the inner-city pupils in our schools.

Inner-city Jackie's battle with reading is his or her Achilles' heel. But this problem may result from overlooking the strengths Jackie brings to school. These strengths are not measurable by readiness tests or other criteria usually used to assess readiness, but they can be determined through cognitive style mapping.

Cognitive style mapping is a process in which the individual is assessed for his or her most comfortable manner of learning—visual or auditory, independent or in a group. Evidence from cognitive style mapping indicates that inner-city children learn more effectively when physical and oral involvement are present (Cureton 1977).

Evidence from teachers confirms this. While the term cognitive style mapping may be new in educational literature, the practice is not. A group of successful primary grade teachers from inner-city schools, for example, combine learning with pleasure.

Only on Wednesday

The "how" for inner-city teachers varies, of course, from class to class. But one "how" that has worked for many combines, as it were, business with pleasure. If these teachers are observed, it is difficult to determine when the game is over and when learning takes place. They use a phonics approach to teach reading because they have found that their students are better able to cope with a program that is heavily based on phonics than with a program that places more emphasis on sight words. With a phonics program, they can provide more action, more fun, in contrast to the quieter setting of the traditional classroom, a setting which is not characteristic of the inner-city child's daily life.

Inner-city children, although used to talking a great deal, often come to school with a poor auditory set. They are not accustomed to listening for long periods. The action approach to learning, which demands continuous participation by the children, also teaches them to listen as they learn, for their participation is in response to questions from the teacher, questions that must be listened to and understood before they can be responded to. That the action approach works, and that acquisition of knowledge does take place, are attested to not only by the teachers' evaluations of their students but also by these children's scores on standardized reading test.

Putting Sounds Together

In a first grade classroom where the action approach is being used the teacher develops the concept of blending by having the children slide around the room. This is done to demonstrate physically how letters and sounds are blended together into words. This psychomotor technique makes the concept of blending letters meaningful, especially when the teacher says, "Slide the sounds together." To further reinforce the skill of sliding or blending the teacher has the children "slide" the initial sounds in their names together to produce a word. For example, Mary muh, Albert aah, Pam puh, would produce the word "map." (In sliding sounds, the teacher always leads the children through three steps: the separate sounds—muh, aah, puh; the sounds joined together—muhaahpuh; and the word with no distortions—map).

Another way in which the concept of blending is reinforced is to have children slide objects or pictures of objects together on a table. As they slide a bar of soap, an apple, and money together, they blend the word "Sam." Teaching the skill of blending in a concrete manner before applying it to letters brings the concept to life and allows it to make sense to the children. The transition from object to letter is a natural progression and far less frustrating than starting with putting letters together to make words.

The last stage of the acquisition of blending skills is seen as the class plays a game. The teacher calls out a series of code words, and the students synthesize into words the sounds these code words stand for. For example, the teacher calls out, "soap, money, apple, shoe," and the class responds with the word "smash." The game has two main purposes: to help develop listening skills, and to give students a background—a frame of reference—to call upon when they apply the concept of blending to the abstract symbols of the alphabet. This happens later, as the teacher systematically replaces the objects with the letters that represent them. Using this concrete approach to blending eliminates the problem most discussed in teaching with a phonetic approach, getting the children to put the sounds together.

As the children master the concrete representations of the alphabet and of letter combinations, the teacher will play the game again, but this time the students will have to write the letter representing the code. Use of the code not only facilitates the decoding process but also aids those children who have difficulty in hearing the difference between similar sounds, for example, between the short *i* and short *e*. The picture of itching (a girl scratching an itch) which represents the short *i* sound and the picture of another girl named Ethel which represents the short *e* sound make the difference between the two concrete and unforgettable.

During the teaching of skills, this first grade teacher has everybody in the class participating simultaneously in answering questions. The purpose of this choral response mode is twofold: to keep everyone alert and to build confidence. Children are able to make a wrong response and have it blend in with the correct one and not be embarrassed. The choral response also gives security to the shy child. Many questions are repeated and responded to several times so that children who are unsure the first time can respond correctly the next.

In this class, both teacher and children stand during the presentation of new skills; the teacher moves around the room, drawing every eye. This strongly teacher-centered approach might be frowned on in some schools as being too authoritarian and uncreative. However, as one teacher put it, "Creativity will become part of the children's learning styles when they have mastered the basics."

Furthermore, it works. The children, far from feeling cramped or frustrated, are eager to learn. The pace and the action of the class, and the accomplishment they feel as they acquire new skills and review earlier ones, make them look forward to reading.

Can individualized reading programs be successful in inner-city schools, where the learning style of the children favors teacher-centered instruction? The answer will depend somewhat on what is meant by individualized programs. Research by Amidon and Flanders (1963) suggests that the achievement level is higher where there is interaction between teacher and student. As one of my students declared after a year of using an individualized program, "I need a teacher who will make me learn."

The foregoing paragraphs describe a learning style that results in reading achievement at the primary level. The next question is how to solve the perplexing problem of maintaining this achievement. Research indicates that by the time most inner-city children reach the fourth grade level they have lost from a few months to a year in reading. Why?

One reason appears to be the nature of the tests measuring reading achievement. The questions on intermediate grade tests require critical thinking rather than simple recall. Teachers who have been successful in maintaining inner-city children's reading achievement have, therefore, devoted large portions of time to the development of interpretive skills.

One such teacher points out that development of comprehension skills with her inner-city children is a persistent search for "why." In this search, oral discussion is essential. The student must give reasons why one answer is better than another and must defend that answer with proof. The proof may come from the story or from his or her experience. In order that the "give up" syndrome does not creep into the children's desire to go after the problem, the teacher never says a child's answer is wrong. Instead, the teacher responds to the students with something like, "Now that's thinking. But is there another answer even closer to the problem?" (Such a discussion does not always have to be the outcome of a reading lesson. It could also result from work on an oral puzzle, which allows for participation of the entire class.) Such teacher interaction with the students may take a great deal of time, but it is time well spent, for it builds enduring patterns for students' thinking.

Another way to ensure participation is to have the students act out the passage they have been reading. In this way, emotion and feelings can play a role in comprehension.

Taking Tests

These techniques have been very helpful in building comprehension skills. But many children do not transfer the acquisition of these skills to testing situations. To correct this, we must make students test-conscious and test-wise and point out the "trickery" of some test questions and the ways in which some test authors try to get students to choose wrong answers. Alerting students to these techniques ensures careful reading of each test question and also helps to build critical thinking skills. Again, this is done through teacher-student interaction.

Why so much emphasis on oral interaction between student and teacher? Simply because of the student's oral background. As one student pointed out, he could see the causal relationship in the story better when the choice of best answers was determined in class discussion. The inner-city student's learning style depends on oral involvement. The student needs to talk out, with a group, the rationale for a particular choice. This oral exchange of reasons and answers also helps to provide the less apt student with strategies for selecting answers. Most "individualized" programs cannot provide this kind of support.

Computer assisted instruction is a case in point. The machine does not help show why a chosen answer is wrong. The cold response "incorrect, read again" leads to guessing—and a disdain of the computer. To be sure, some self-directed students enjoy the instruction the computer offers and seem to profit from its use, but they feel that they work better when the classroom teacher is in the computer lab to praise their achievement and to record their progress. Even though the machine keeps an accurate account of their answers, the students want the teacher to write the percent of correct responses in a record book.

Interaction between teacher and student plays a particular role in helping students prepare for standardized tests. When the teacher has interacted with the students all through the term before they are tested, the students take this involvement with them into the test-taking situation. As they take the tests and choose their answers, they can "hear" the class discussion.

Test taking is something many of us dread, and for the inner-city child it is an especially traumatic experience. An effective way to lessen this fear is to place students in as many testing situations as possible, to give them practice in taking tests. This is particularly important in the area of reading. In content areas such as mathematics, science, and social studies, students know essentially what the content of the test will be, and they can prepare for it. In reading, however, they have no clue as to the content of the passages they will be asked questions on. This content may be totally unrelated to their daily lives and experiences. Thus it seems mandatory to provide ample preparation, again using the teacher-student interaction learning approach.

When inner-city students who have been given practice in test-taking situations are given standardized tests, they seem to perform better than students who have not had this kind of practice. Perhaps one more reason for this increased performance is that these students have learned to work against time. Because inner-city students are often disturbed by the pressure of time, practice in test taking reduces this anxiety.

Is there a black learning style, a learning style especially suited to inner-city students? I believe there is. Use of such a style does not mean lowering standards or expectations; however, it does mean recognizing the students' strengths and utilizing them to help these students learn to read. This learning style has been successful in rural, suburban, and small city settings with students from many ethnic backgrounds. All of these students, however, share many characteristics of inner-city children.

Teachers must attune themselves to the learning styles of the many inner-city Jackies so that these students' fullest potential may become visible on standardized tests. This is as true of students of secondary school and college age as it is of beginners. To develop the use of this learning style, the teacher need only create an interactive learning environment.

References

Allen, Carolyn. "Cureton vs. Non-Cureton Readers." Masters thesis, Keane College, Union, N.J., 1975.

Amidon, Edmund J., and Ned A. Flanders. *The Role of the Teacher in the Classroom: A Manual for Understanding and Improving Teachers' Classroom Behaviors.* Minneapolis, Minn.: Amidon and Associates, Inc., 1963.

Atwood, Beth S. "Helping Students Recognize Their Own Learning Style." *Learning* 3 (April 1975): 72–74.

Cureton, George O. *Action Reading: The Participatory Approach.* Boston: Allyn & Bacon, 1977.

Hoover, M. R., Robert L. Politzer, and O. Taylor. *Bias in Achievement and Diagnostic Reading Tests: A Linguistically Oriented View.* Unpublished manuscript.

McPhail, Irving P. *Test-Wiseness Curriculum.* Randallstown, Md.: Kamilah Educational Enterprises, 1978.

Reissman, Frank. *The Inner-City Child.* New York: Harper & Row, 1976.

Teaching Minority Children to Read in Elementary School

Constance J. Batty
College at Old Westbury, SUNY

Beauford R. Batty
Island Park Schools, New York

In 1974 the state of New York sponsored a research study in order to identify those school factors which influence student reading achievement. Two New York City elementary schools were selected for an in-depth examination. The population of one school consistently achieved high reading scores while the population of the other school consistently achieved low scores. The schools were matched on the basis of economic, social, and racial characteristics of the student population.

The results of the study showed, among other things, that "The differences in student performances in these two schools seemed to be attributed to factors under the schools' direct control" despite the fact that "Many professional personnel in the less effective school attributed children's reading problems to nonschool factors and were pessimistic about their ability to have an impact, creating an environment in which children failed because they were not expected to succeed. However, in the more effective school, teachers were less skeptical about their ability to have an impact on children." (*School Factors Influencing Reading Achievement 1974*, vi-vii.)

This study suggests that the factor which had the greatest impact upon the reading achievement of the student population in the two schools was the *attitude* of the classroom teacher. Findings of other research projects have supported this notion (Rayner and Schumer 1976; Quarles 1976; and Rist 1970).

It is well known that many minority children in the elementary grades are not making sufficient progress in learning to read. This crucial problem has attracted the attention of researchers in various disciplines as well as that of the educators who are intimately involved.

While many variables which contribute to the problem have been identified, most informed persons agree that the classroom teacher is the important factor in a child's success in learning to read.

Recommendations

The attitude, motivation, and expectations of the classroom teacher can affect the teacher-pupil relationships, distribution of teacher time, and teacher evaluation of student progress. These factors affect all children's performances in reading. However, they may have a greater effect on children who represent minority groups and who may have low self-concepts.

Teachers who work with minorities, especially black children, should develop an understanding of the pluralistic nature of society and the worthiness of each group in that society. These teachers need to know and appreciate the life-styles of the children and most importantly, they must believe that all children should be respected and are entitled to be educated. The teachers must convey these beliefs to the children with such fervor that the children will know that the teacher expects them to succeed.

Interpersonal relationships should be emphasized. Through informal talk, teachers should identify children's interests and discuss non-school related activities with them. An occasional pat on the shoulder indicates the teacher's awareness of the children's efforts. This may take a few minutes, but the rewards for both teacher and pupil will be well worth the effort.

Teachers can build on the strengths of the children's families and communities. Parents can be asked to read stories to the class or group and under the direction of the teacher, they can work with individual children. The teacher can have the children read stories revolving around activities and events in the local community. When possible, the teacher can provide appropriate challenging reading material that reflects the interests and life-styles of the children.

It is necessary for teachers to monitor the amount and quality of reading instruction time given to each child or group of children. Studies have revealed that, although it may be unintentional, teachers do spend less time teaching the less able readers. Therefore, an effort should be made to maintain consistent teacher-pupil interaction with an emphasis on high standards and expectations. Throughout these relationships, the teacher must allow each child to experience daily success. Subsequently, appropriate praise should be freely given.

In addition to establishing a positive and effective teacher-pupil relationship, teachers should plan *each* reading lesson carefully. Plans should include opportunitites for individualized instruction, discussion, explanation, and various types of questioning techniques. This is particularly important for students whose background or experience may be dissimilar to the content of the reading selection. Teachers should eliminate oral reading lessons that consist solely of one child after another reading aloud with no opportunity for silent reading, sharing, or building bridges between the child and the content of the reading selection.

Furthermore, Goodman states that "Meaning is embedded not in individual words but in the whole context" (1976, 2). Goodman believes that if children get meaning from the printed page then the dialect used during oral reading is relatively unimportant. Further, he states that it is possible for children to read and understand standard written language although orally using a nonstandard dialect.

Weber (1973) described a study of oral reading "errors" by black children who spoke black English. She identified some reading "errors" as based in speech patterns. Weber stated that these "errors" can be attributed erroneously by teachers to a lack of comprehension. A misunderstanding of dialect use may result in an inaccurate assessment of reading achievement. Thus, teachers should place more emphasis on comprehension than on oral reading.

Indeed, oral reading should be minimized in preference to both short and sustained periods of silent reading. Teachers should serve as models and read with the children during this time. Following silent reading, children should have the opportunity to retell, dramatize, or discuss the selection comfortably in their own language style. These kinds of activities will provide the teacher with opportunities to assess each child's level of comprehension. If children are successful in such activities, then indeed, reading comprehension has occurred.

Speakers of black dialect should be introduced to all the varied word recognition skills. The ability to use context clues strengthens comprehension as well as word recognition. A simple questioning technique such as "Alicia, what word do *you think* should be there?" may suffice. In any event, the teacher should remember that misrepresenting one or two words may *not* reduce the reader's overall comprehension of the selection.

Teachers should consider the use of the Language Experience Approach (LEA) to reading. The LEA uses the language and experiences of the children when creating materials for reading instruction. In this method, children dictate and teachers record a story (Aukerman 1971). Research studies have suggested that the Language Experience Approach is no less effective than the basal reader or other approaches to reading. However, the approach offers some social and psychological benefits to the reader. LEA eliminates the possible mismatch between the language of the reader and the print. Further, it allows the child to incorporate his own experiences and thoughts into the reading program. It personalizes reading instruction and in turn, may foster a positive attitude toward reading.

Currently, some basal readers reflect society's pluralism. Literature books containing black characters are available as well as history and science textbooks which contain black representation. However, teachers must concern themselves with the quality of this representation. Baronberg (1971) surveyed fifty-six picture books involving black people and found "(1) almost half only portray black people. . . . It is certain that to label them "integrated" or "multiethnic" as they are commonly called is inaccurate and misleading; (2) of the books which show both black and white people, the illustrations in at least half of them make skin color indeterminable; (3) with one or two exceptions, none of the books mention race. . ." (1971, 2).

Agree (1976), in her dissertation study which involved literature books published for children between 1950 and 1970, concluded that "most of the books in the sample (each contained at least one black character) would fail to enlighten either the black or white child as to the causes and background of the racial situation in the United States. Earlier derogatory stereotypes of black Americans appear to have been replaced by middle-class black characters lacking in significant ethnic authenticity. The books also failed to depict the variety of personal and socioeconomic life styles of black Americans" (1976, 6).

Teachers need to examine the new, multiethnic books and discard them if they include white individuals as the all-understanding benefactor of a single black or blacks who are not in control of their own lives. In addition, it is suggested that teachers de-emphasize some of the European folk tales (e.g., Goldilocks, Snow White) and include some folk tales from Africa and Asia, for instance, as well as native American folk tales. For criteria to use when selecting appropriate books for all children, we refer the reader to "Ten Quick Ways to Analyze Books for Racism and Sexism" (1974).

Finally, it is suggested that teachers should create a reading environment. They should read to the children, provide adequate time and books for the children to read, and build bridges between the world of the writer and the reader.

Conclusion

If teachers are to succeed in creating a positive and meaningful educational experience, they must learn about the children they teach. Family, home, and community are a part of the child, and it is all of these facets in concert that the child brings to school. Teachers should maximize their efforts toward developing an understanding of the culture of minority groups represented in the class. However, similar efforts should be expended toward a nonjudgmental understanding of the individual. Children should be allowed to accept themselves, and it is incumbent upon the teacher to maximize opportunities for each child to have some success each day. Each child needs concrete evidence of success. Children can sense meaningless, unwarranted platitudes from well-meaning teachers. Teachers should structure the learning environment so that reading failure is minimal, and if it occurs, it should be private.

We are aware that many issues concerning reading failure among minority children were undiscussed in this paper. The pervading factors of racism, unequal distribution of educational opportunity and financing, unequal minority representation in policy-making bodies, unequal representation of minorities in the education milieu, the entire area of IQ testing, and tracking are but a few of the issues that have an effect upon the failure of minority children. However, it is the writers' hope that the reader has acquired some additional insights and food for thought.

In summary, the writers feel it would be particularly helpful for those concerned with the education of minority children to remember these points.

1. The problem of academic and reading failure cannot be laid at the doorstep of the victim. Schools and teachers can make a difference.

2. Teachers must examine their own attitudes and study ethnic groups other than their own with the goal of becoming more knowledgeable, understanding, and sensitized concerning differences.

3. Appropriate training of teachers should include more extensive preservice and inservice content pertaining to language acquisition and reading.

4. Black children live in a verbal environment, and their speech is meaningful, functional, and appropriate in their environment. Their language is not primitive.

5. Children with nonstandard speech patterns can probably acquire meaning from standard orthography with the same degree of success as the general population.

6. Basal readers and other educational material should appropriately reflect the cultural pluralism of our society and reflect the contributions which members of various ethnic groups have made.

Teachers of black children, regardless of their own ethnicity, must be sensitive to the problems of black people. Many black children will succeed in spite of the teachers; many others will fail because of them. A reduction in the number of failures is our goal.

References

Agree, Rose Hyla. "The Black American in Children's Books: A Critical Analysis of the Afro-American as Delineated in the Contents of a Selected Group of Children's Trade Books Published in America from 1950 to 1970." (Dissertation abstract. In *Research in Children's Literature: An Annotated Bibliography,* edited by Dianne L. Monson and Bette J. Peltola. Newark, Del.: International Reading Association, 1976.

Aukerman, Robert C. *Approaches to Beginning Reading.* New York: John Wiley & Sons, 1971.

Baronberg, Joan. *Black Representation in Children's Books.* Urban Disadvantaged, No. 21. New York: Columbia University, 1971.

Fromkin, Victoria P., and P. Rodman. *An Introduction to Language.* New York: Holt, Rinehart & Winston, 1974.

Goodman, Kenneth. *Reading: A Conversation with Kenneth Goodman.* Scott, Foresman & Co., 1976.

Hockman, Carol. "Black Dialect Reading Test in the Urban Elementary School." *The Reading Teacher* 26 (March 1973).

Rayner, James, and Harry Schumer. "Reading Achievement Gains as a Function of Teacher Predictions." *The Journal of Education Research* (February 1976): 232–35.

Rist, Ray. "Students Social Class and Teacher Expectations: The Self-Fulfilling Prophecy in Ghetto Education." *Harvard Educational Review* (August 1970): 411–49.

Quarles, Royce. "Teacher Incentive through Performance Contracting: A Programmatic Approach." *Reading Improvement* 11 (Fall 1974): 10–12.

Smith, E. B., K. S. Goodman, and Robert Meredith. *Language and Thinking in the Elementary School.* New York: Holt, Rinehart & Winston, 1970.

Weber, Rose-Marie. "Dialect Differences in Oral Reading." In *Language Differences: Do They Interfere?* edited by James L. Laffey and Roger Shuy. Newark, Del.: International Reading Association, 1973.

School Factors Influencing Reading Achievement. Research report. New York State Board of Education, 1974, pp. vi–vii.

"Ten Quick Ways to Analyze Books for Racism and Sexism." *Bulletin* 5 (1974).

Closing the Generation Gap and Turning Students On to Reading

Ire Adams Page
Hampton Institute, Virginia

In the summer of 1975, it was my good fortune to teach a group of high school students who were enrolled in the Upward Bound program at a northern university. The program sought to raise the academic level of those students whose potential was greater than their performance. While black students were in the majority, a small percentage of white and Spanish-speaking students were enrolled in the program. All of the students assigned to my reading class were black, and all of them met the established low socio-economic criterion. Largely, they were reserved about reading or, more precisely, "turned off" to it.

My previous teaching experience included high school home economics and developmental and remedial reading in the elementary school. At the time of this experience, I was a doctoral candidate in education with a specialty in reading. I was born in the South and spent most of my life there. My background, therefore, bore some similarities and some differences to that of my students. Our heritage as black Americans was the same, but I was a southerner, and they were not. Moreover, we were in different generations.

During this seven-week period, my primary charge was to develop reading skills. The purpose of the program was for students to receive intensive instruction to advance existing skills and possibly generate new ones. Thus, I planned a highly structured skills-oriented curriculum with provisions for informal reading periods after instruction was completed.

A Need for Change

In spite of my preparation, the students responded to my curriculum with only moderate enthusiasm and even less initial success. I needed a new approach! Several questions surfaced immediately. First, how

115

could I stimulate the interest of the students and still maintain a leisurely, provocative atmosphere? Second, what would produce the most results for the students—a skills program or an interest-oriented one? In answering these questions, I decided to focus on the students' interests. This decision generated another question. How could I capitalize on the similarities in our backgrounds? Or better yet, how could I give the students an appetite for reading?

Deciding to make procedural rather than content changes immediately, I altered the format. On the next day, instead of our usual routine, we began our class period in the informal area of our room where there were couches, chairs, and pillows. The "new" day started with some discussion about "What" we were going to do and "Why." We would listen to and read some poetry written by a black poet, Paul Laurence Dunbar (*The Complete Poems*, Dodd, Mead & Co., 1972). Surely, I thought, this would spark enthusiasm since we were of the same ethnic background. So, I began reading aloud a favorite of mine, "In the Morning."

> 'Lias! 'Lias! Bless de Lawd!
> Don' you know de day's erbroad?
> Ef you don' git up you scamp,
> Dey'll be trouble in dis camp.
> Tink I gwine to let you sleep
> W'ile I meks yo boa'd an' keep?

Expecting signs of appreciation from the students, I looked up and found bewildered stares instead. In response to my queries about their reception of the poem, I was met with "What is that all about?" and "I don't understand it." The students were not familiar with the language—the dialect. They couldn't relate to the symbolism nor to the rhythm. And, to compound it all, their verbal responses revealed an indifference, even antagonism to poetry—at least the kind they had been exposed to previously. Since this was poetry, it met the same fate. The fact that this poetry had a black orientation made no difference at all. Intent on making this an effective lesson, I decided to explain the language of the poem in detail—the vocabulary, word and phrase meanings, the pronunciations, and the story the poem was telling:

gwine/going

hyeah/hear

Lawd/Lord

scamp/rascal

day's erbroad/the sun is up

trouble in dis camp/trouble in the home (he would be spanked)

boad an' keep/food, shelter and care

In the course of our discussion, I stated that the language was a part of my heritage—sounds heard in my youth. I could relate to it as perhaps some of their parents could because, like me, they possibly had heard the language spoken or had studied Dunbar's poetry in school. This created interest on the part of the students that was different from what I intended. They wanted to know more about "me"—who I was, where I had come from, and what I was doing with my life. They had perceived me as different from them, since my language was not like theirs and since I represented an older generation. I told them about my life, about my schooling, about my dreams, of persons who had inspired me and of why I spoke in standard English. After I explained my background and "where I was coming from" to their satisfaction, and after they saw I was "for real," they began to warm up. They realized that we had a common bond because some of my past experiences were identical to theirs. Now they were willing to cooperate.

Success at Last

Returning to the poem, we took turns reading individually and in groups. It was an enjoyable experience—interest was aroused and comprehension was evident. They began to relate their experiences, to understand the poem in its context, and to appreciate it.

Having met with a degree of enthusiasm, I started the next session with the reading of excerpts from a short novel by Mary Elizabeth Vroman, another black writer. The book was *Esther* (Bantam, 1963). This book deals with the pain and frustration of a young black girl growing into maturity long before her childhood is over. I felt that it presented more life experiences with which we could identify.

> "Munsie Atwater is 'bout to have her baby. . . ."
> Esther leaped out of bed. She had never imagined that Grandear would ask her along on a case, at least not before she was sixteen or so. To see a real baby born! . . .
> Lucy followed Esther into the bathroom. "You mean you really want to go?" she asked incredulously. . . . Esther nodded. "But it's awful! A whole lot of blood, and they screams and screams!" Esther spat joyously. "Sure; because it hurts, until it's over. Anyway, there's not all that much blood."

"And you don't mind seeing people hurt?" There was reproach in
Lucy's tone.
Esther paused her washing. "Of course I mind, Lucy. But I'm
going to help Grandear. Folks in pain need people to help them.
But I do want to see it. There are two things I've always wanted
to see—somebody borning and somebody dying" (p. 16).

The students were enthralled and the discussions which followed
revealed the depth of their involvement. "What was it like to give
birth?" "What was the father's responsibility during the birth process
and afterwards?" "What was it like to see a baby being born?" They
injected their own feelings and experiences about the birth process.
This reading session was followed by a request (from one of the most
avowed nonreaders) to take the book to the dorm. I was sure then
that appetites had been whetted. Subsequently, I was told the book
passed among the students and remained visible throughout the
summer. After that, the students brought in plays and other readings
which we shared. These young adults later intimated that the best
part of the reading class was hearing me read. They wanted to be
able to read like that (the teacher-modeled reading behavior). The
nonreading student said that she had always hated reading but now
she was really "turned on." It was evident, too. The "teachable
moment" had occurred and it was a beautiful happening. From that
point on, we moved toward the specific goals that I had established
at the outset of the summer.

Outside readings were shared through written summaries and
reactions. The summaries included the main ideas, supporting details
and vocabulary. The reactions to the reading selections were very
personal. They included *what* the readings meant to them and *why*
they were appealing. Difficult terms and complex sentence structures
were singled out so that word attack skills could be applied and
meanings could be clarified.

Visual modalities were tapped as the use of diacritical marks and
syllabication were demonstrated. Much discussion was provided in
addition to dictionary usage so that greater understandings were
possible. These activities provided auditory input for this troublesome
area.

The students and I felt good about the learning that was taking
place, about each other and about the relationships among us. I used
this emotional bond to emphasize that certain instructional objectives
had been set for this summer. These had to be met, and there had to
be some visible evidence of the progress being made towards reaching

those objectives. Skill acquisition was extremely important but I did not want to minimize personal reactions. So, outside reading was tied with the published materials.

Our program was operating according to Ausubel's (1963) strategy for teaching students with cultural differences. Ausubel dicusses three factors for effective teaching: (1) the selection of initial learning material geared to the learner's existing state of readiness; (2) mastery and consolidation of all ongoing learning tasks before new tasks are introduced, in order to provide the necessary foundation for successful learning and to prevent unreadiness for future learning tasks; and (3) the use of structural learning materials optimally organized to facilitate efficient sequential learning."

The commercial materials we used were: the *Reader's Digest Skill Builders*, Laidlaw Brothers' *Target Reading Series*, and Walter Pauk's *Six-Way Paragraphs* by Jamestown Publishers. These materials helped to develop students' comprehension, vocabulary, and word attack skills. The students and I could see evidence of progress because the exercises provided feedback in several ways. All of the materials had reading selections and questions at the end. Pupils could (1) read and answer the questions, (2) re-read and check for specific details, (3) re-read and think through inference-type questions, and (4) use the answers provided as a basis for assessing their own answers. The students even asked questions of their own when they were particularly interested in the stories. The *Six-Way Paragraphs* also included a chart for recording and following progress. After reading and discussing assigned activites, pupils noted their errors and entered the results on a graph. They worked toward making fewer and fewer errors. The work was rewarding to the students through this positive reinforcement. By this time, a library of paperback novels had been provided. The students used these for preferred reading.

Implications for Teaching

I learned and relearned a great deal that summer and drew a number of conclusions. These conclusions are the result of much reflection and hindsight, but they are based on learning theory and research. They include implications for teachers who have the same kinds of learners. Why was I able to motivate these students and gain acceptance? The answer is contained in the following observations:

My own reading interests were used to capture attention. The subject-matter of those interests stirred the students' curiosity. As they listened, the students developed an appreciation for what they heard, and they agreed to participate.

The reading act was demonstrated. The students saw how pleasant reading could be. Ausubel says that cognitive drive or intrinsic motivation to learn is probably derived in a general sense from curiosity tendencies and from inclinations to explore, manipulate, and cope with the environment. He cautions, however, that these tendencies are activated only in satisfactory encounters with the values of persons with whom the learners identify.

The reading teacher, the model, was a person who identified with the students. No longer an outsider, alien to their world, I became part of the group. I belonged because I had shared my world with them, and they related to it.

Studies have shown that observers learn to imitate models more readily if the behavior to be modeled has novel features (novel meaning, in some way related to the observer's needs). This is conditioned, however, by the desire or need to reproduce the behavior of the model. Robert Travers (1972, 419–20) supports this position, and Miller and Dollard (1941) have said that the value of the demonstration is generally highly dependent upon the ability of the observer to imitate. This ability is a learned phenomenon. Gage (1972) added, "The characteristics of the model are extremely important. The model must have prestige and must be seen as a source of reinforcement for given kinds of behaviors." As was stated previously, the students wanted to be able to read like me. They had a felt need.

Ralph Tyler (1971), in discussing learning, said: "Given a learner whose interest has been aroused, the next thing is to find the skill level at which the learner can experience a good degree of success. . . . The instructional material must be relevant (seen as important) to his current needs and interests, must demand a new kind of performance yet to be attainable." As for the transfer of learning, he added, "part of a good theory of learning is seeing to it that the learner has opportunity to practice. . . . Without the ability to transfer learning, the child tends to think of learning as what we do in school but not anywhere else." The students viewed the instructional materials we used as worthwhile for practice activities. This learning was applied to their personal reading. The discussions about this reading tied everything together. Because I was there to guide, to correct their work and to encourage, it was a shared experience.

The shared experience, one in which everybody took part, was self-enhancing. There was so much to talk about—to give—and so we all learned. What were we talking about? The content of our reading as it influenced our lives.

Conclusions

Success is evident only after interest is tapped. Inherent in this interest is the factor of relevance—what the learners saw as real and important. Relevance gave the reading a reality that was based upon the value systems of the learners and upon their own experiences. Once motivated, they began to demonstrate an awareness that what was of interest and what was of value could be reconciled by using their reading skills. This was their step toward independence.

What had originally been perceived as a situation involving "turned off" kids was really one with a "tuned out" teacher. When efforts were made to stimulate the students, new understandings and appreciations evolved. We found the area where our lives and experiences overlapped, that is, where the learner's reality and the teacher's reality showed a commonality. The "oneness of reality"—acceptance of the other's value systems, brought forth more positive attitudes and acceptance—each for the other. We then moved towards obtainable goals in a warm and self-actualizing climate.

The incidence of race was circumstantial rather than necessary. I feel compelled to suggest that in any teaching/learning situation, when efforts are made to unify the interests of the teacher and learners, the teacher and the learners may then be "turned on" and "tuned in."

Questions are asked at the start of the program regarding the measurement of progress were not—and could not—be answered singularly. Much that was learned could not be measured. A testing program using a standardized instrument was on ongoing procedure of the Upward Bound program. I hope that improved performance was evident in that assessment; however, it was more significant that the students now had a desire to read. It was, and still is, my hope that they maintain that desire to read and that they continue to discuss ideas.

References

Ausubel, David P. "A Teaching Strategy for Culturally Deprived Pupils: Cognitive and Motivational Considerations." *School Review* 71 (Winter 1963): 454–63.

Gage, N. L. *Teacher Effectiveness and Teacher Education.* Palo Alto, Calif.: Pacific Books, 1972.

Miller and Dollard. "Social Learning and Imitation." *Grade Teacher* (May–June 1941): 46–48.

Travers, Robert. *Essentials of Learning.* 3d ed. New York: Macmillan, 1972.

Tyler, Ralph. "Theory and Practice: Bridging the Gap." *Grade Teacher* (May–June 1971): 46–48.

Instructional Strategies for Teaching Test-Wiseness

Irving P. McPhail
Baltimore Public Schools, Maryland

The prevalence of testing in schools, particularly minimum competency testing as a prerequisite for graduation, has alerted educators to the importance of test-taking skills (Downey 1977; McPhail 1979). This raises three important questions: What are the skills? Can they be effectively taught? How should they be taught?

Test-wiseness has a relatively short history in educational research. The theoretical work of Millman, Bishop, and Ebel (1965) is regarded as the classic in the area. They maintained that,

> test-wiseness is defined as a subject's capacity to utilize the characteristics and formats of the test and/or the test-taking situation to receive a high score. Test-wiseness is logically independent of the examinee's knowledge of the subject matter for which items are supposedly measured . . . it will be restricted to the actual taking of (not preparing for) *objective* achievement and aptitude tests (1965, 707).

Perhaps the most important contribution of Millman, Bishop, and Ebel's work is their comprehensive taxonomy of test-wiseness, a list of principles students should apply in taking tests. This list was synthesized from test construction principles and problem-solving styles of test takers. It was intended as a framework for empirical study, but teachers can use portions of it as a guide to test-taking strategies that might be taught to students. Figure I presents sample items from "An Outline of Test-Wiseness Principles."

For example, a teacher could easily find examples, from his or her own past objective tests, of test items that illustrate varying lengths of the answer options. Even young children can be taught to perceive these cues. Examples of the generalization cue are also readily available, but since generalization is more difficult to perceive, it might be taught later or with older students.

123

Why Teach Test Wiseness?

Given that tests are commonplace, there are good reasons why students should be taught how to pass them. Fortunately, there is objective evidence that test-wiseness can be taught at all educational levels (McPhail 1979; Sarnacki 1979). Here are two reasons for doing so.

The Validity of Test Results

Much research in test-wiseness has focused on the "cue-using strategy." This presupposes that there are flaws in the construction of test items, e.g., leads (item stems) based on incomplete statements, specific determiners that tend to appear in the correct answer alternative, grammatical inconsistencies between the lead and alternatives, or a correct alternative that is longer than any of the incorrect alternatives.

There are, clearly, two ways to avoid bias against students who have not learned to respond successfully to item writing faults (secondary cues). The first is to construct tests that are free from secondary cues. The second is to teach all students a cue-using strategy in order to equalize this knowledge among all groups.

Teachers should identify students who are not test wise and teach them how to take tests. Otherwise, the validity of these students' scores is impaired. For example, if students do not know how to allot their time during a timed test, their scores will not reflect their true abilities.

Perhaps it is even more critical to teach students how the structure of a test provides a frame of reference for selecting answers. For example, *Test-Wiseness Strategies for Reading Comprehension Tests* (McPhail 1978a) can show students (under General Procedures) that they should preview a reading passage on a test and look over the first few questions before they read the full passage. This technique provides them a prereading organizer. The technique also alerts them to the fact that it is usually the first two or three questions that deal with the central idea of a passage. Teachers can alert students to specific wording that is a cue to a certain type of test question, and they can show students specific steps for solving these test items. Figure 2 illustrates the use of this strategy for inference items.

Equal Education, Employment and Promotion Opportunity for Minorities

Most minority students score lower on achievement and aptitude tests than the population at large. A plethora of "deficit" views, e.g., that a flaw in black genes is responsible for low black test scores, and "difference" views, e.g., that blacks are so different in their language and culture that they cannot learn, or that they require a "special" nonacademic education, have been offered as explanations for the variance in test performance between minority and majority students. At the same time, there is voluminous evidence in the literature of cultural, linguistic, and other forms of test bias that operate as delimiting factors in the test performance of minority students. Yet, the educational research and testing industries continue to produce spurious, pseudo-scientific arguments to justify the testing and the interpretation of test results of minority students. Consequently, tests have taken on a sinister quality in certain minority communities in the areas of education, employment, and promotion. Many suspect that tests are used to screen out minorities from access to equal education, employment, and promotion opportunity (Ristow 1978; Word 1974).

The recent experience of Florida illustrates the growing attack on equal opportunity being waged by the educational testing industry. Most of the students failing new minimum competency tests in English and mathematics were black and Hispanic, raising serious questions about whether the tests and the program as a whole were discriminating against minority students.

Given the evidence, it is ironic that only limited attention has been focused on the role of test-wiseness in the test performance of minority students. Looking at seventy-six fifth and sixth grade inner-city children, Diamond et al. (1977) determined that the children knew the cues of answer length and of association between the item stem and certain answer options. However, no significant relationship was found between knowledge of these cues and standardized reading test scores. More work is needed on a wider variety of test-taking skills to determine whether a relationship does exist.

Four attempts to teach selected test-wiseness principles to minority students have been reported (McPhail 1978b; 1979). In three studies, students demonstrated several patterns of improvement in test-wiseness. The fourth study concluded that short-term "coaching" for the Scholastic Aptitude Test (SAT) was not successful, but it should be observed that the course on test-taking skills did *not* "try to help the student to learn the 'tricks' of the test-maker" (Roberts and Oppenheim 1966, 46). As such, the course on SAT test-taking was narrowly defined and did not include many important aspects of test-wiseness.

Informal reports from classroom teachers who have taught test-wiseness systematically to minority students have been encouraging.

This informal data, together with the limited empirical data on teaching test-wiseness to minority students, suggest that these students can be taught to be test-wise and can improve their performance as a result. Future research on these hypotheses, and on which skills to teach, is a critical need.

Approaches to Teaching Test-Wiseness

Research has shown that test-wiseness has only a negligible relationship to a student's general cognitive ability (Diamond and Evans 1972). However, the sort of analysis required by some activities used to teach test-wiseness seems likely to strengthen students' critical thinking.

It is important to distinguish here between two ways of learning test-wiseness: associative learning and problem-solving. Associative learning means learning from being told and from practice and drill. Test-taking skills can be mastered effectively through associative learning.

In the problem-solving approach, students search for a pattern; they are presented with evidence and are asked to investigate the data and draw conclusions. Of course, problem-solving calls upon earlier associative learning in the process of searching for patterns.

The Test-Making Activity is a series of experiences in test construction designed to teach students test-wiseness through an inductive, problem-solving approach (McPhail 1978a). It has been used with inner-city high school students (McPhail 1978b) and other grade levels. Each stage prepares students for the next. Working in small heterogeneous groups, the students learn how a test is built. At the last stage, they deliberately rewrite items to include secondary cues. The assumption is that anyone who can build a faulty item can also recognize one. Figure 3 presents the four stages in the Test-Making Activity.

Conclusions and Recommendations

Although we are still in need of more empirical evidence, it appears that test-wiseness training develops important test-taking skills and helps to negate the problems associated with individuals who are low in test-wiseness. This is important both for the individual whose life is influenced by the testing and for educators who want test results to be as valid as possible. At the same time, if test-wiseness training helps develop students' critical thinking skills, especially at the level of analytical problem-solving, we have gained a valuable instructional tool.

Test-Wiseness Principles

I. Elements independent of test constructor or test purpose.
  A. Time-using strategy
   1. Begin to work as rapidly as possible with reasonable assurance of accuracy.
   2. Set up a schedule for progress through the test.
   3. Omit or guess at items (see I.A.4. and II.B.) which resist a quick response.
   4. Mark omitted items, or items which could use further consideration, to assure easy relocation.
   5. Use time remaining after completion of the test to reconsider answers.
  B. Error-avoidance strategy.
   1. Pay careful attention to directions, determining clearly the nature of the task and the intended basis for response.
   2. Pay careful attention to the items, determining clearly the nature of the question.
   3. Ask examiner for clarification when necessary, if it is permitted.
   4. Check all answers.
II. Elements dependent upon the test constructor or purpose.
  A. Intent consideration strategy.
   1. Interpret and answer questions in view of previous idiosyncratic emphases of the test constructor or in view of the test purpose.
   2. Answer items as the test constructor intended.
   3. Adopt the level of sophistication that is expected.
   4. Consider the relevance of specific detail.
  B. Cue-using strategy
   1. The correct answer is longer (shorter) than the incorrect options.
   2. The correct answer is qualified more carefully, or represents a higher degree of generalization.
   3. The test includes more false (true) statements.
   4. The correct answer is in certain physical positions among the options (such as in the middle).
   5. The correct answer is in a certain logical position among an ordered set of options (such as the middle of the sequence).

Figure 1. Sample Items from an Outline of Test-Wiseness Principles. From "An Analysis of Test-Wiseness" by J. Millman, C. H. Bishop, and R. Ebel, *Educational and Psychological Measurement*, Vol. 25 (Autumn 1965), 707–26. Copyright 1965 by *Educational and Psychological Measurement*. Reprinted by permission.

Test-Wiseness Strategies

Inference

Inference items range from implied meaning to author's intent. They
are questions which go beyond the literal level of comprehension.
Inference items are generally worded as follows:

> The chief purpose of this selection is to . . . .
> The writer implies that . . . .
> The tone of the passage is . . . .
> The writer is probably most interested in . . . .
> It can be inferred that . . . .
> A conclusion that can be drawn from this selection is . . . .
> The story suggests . . . .
> The attitude of this story is one of . . . .

How to Answer an Inference Item

1. Select two or three possibilities from the multiple-choices.
2. Test each possibility by rereading the paragraph(s) with that
   one inference in mind.
3. When or if a phrase or sentence seems to contradict that inference, stop reading the paragraph and start again with another
   inference in mind.
4. Select the one that best answers the question.

Figure 2. Sample Test-Wiseness Strategies for Reading Comprehension Tests. From
Test-Wiseness Curriculum by I. P. McPhail, p. 24. Copyright 1978 by Kamilah Educational Enterprises. Reprinted by permission.

Test-Making Activity

1. Read each passage. Then read each question about the passage. You are to find the best answer to each question. Place an "X" mark in the box before the option containing the most complete or most accurate answer. (Work in small groups.)

2. Read each passage. Then read each question about the passage. For each question, make up four statements. One statement should be the most complete or most accurate answer to the question. The remaining three statements should be attractive but incorrect answers to the question. Place an "X" mark in the box before the option containing the most complete or most accurate answer. (Work in small groups.)

3. Make a reading comprehension test based on each of the following passages. Compose 10 questions (stems) with five options (statements) each. Two questions each should be based on the following five comprehension skills: (1) main idea, (2) supporting details, (3) vocabulary in context, (4) inference, and (5) drawing a conclusion. Place an "X" mark in the box before the option containing the most complete or most accurate answer. (Work in small groups.)

4. Rewrite the following questions and/or statements so that the correct answer is signaled by test-wiseness cues. Utilize each of the following test-wiseness cues at least once in rewriting questions and/or statements: (1) *association* between stem and alternative, (2) the use of *specific determiners* in the distractors, (3) the use of *correct alternatives which are longer* and in some cases more specific than the other distractors, and (4) the use of *grammatical clues* in the stem. (Work in small groups.)

Figure 3. Stages in Test-Making Activity. From *Test-Wiseness Curriculum* by I. P. McPhail, pp. 26–51. Copyright 1978 by Kamilah Educational Enterprises. Reprinted by permission.

References

Diamond, James J., James Ayrer, Roger Fishman, and Paul Green. "Are Inner-City Children Test-Wise?" *Journal of Educational Measurement* 14 (Spring 1977): 39–46.

Diamond, James J., and William J. Evans. "An Investigation of the Cognitive Correlates of Test-Wiseness." *Journal of Educational Measurement* 9 (Summer 1972): 145–50.

Downey, Gregg W. "Is It Time We Started Teaching Children How to Take Tests?" *American School Board Journal* 164 (January 1977): 27–30.

McPhail, Irving P. *Test-Wiseness Curriculum.* Randallstown, Md.: Kamilah Educational Enterprises, 1978a.

———. "A Psycholinguistic Approach to Training Urban High School Students in Test-Taking Strategies." *Journal of Negro Education* 47 (Spring 1978b): 168–76.

———. "Test Sophistication: An Important Consideration in Judging the Standardized Test Performance of Black Students." *Reading World* 18 (March 1979): 227–35.

Millman, Jason, Carol H. Bishop, and Robert Ebel. "An Analysis of Test-Wiseness." *Educational and Psychological Measurement* 25 (Autumn 1965): 707–26.

Ristow, W. "Larry P. versus I.Q. Tests." *The Progressive* 42 (November 1978): 48–50.

Roberts, S. O., and Don B. Oppenheim. *The Effect of Special Instruction upon Test Performance of High School Students in Tennessee.* Princeton, N.J.: Educational Testing Service, 1966.

Sarnacki, Randolph E. "An Examination of Test-Wiseness in the Cognitive Test Domain." *Review of Educational Research* 49 (Spring 1979): 252–79.

Word, Carl. "Testing: Another Word for Racism." *Essence* 5 (October 1974): 38.

Implications in Personal Construct Theory for Teaching Reading to Black Students

Miriam T. Chaplin
Rutgers University, Camden, New Jersey

Reading is a mental transaction between two persons. Though separated by time and space, these persons are linked together through a text—a symbol of a writer's conceptualization of reality. Regardless of the subject, a text is always subjectively influenced by its author. The choice of words, the mode of presentation and the selected voice are all representations of a particular personality actively communicating with a preconceived audience. On the other hand, the readers who comprise the audience do not passively receive the message. Each reader's attention to the text is motivated by a dynamic force of expectations and is maintained by the reader's emotional involvement. The purposes for reading will differ from one situation to another and this may lessen or intensify the reader's involvement with the text. The reading behavior, however, is always affected by the reader's personality enmeshed as it is with past experiences, present realities and future possibilities.

Therefore, the reader's interpretation of the writer's message is as dependent on his or her unique characteristics as was the writer's when the words were recorded. There is no one correct interpretation; there are as many interpretations as there are readers. It is in these diverse interpretations that we discover the mystery of the written word and the heterogeneity of human personalities.

George Kelly (1955) has written extensively about the human personality. He developed his theory for use in psychotherapy, but its value and utility far exceed a particular reference. The primary emphasis in the theory is placed on the *meaning* one gives to events as they occur rather than the behavior that is displayed as a result of an event. Kelly says that "if we reach an understanding of how a person behaves, we discover it in the manner in which he represents his circumstances to himself" (Kelly 1955). In the light of this view, behavior becomes a means to an end and not an end in itself.

While this observation is generally applicable to human behavior, it can be particularly helpful in understanding some of the problems that black students exhibit as they read. It is well known that large numbers of black students fail to achieve the levels of competence in reading that educational institutions require of them. These failures have been attributed to inferior intelligence, poorly developed basic skills, hostility, and/or lack of interest. While is is possible that any one of these factors may interfere with the academic performance of specific students, it is unlikely that that same factor could be used to explain group behaviors. The failure of many black students to succeed in reading may be more deeply rooted in their perceptions of themselves which have evolved out of cultural and historical realities they have experienced. If this is true, a cursory analysis of George Kelly's *Psychology of Personal Constructs* will reveal theoretical concepts that can be practically applied to reading instruction for black students.

The Control Factor in Reading

Kelly regards all people as scientists who are primarily interested in predicting and controlling their environments. He does not believe that behavior is a response to a stimulus because this view implies that people are inert objects propelled into action by energy external to themselves. Nor does he propose that behavior is motivated by drives because this assigns energetic properties to internal needs. Indeed, he dismisses these theories as "push" and "pull" explanations for human behavior. (Kelly 1955).

According to Kelly, human beings psychologically represent each external situation that confronts them. The representations emanate directly from an internal construct system which has been formed on the basis of past representations. The construct system is not static. As an event occurs, the person attempts to fit the representation of it into the existing system. If it conforms to the system, it is retained; if it does not conform, a decision must be reached. Either the system must be reconstructed to accommodate the new representation or it must be rejected. Kelly calls this process "constructive alternativism" and it is the keystone of Personal Construct Theory. It explains the exalted position of the human personality as the controlling factor in all behavior. Since the construct system is built on an individual pattern of expectations, the person can select those aspects of reality to which she or he will respond. Thus, construction decisions are personality specific. Moreover, these decisions are not binding; they are reflective of the system at a given time. Hence individuals are restricted in their construct selections only by the system they erect for themselves.

Reading a text is an event which demands action on the part of students. They must process the written word as they impose their own interpretations on it. The fate of a text depends entirely on the interpretation and subsequent reaction on the part of its readers. This makes a text fair game for the universe of readers. An author's message can be broadened or shortened as it is applied to different circumstances. Once an author has released his or her work for publication, it belongs to the world. Copyright laws will protect its duplication but nothing can protect its interpretation. From the ideas as presented by the author, readers are free to draw their own conclusions. The skill of readers depends on their abilities to elaborate ideas rather than to recall them. It is on this basis that students are judged as poor, good, or superior readers.

This act of interpretation, however, requires that students realize their power to control the text. This creates a dichotomy for some black students. The compelling natural desire to control the environments, of which Kelly speaks, conflicts with the powerlessness which they have learned to accept. Black students are unable to view the word as a subject under their dominion because they cannot conceive of themselves as controlling agents. Economically, politically, and socially, they find themselves at the lowest rung of the ladder and in a stratified society, one learns that this means a subjection to the will of others. Even the language they use is deemed inferior, and they are urged to discard it in favor of the language of the text. It is a formidable lesson to black students that words are forces of enslavement rather than emancipation.

For many black students, reading is a superficial act in which foreign ideas are forced upon their intellects and wills. They make no attempt to grapple with the ideas embedded in the written word or immerse themselves in them. They simply accept what is written as they have learned to accept other circumstances which they believe are beyond their control. This air of resignation is reflected in their responses to test questions, written reports and in class discussions. These exhibited behaviors cause teachers to view black students as mediocre or dull.

More importantly, many black students internalize a negative perception of themselves. It becomes what Kelly calls a "superordinate" construct and all other constructs become subordinate to it. The students' psychological processes become the mechanisms which guide their actions and all events including the written word are processed in the light of this perceived insignificance. The behaviors which teachers observe in these students may not be true indicators of their real abilities; nevertheless, they are true indicators of the students' concepts of themselves in the world. Their behaviors reflect their construct systems and as long as these systems remain intact, the students are trapped in a web of convictions which impedes growth. In Kelly's words:

> Ultimately a man sets the measure of his own freedom and his own bondage by the level at which he chooses to establish his convictions. The man who orders his life in terms of many special and inflexible convictions about temporary matters makes himself the victim of circumstances (Kelly 1955).

The students' perceptions may not interfere with their reading behaviors in the early grades when there is a preoccupation with mechanical decoding skills. More black students succeed at this level than at any other. However, as the task becomes more demanding of the students' total emotional and cognitive involvement, black students experience increased difficulty. In some cases, even when they have mastered the basic skills of decoding, they are unable to move beyond the literal to creative interpretations.

Implications in the Theory

The overwhelming appeal of Personal Construct Theory is that it offers hope to these black students and to the teachers who work with them. Kelly says that "man to the extent that he is able to construe his circumstances, can find for himself freedom from their domination" (Kelly 1955). Therefore, the students' faulty constructs can be discarded and replaced with newer more profitable ones if they are willing to reorganize their systems. This reorganization is a personal task that teachers cannot orchestrate, but teachers can assist the students' efforts. First, teachers must comprehend the complexity of the reconstruction process and second, they must be able to divert their own attention away from the actual behaviors which students exhibit to the possibilities that lie within.

Reading instruction for black students must be holistic rather than atomistic. An identification of the author's main points should be coupled with a personal interpretation and application. Inherent in this process is a manipulation of ideas; this is the first step toward control of them. Students must be encouraged to create the meaning of the text rather than to discover it. This is a trial and error procedure in which students are allowed to pursue many possible avenues of interpretation until one is found to which they can relate.

Prediction through questioning is the first step in this venture. Students should be taught to formulate their own questions before they read in an attempt to predict what will be learned. If predictions are not validated, the process of determining why is a valuable learning experience. When predictions are accurate, however, students will gain confidence in their own abilities.

It is equally as important for students to pose questions after they have read a text. When given an opportunity, students will question those ideas which are important and of the greatest interest to them. "Predigested" questions, on the other hand, (those formed by the teacher or another person) can only identify what seemed important to that person. Very often, these external questions do not correspond to the value of the material as seen by the students. If reading comprehension is evaluated solely by student responses to external questions, the students' potential for comprehending material on their own terms may never be realized. The students will always believe that they must conform to the thoughts of others. Therefore, in order to help black students to acquire experience as authorities of their own interpretations, teachers should provide many opportunities for self-imposed questioning.

External questions, however, do serve a purpose in instruction. They are useful in helping students to see another's point of view. To maximize this utility, these questions should be asked more than once. This might be accomplished by having students read a selection or a text at the beginning of a term and respond to external questions. The responses are retained and the same material is assigned toward the end of the term. The response at the end should be different because as students acquire more knowledge, their powers of interpretation are intensified. They acquire newer frames of reference and are able to make more applications. This may lead to a revision of their basic construct system. If this happens, students will realize that ideas that are firmly entrenched can be discarded if newer ideas are more palatable. This kind of concept manipulation is necessary for black students because it provides practice in using new knowledge to effect change in basic perceptions.

Teachers who invest their time in the careful planning of instructional strategies geared to specific learners will find these activities are far more effective in producing good readers than are reading skill exercises. This does not minimize the need for all students to learn basic skills. Rather, it accentuates the view that skills are more easily learned when they are woven into relevant content. This facilitates the application of skills as they are mastered. It can also lead to an interdisciplinary approach to learning if techniques are used to help students to make connections in thought processes. For example, students can be asked to locate information on a particular topic. After reading this material, students can discuss what they have read as if they were someone other than themselves. They might assume the role of political scientists, sociologists and psychologists and define "democracy" from those perspectives or discuss teenage pregnancy as if they were parents, school counselors, or tenth graders. The interdisciplinary approach can also be emphasized by allowing students to complete the assignment for more than one course.

If a term paper or written term project is assigned in history, sociology or psychology, students can select one topic that can be used in each of those courses simultaneously. The research and the focus will be different in each course, but the students will clearly see the comparisons as well as the contrasts. It appears that Kelly's theory supports this practice. He writes:

> Events upon which facts are based hold no institutional loyalties. They are in the public domain. The same event may be construed simultaneously and profitably within various disciplinary systems (Kelly 1955).

Helping students to comprehend content material from different vantage points develops their ability to scrutinize their own ideas. This increases their powers of abstraction, which allows them to step outside themselves and peer in again at their own construct system for purposes of analysis. The students can then infuse new ideas that are met in reading without the fear of destroying the system because as new ideas are added, less productive ones are destroyed in the reconstruction process.

In these learning experiences, each student will progress at a different rate because the starting points are not the same. Some students have built stronger construct systems than others and are more entrenched in their own beliefs. Teachers should not be discouraged by this mark of individuality. On the contrary, it should cause them to increase their efforts to attain objectives by acquainting all students with an ever widening range of materials with varying viewpoints. Even though some students will find more digestible ideas than others, the exposure stirs the digestive activity. If teachers exercise restraint and "prod" cautiously, even the most hesitant students will develop a willingness to accept new ideas and make them their own.

This mode of instruction does not lend itself to prescriptive teaching because it is more subjective than objective. Nevertheless, it helps students to understand that personal interpretation is a valued undertaking. Through this revelation, reading becomes an experience which helps students to organize reality instead of a means of reacting to it. This is consistent with Kelly's belief that learning *is* the reconstruction of ideas. The control tower of learning is occupied by the student. What is actually learned in a classroom is dependent on the constructions that students place on what is encountered. All that is heard and read in and out of the classroom serves as a springboard for new knowledge, but where the students will land intellectually as a result of their leap cannot be accurately determined by the teacher. Teachers who embrace this approach must believe that the "journey" along the road of ideas is more important and valuable than the "destination."

The approach is facilitated by idea exchanges through interpersonal relations in the classroom. If through reading students can understand their own construct systems, they can develop an empathy and appreciation for the ideas of others. This does not necessitate conformity, but it insures inter-group communication. It allows reading to lead the way from personal introspection to group participation. It provides an opportunity for students to communicate with authors who are physically removed from the environment, and this gives them more confidence in relating to those who are accessible to them. Reading, then, becomes a means of helping students travel to the depths of their own perceptions and to understand more about the perceptions of others.

Finally, Kelly frees students from the strongholds of their pasts. His assertion that "no one is a victim of his biography" (Kelly 1955), is powerful when applied to the education of black students, destroying in one fell swoop all of the myths that abound in education about the inability of these students to "rise above" their assessed abilities.

Reading is the most assessed skill in the educative process. Reading scores haunt black students from the earliest grades to places of employment in adulthood. However, tests can measure only what students are willing to reveal, and black students often respond in a chameleon way to test questions. Moreover, the objective nature of standardized tests can only measure past performance. Kelly posits that behavior cannot be assessed from past performance alone, for it is at once a manifestation of the past, present, and future. The evaluation and labeling of black students on the basis of data gathered from achievement tests leads to stereotyped conclusions about them. This practice is deeply rooted in all levels of education.

Adherents of Kellian theory, however, will support the position that students' destinies are in their own hands and not in percentile ratings. Indeed, there are factors of life for black students and these can have an effect on performance ability. If one holds with Kelly, however, it is the manner in which students perceive these realities that will determine their ability to overcome them. Learning experiences similar to the ones mentioned above can help students to use the disadvantaged condition as a bridge to success rather than as a mountain to impede its attainment.

Conclusion

This discussion enhances the need for black students to develop improved self-concepts and confidence in their own abilities. These perceptions should also be internalized by their teachers, who should constantly emphasize the possibilities for growth and further development. It is through reading that students can capture bits of reality to embellish the constructs they have formed through experience. If those who work with black students will internalize Kelly's conviction that personality orchestrates human behavior, reading instruction can become the means whereby students are introduced to ideas which can have a positive effect on their performance. Teachers who accept this challenge can face students unmoved by reading tests scores or unfortunate circumstances of birth. They can meet students as "scientists" who must enter the laboratory of life determined to hypothesize and experiment until weak constructs are eliminated and are replaced with stronger, more durable ones. These students may not transform the world, but the systems they build for themselves will be bold enough to meet it head on and efficient enough to assimilate its realities without being destroyed by them.

References

Kelly, George A. *A Theory of Personality: The Psychology of Personal Constructs.* New York: W. W. Norton & Co., 1955.

Reading Materials

Dolores Straker
New York College, CUNY, Jamaica, New York

Slow progress by black children during the early school years has caused a great deal of concern on the part of linguists and educators. Some of these professionals believe that at least a part of the difficulty these children face in learning to read stems from the disparity between the oral language they speak (black English) and the printed variety (standard English) they encounter in school. The interests of these professionals has led to the development of beginning reading materials, theoretical positions and instructional techniques geared specifically to children who speak black English. While there has been little research to support these approaches, it is important to look closely at them in order to identify inherent strengths and weaknesses in their ability to effect positive changes in black children's reading performances.

There are basically three approaches for which there exist reading materials: (1) dialect readers, (2) oral language development programs, and (3) programs emphasizing teacher awareness of black English.

Dialect Readers

Experimental readers published in 1969 by the Educational Study Center in Washington, D.C. and the Chicago Psycholinguistic Reading Series developed by Davis, Gladney, and Leaverton (1968) both belong to the dialect readers approach which advocates the use of one's native language for reading instruction. The basic premise is that the grammatical mismatch between the child's spoken language and the beginning reading materials can be minimized if the reading materials are structured to be relevant to the background and experience of the learner as well as to reflect the student's grammatical patterns. Both series focus on the grammatical mismatch between

139

Standard English (SE) and Black English (BE) by utilizing the comparative approach and presenting identical stories in two language varieties: everyday talk and school talk. Everyday talk is supposed to represent a variation of black English while school talk is representative of standard English. Three major problems with these series can be identified: (1) the texts reflect the difficulty in translating from BE into SE, (2) even when the match between BE and SE features can be controlled, the BE features are overused to the extent that they occur more frequently in print than they naturally would in oral language, and (3) the BE features are awkwardly combined with SE constructions, causing the language flow to appear quite unnatural.

Problematic Translations

    Experimental Series—"Ollie"

Everyday Talk	School Talk
Ollie *have* a big family.	Ollie *has* a big family.
He *have* three sister.	He *has* three sisters.

    Chicago Psycholinguistics Reading Series—"My Family"

Everyday Talk	School Talk
I got a mama.	I have a mama.
I got a daddy.	I have a daddy.
I got a sister.	I have a sister.

    In the Experimental Series the contrasted features are "have" and "has," while in the Psycholinguistic Series, the contrasted features are "got" and "have." There is no reason why the BE (Everyday Talk) sentence in the Experimental Series could not have been "Ollie got a big family." Both "Ollie got" and "Ollie have" are BE forms that translate into "Ollie has."

Overuse

    Experimental Series—"Ollie"

    Everyday Talk

    Mamma *she* go to work.

    Big Mamma *she* take care of Ollie . . .

    Ollie tell Leroy, *he* say, "I want some soda."

    And Leroy *he* say, "I want some soda too."

This appositive type structure is certainly characteristic of BE but it does not occur as frequently in speech as it occurs in this short passage.

Awkward Construction

Psycholinguistic Series—"My Family"

My daddy good.
My *strong* daddy good.

My mamma funny.
My *pretty* mamma funny.

My grand mamma pretty.
My *old* grand mamma pretty.

My family funny.
My *loud* family funny.

The omission of the verb "is" occurring with the subject adjective is an awkward construction. The omission is repeated so consistently that it does not help to reinforce the use of the subject adjective, the apparent goal of this particular lesson.

Two final criticisms of these materials are in order. First, the Experimental Series seems to try to use the syntactic patterns of beginning readers, but as the story progresses, some of the syntactic structures become quite complex. Unlike the Chicago Psycholinguistic Series, there is no focus on the comparison of one feature at a time. The syntactic features are not systematically controlled with respect to occurrence of difficulty. Second, the Psycholinguistic Series, on the other hand, does control the difficulty of the text and the occurrence of the features they wish to expose to the students but, in doing the latter, the materials do not reflect the same kind of variation that occurs in the spoken language. A study conducted by one of the authors of this series demonstrated that the program seemed to be successful with boys who scored in the lowest quartile on reading readiness tests given at the beginning of the first grade. However, it is difficult to determine the specific population the materials might benefit because they do not accurately reflect the children's actual word patterns or grammatical structures.

Teacher Awareness Approach

The Bridge Cross-Culture Reading Program, developed by Simpkins, Simpkins, and Holt (1977), includes dialect readers, but another primary objective is to increase the awareness of teachers who work with BE speakers. The latter approach advocates making teachers aware of BE so that they will not confuse its use with real reading problems. This program, like the Experimental and Psycholinguistic Series, makes use of the comparative approach. It employs three language forms—standard English, a transitional form and black English. This reading series is aimed toward the older reader at the junior and senior high school level who has exhibited previous reading difficulty. According to the authors, the stories "are about realistic, contemporary black characters and are set in surroundings that most black students know." The Bridge Series places emphasis on language skills already in the students' repertories using materials representative of their cultural experiences. The pedagogical philosophy underlying the Bridge Series is that it starts where the student is by building on his or her cultural linguistic knowledge. Using these primary language skills as a foundation, the program enables the student to develop a sense of competency in reading the dialect materials and to transfer this reading competency to materials written in standard English.

The series consists of five booklets that initially have stories written only in black vernacular and gradually move to stories written only in standard English. Many of the stories in the vernacular are tape-recorded and others in standard English also have recorded introductions. Each study booklet in the series is accompanied by its own teacher's edition, which provides story questions (and answers) and the nine comprehension skills focused on throughout the series. These skills include determining meaning from context, recognizing figures of speech, key words, word order, time order, word parts, making inferences, finding the main idea, and identifying causes and effects.

While there are no data to attest to the effectiveness of the Bridge Series, it is to be commended for several reasons: (1) The stories that are written in the vernacular are representative of folklore and are presented in a fashion that is not awkward for the reader. Additionally, there are taped versions and brief introductions. (2) The series is specifically targeted at an identifiable reading group and makes a sincere effort to provide positive motivation and a successful reading experience. (The materials are organized such that seeing and reading the stories in the vernacular does not arouse those negative attitudes evoked when language is not appropriately suited to the context.) (3) The series and its teacher's manual are well organized. The teacher's manual outlines: (a) the introduction to the program, (b) the program's philosophy, (c) who will benefit from the program, (d) a teaching-learning strategy for using the series, (e) student selection procedures, (f) a full description of the materials, (g) the teacher's role in instruction, (h) an explanation of peer control reading, (i) a master lesson plan, and (j) some background material on black vernacular. It does not threaten the teacher who is unfamiliar with the BE speech community, and there is enough information to help the unfamiliar teacher become comfortable with the materials and with implementing them. (4) Finally, the basic principles and concepts are identical to those found in other widely used programs.

Oral Language Approach

One program that does not teach reading specifically but stresses teacher awareness of cultural factors is the Cultural Linguistic Approach, an early childhood educational program specializing in culture-based materials and methodologies for black children. These materials were developed by the Center for Inner City Studies at Northeastern Illinois University. This approach to teaching "requires that teachers recognize and accept the ethnic heritage of their pupils and build the instructional program around that culture base. Culture based instruction demands that curriculum content and teaching strategies be designed and implemented to enhance the child's social, physical and .ultural environment. The curriculum must build on those positives the children bring with them (to school)." The program manuals used to implement instruction cover the areas of oral language, social studies, science, mathematics, and physical education. Each manual offers several units with concepts, performance objectives, vocabulary, and sample lessons.

Since this is not a reading program, the Cultural Linguistic Approach does not provide a reading manual. The schools that use the culture based materials have their own reading programs. While the consultants of the program do not endorse or recommend any particular basal reader, they do encourage the schools to use a total reading program, and they emphasize the value of the language experience approach as part of this total reading program.

It is especially interesting to note that the oral language instructional sequence focuses on many of the skills that are necessary for successful reading. For example, the kindergarten/primary manual is organized into three sections. The first section concentrates on developing a descriptive vocabulary stressing the following concepts and activities: attributes, temporal and spatial relationship of oral speech to its written counterpart, expanding word meaning, and basic sight word understanding. The second section concentrates on developing a cognitive vocabulary stressing the cognitive processes of observation, classification, association, cause and effect, sequence, conclusion, and influence and on solving intellectual and social problems. Finally, the third section concentrates on developing an expressive vocabulary. The children are encouraged to explore and express their inner feelings and to learn several ways to convey thoughts and emotions. Hall (1979) suggests that familiarity with a variety of vocabulary words and consequently a variety of concepts helps young children to become more adept at being effective communicators in contexts other than home and family. This observation is consonant with the Cultural Linguistic Approach.

Like the Bridge Series, the materials for the Cultural Linguistic Approach are well organized. The staff of the Center for Inner City Studies provides inservice training directly for the teachers, paraprofessionals, parents, and for school as well as program administrators.

The Curriculum Research Project at Brooklyn College organized by Carol Reed and Milton Baxter offers contrastive materials to teach college freshmen English composition as a second dialect approach (one aspect of the oral language approach). These materials permit one to examine both BE and SE linguistic systems by emphasizing the systematic nature of both and explicating the points of contrast between the two. The materials aim to develop the students' consciousness about their dialect so that they are better able to understand and recognize the points of contrast and interference between this dialect and the SE encountered in the classroom. Additionally, the program is designed to help the student develop the composition skills necessary for effective written communication in the academic environment. Students are placed into this particular composition sequence based on an English composition entrance examination administered to all incoming freshmen students. The students are required to accomplish the traditional tasks of English composition classes, but they are also exposed to BE as an oral tradition. An effort is made to identify the specific points of grammatical contrast between BE and SE which interfere with the students' achieving functional competence in standard English and it emphasizes the notion that language (written or spoken) must be appropriate for the context in which it is used. While the materials for this program are not published, Reed and Baxter do hold workshops for those composition instructors interested in using the materials. In these workshops questions are posed, private techniques are shared and many unanticipated problems are worked out.

Even though the Curriculum Research Project is designed to teach composition rather than reading, the two skills are closely related and many of the students who are placed into this type of English sequence also have poor reading skills. It is similar to the Bridge Series in that it utilizes the skills the students bring to the learning situation. This type of strategy seems to come closer to achieving the primary goal of written communication because it enhances those learning strategies the students have already internalized. There are no subtle implications in this program that the student or the student's language is inferior.

Summary

It can be concluded that there are promising ways to use BE as a pedagogical tool to advance the reading capabilities of the students who participate in this language tradition. The Bridge Series, the Curriculum Research Project and the Cultural Linguistic Approach are cases in point. Some of these materials combine approaches while others add a new dimension. The Bridge Series utilizes BE folktales and other stories printed in BE dialect. With the tapes and introductory notes provided, the use of the dialect in this context does not appear awkward, unusual, or offensive. The Curriculum Research Project, in its comparative approach to grammar, tries to make students more sociolinguistically aware of the relation between language use and context-appropriate situations. Because it is a tool for English composition, it cannot be identified as an approach to reading instruction. However, since it relies so heavily on contrastive analysis, it is closest in theory to the oral language approaches that stress bidialectalism. It adds a new and positive dimension to this approach because its emphasis is on a sociolinguistic understanding of language rather than an oral language skill. The oral language sequence of the Cultural Linguistic Approach emphasizes the need to develop effective communication strategies in students and does so in a twofold manner. The child's culture and language are used as a base from which those concepts crucial for successful reading are introduced and reinforced. This method also is an extension of the oral language development approach. It focuses, however, on conceptual development rather than on eventual changes in the speaker's syntactic patterns.

Although research data supporting the effects of these approaches are lacking, these programs have potential because they stress respect for the learner and his or her innate strengths and competencies. Each program in some manner tries to build on these strengths and broaden the competencies. Therefore, these programs provide the students with positive learning contexts and emphasize to the teacher and the researcher how crucial it is to understand fully the underlying factors of a learner's use of language.

References

Davis, Olga J., M. R. Gladney, and L. Leaverton. *Psycholinguistic Reading Series.* Chicago: Board of Education, 1968.

Hall, W. S., and W. E. Nagey. *Theoretical Issues in the Investigation of Words of Internal Report (Technical Report No. 146).* Urbana, Ill.: Center for Study of Reading, University of Illinois, 1979.

Simpkins, Gary, C. Simpkins, and G. Holt. *Bridge: A Cross-Culture Reading Program.* Boston: Houghton Mifflin, 1977.

III Writing

Introduction: Writing

Delores Lipscomb
Chicago State University, Illinois

When I write, I feel as though my pen can't move fast enough. My thoughts fly, and I try to catch the good ideas by writing them down. When I really get into what I'm writing, I feel as though my thoughts will never end.

Christine Lee, Age 11

When I write, I go through this search for words and ideas that I sometimes can't find. Sometimes, I'll spend a long time trying to fix an idea. I might add a sentence or take one away. Then, I look again, and the whole thing seems exaggerated and doesn't say what I mean. So I try again. I look at the sentences and try to match them with my imagination—with the story I'm trying to tell. Maybe this time it says exactly what I mean to say.

Norma Johnson, Age 12

Those youngsters' views of the composing process contrast sharply with the traditional conception of how black students should be taught to write. Many teachers equate the teaching of writing with the eradication of deviant language patterns. Unfortunately, for them, writing has become synonymous with teaching grammar and those surface features of the language which are not composing. This confusion over the composing process has led many teachers to exclude those strategies that encourage written language growth.

Research now demonstrates that the composing process is cyclical or recursive, involving many stops, conscious readings, rereadings, and revisions occurring repeatedly until the message is fully developed. Of course, this description of the composing process is somewhat simplistic and narrow and does not fully explain the complex operations that occur. What is to be emphasized is that writing necessitates deliberate thinking and planning. The student receives some form of stimulus and initiates the writing act. The writer first engages in mental activities that lead to discoveries about the intended message. In doing so, the writer examines his or her experience and knowledge, frequently grasping a new concept or giving a free treatment to an old thought. But the writer's discernments do not end here. Other discoveries are made about the numerous relationships existing between language and the message. As choices in terms of purpose, audience, and style are made, the writer learns something about the limitations and restraints imposed by each one. These discoveries may in turn necessitate a series of subsequent stops, changes, and revisions. These speculations and explanations into the broader dimensions of language and the message recur until no new discoveries are made. Sondra Perl (1980) observes that discovery in writing means that "we end up with a process that teaches us something that clarifies what we know . . . , and that lifts out or explicates or enlarges our experience." Clearly, writing enlarges the students' writing experiences in numerous ways.

Through writing students can practice the subtleties of language. They write poems, scripts or fashion raw materials from their observations into a narrative or an expository commentary. Through writing in its various forms, students can also be led to think more critically about what they read or hear. Writing is a vital part of the language development process. It enables students to explore their ideas and fantasies, to seek out and express themselves as human beings.

The teacher, of course, has the responsibility of providing experiences that enhance language growth. But how is this to be done? Drills and excessive pattern practice in language labs or other isolated situations, in addition to being dull, have not proved to be effective in changing language behavior. Regardless of how they are approached, these drills do not occur in response to any real purpose such as conveying an experience, option or emotion. True language learning never occurs in a void; it always occurs in the context of an audience, situation and purpose. The aim, it seems, should be to teach black students to use language in a variety of situations and in a variety of styles to use language fully and richly whenever and wherever the need for communication arises. The focus then is not placed on errors and dilectual differences, but on enlarging the students' capacity to adapt written language for multiple uses.

If writing affords so many opportunities to learn and discover things about one's self, the topics, and language, what can teachers do to produce effective writing experiences? First, they can develop relevant and meaningful writing assignments. The assignments should be carefully sequenced and planned so that simple tasks lead to more complex ones, while brief papers and personal commentaries lead to longer essays with challenging topics. All assignments must embody critical thinking with analysis and synthesis of the subject matter. This approach does not consist of teaching pure logic or syllogistic reasoning nor is it solely introducing students to the theoretical modes of discourse. It is a commitment to designing writing tasks that reflect real situations involving audience, purpose, and other strategies underlying everyday communication. Above all, these assignments must highlight the various aspects of the writing process and supply ample opportunity for practice.

Second, each piece of writing must be accepted with understanding and respect for the writer. Each piece of writing is an expression—an act of communication from one human being to another. In an atmosphere of mutual respect and encouragement, writing principles can be established and discussed in terms of how well they were accomplished. In such an environment, critical comments from the teacher or peers do not alienate students but are accepted as guidelines for improving their written language. It is primarily through this kind of exposure to practical writing assignments and the process of composing that students can compose freely and earnestly, acquiring skills that "clarify and explicate their experiences."

Janis Epps discusses the teaching of composition and its effect on millions of black American students. In her view, composition courses for black Americans and the working-class poor do not contribute to students' growth as thinkers, writers, or individuals. Rather, these courses are debilitating experiences that perpetuate the inequalities in the American school system by maintaining blacks in an impoverished, oppressed state. The Epps article serves both as an introduction to this section and as a warning regarding what can happen when students are not taught properly. It is followed by practical teaching suggestions.

Jacqueline Royster reassesses the teaching of composition maintaining that, although research has created a large data base, much more information is needed so that black students are no longer viewed as atypical. Her essay concludes with two process-oriented inquiry teaching techniques.

Poet/publisher/essayist Haki Madhubuti (Don L. Lee) examines his own experiences as a writer of poetry. He explores such principles as triteness, originality, details, and color imagery and concludes with some hard advice as to how young writers can improve their craft and use writing as a tool to serve the interest of black people.

Paul Ramsey describes his experiences in training graduate students to teach writing to dialect speakers. His emphasis on pedagogical issues and teachers' attitudes rather than dialectal differences sets the tone for the rest of the articles. Robert Fowler's article investigates the composing process of black dialect users. The paper demonstrates the naturalness of composing and the fact that these composers, like others, utilize strategies in a consistent manner. More important, Fowler's article discusses those factors that may impede writing growth.

Vivian Davis, using student conferences, illustrates the role of revision in the writing process and stresses the need for the teacher to act as editor. In this role, the teacher shows the student how to become a confident writer. She urges teachers to avoid focusing on errors and to help the students to intuit the problems and to make decisions about how to improve writing. A similar conference approach is used by Barbara Hunt as she outlines a student-centered course that integrates reading and writing and oral language skills.

Using a combination of student conferences and laboratory approach, Carolyn Drakeford portrays an individualized approach that utilizes drills and exercises while exposing students to composing numerous forms of discourse.

Ernest Bradford and Ethel Taylor argue that composition must ultimately be extended beyond the composition classes. They describe a two-semester freshman composition course that involves faculty from other departments and utilizes resources in the community. With the primary purpose of enabling students to see the relationship between writing and the outside world, students were introduced to oral history research techniques and business writing. The authors discovered that students in the program more readily assumed responsibility for their own writing growth. Edward Anderson addresses the rich oral and folklore tradition that black students have inherited. He discusses oral strategies existing in black culture and demonstrates how they can be used in composition classes to teach exposition and argumentation.

In my paper, I discuss some strategies for teaching writing to gifted black junior high school students.

This section concludes with Arthuree McCoy and Linda Kumi setting forth procedures for teaching early reading and writing skills. The approach utilizes the children's prior knowledge and relies heavily upon numerous oral language experiences and games that set the stage for the acquisition of reading and writing skills.

References

Emig, Janet. "Writing as a Mode of Learning." *College Composition and Communication* 28 (May 1977): 122–28.

Larson, Richard L. "Selected Bibliography of Research and Writing about the Teaching of Composition, 1977." *College Composition and Communication* 29 (May 1978): 181–94.

Sommers, Nancy. "Revision Strategies of Student Writers and Experienced Adult Writers." *College Composition and Communication* 31 (December 1980): 378–88.

Perl, Sondra. "Understanding Composing." *College Composition and Communication* 31 (December 1980): 363–69.

Moffett, James. *A Student-Centered Language Arts Curriculum, K–13: A Handbook for Teachers.* Houghton Mifflin, 1972.

Killing Them Softly:
Why Willie Can't Write

Janis Epps
Atlanta Junior College, Georgia

A wholesale slaughter of Afro-Americans is taking place in this country every day! It is a massacre more complete than America's eradication of the American Indian, more devastating than Hitler's mass murder of the Jewish people, and more dehumanizing than American slavery. Black students are, in effect, being murdered in classrooms throughout this country. No guns, knives, lynch ropes, or drugs are necessary. The minds of black students are robbed and mugged on a daily basis because they are not being taught to read and write so that they can determine the course of their own lives.

Many people may view the above statements as harsh and exaggerated. Can the literacy crisis affecting black Americans be compared to the horrors of slavery and the holocaust? I think so. The tragedy concerning the illiteracy of black Americans may not be as graphic as bloody bodies lying on a battlefield, but the results are just as terrifying. For not only are the students who sit in those classrooms today affected, but so are generations of black Americans yet to be born.

On the one hand, the American educational system has been proficient in teaching black Americans to be functionally literate. Our people are literate enough to sign their names to checks and to open credit accounts to ensure their indebtedness to the American capitalist economy. On the other hand, they are not literate enough to seize the power of the written word and thus change the course of their destiny.

Paulo Freire, writing in *Education for Critical Consciousness*, says "to acquire literacy is more than to psychologically and mechanically dominate reading and writing techniques. It is to dominate these techniques in terms of consciousness; to understand what one reads and to write what one understands; it is to communicate graphically. Acquiring literacy does not involve memorizing sentences, words, or syllables—lifeless objects unconnected to an existential universe—but rather an attitude of creation and re-creation, a self-transformation producing a stance of intervention in one's context" (1974).

It is Freire's definition of literacy, "a conscious intervention in one's context," which has eluded black Americans and kept us from becoming truly literate. We have not been allowed to acquire true literacy. That acquisition would necessitate an analysis of who we are and would point a critical finger at the continued racist and classist nature of America. Such an analysis would not focus simply on the horrors of slavery, but rather on the horrors of the legacy of slavery in American classrooms today.

During the time of slavery, it was illegal to teach a black person to read and write. Only after the Civil War, during the time of Reconstruction, when it benefited America for black people to participate in the monied economy was the teaching of reading and writing legitimized. Ostensibly, the teaching of reading and writing was legitimized to eliminate illiteracy and ignorance. But realistically, this legitimization was a way of maintaining the superiority of white people and the inferiority of black people.

> If you can control a man's thinking, you do not have to worry about his actions. When you determine what a man shall think, you do not have to concern yourself about what he will do. If you make a man feel that he is inferior, you do not have to compel him to accept an inferior status, for he will seek it himself. If you make a man think that he is justly an outcast, you do not have to order him to the back door. He will do it without being told; and if there is no back door, his very nature will demand one (Carter, Woodson 1933, 84).

In American classrooms one of the major ways of controlling "a man's thinking" and thus his actions has been the American approach to teaching black students to write.

Writing, as it has traditionally been taught in school systems throughout America, continues to be a way of ensuring that those students who have been blatantly misused by American society—the black working poor—will continue to occupy the most powerless position in this nation. To give writing courses so much power is to recognize the phenomenal importance of this one school subject. Composition is the gatekeeper of the inequalities perpetuated in the American system. As it is conceived by the public at large, composition is a skills-oriented, grammar course. By those in the English profession, it is a craft course which help students get ahead in society.

In function, composition instruction is simply the handmaiden of an educational system intent upon maintaining distinct class and racial lines. Privileged youth attend our country's most prestigious institutions where, in their composition courses, they are exposed to ideas and encouraged to respond in writing to those ideas; black and poor youth, on the other hand, are ushered into remedial writing programs where they themselves come to believe that they have no ideas worth expressing and that workbook grammar exercises will lead magically to success in life. The teaching of writing, then, is one of the most effective instruments in perpetuating an oppressed and impoverished status in society.

Rather than a vital course which seeks to aid students in developing skills which will be important to them as individuals, rather than a broadening course which will help them think critically about the world around them and their relation to it, rather than a challenging course which will encourage them to reach their maximum potential, composition is, to most students, a bewildering maze which contributes little to their growth as writers and even less to their growth as individuals. Unfortunately, the main purpose of the composition class, the development of writing skills, is rarely attained by minority and poor students.

While we know that such factors as subject-verb agreement, sentence construction, and punctuation have their place—their vital place in good writing—it is more crucial that we develop within our students critical thinking skills and a respect for their own personal experiences and those of their poeple as well as create opportunities for self-development. Unless writers believe that they have something worthwhile and important to say, unless they feel that they are important enough to say it, and unless they have faith that saying it will somehow make a difference, they may see—and justifiably so—no real need to put forth the kind of effort required to improve their ability in writing.

Unfortunately, most college composition classes are narrow, constricting courses which seek to control thinking rather than expand it. Jeffrey Youdelman, in his insightful article "Limiting Students: Remedial Writing and the Death of Open Admissions" points out the folly of such teaching and shows the necessity of student's making transferences from the "particulars of daily life to the general characteristics of the system in which we live" (Youdelman 1978). After having observed a freshman composition course in which the professor was teaching "limiting topics" as a method of getting started in writing, Youdelman states:

> Yet here was teaching working class students that they must limit themselves and actually fear making connections, for they might fail to do a complete job, get lost, and perhaps worst of all, find while assembling their images and ideas the real need to master an element of grammar and syntax which learning by exercise and rote had never previously made important. This model of essay writing, which discourages students from developing a connected world view, tells them that, since they lack certain grammatical skills, they should handle only the simplest of ideas— if ideas at all. It tells them that until they have mechanically mastered the exercises on subordination, they should not attempt to find the primary and subordinate aspects of two related things (1978, 562).

Herein lies the tragedy of most typical composition programs to which black students are exposed. Little attempt is made to connect the wider reality of the system in which we live to the students' awareness of themselves and their place in the world. Nor are they expected to know how they can use literacy to further social or personal ends in society. Much of what is taught is taught in a vacuum, isolated from the students' lives and from the values of human freedom and truth. Workbook exercises, teacher lecturing, reading from rhetorics without benefit of discussion, and papers written with the teacher as the only audience are all examples of teaching methods which promote feelings of isolation and disconnectedness in the English classroom, and encourage students' beliefs that skills rather than ideas are the "meat" of writing.

Further, the language black students speak and write is thought to be deficient. The language reflects their culture, and it too is thought of as invalid and inferior, Geneva Smitherman, writing in *Talkin and Testifyin*, says that these attitudes toward black language

> generally reflect the power elite's perceived insignificance and hence rejection of Afro-American language and culture. It has as its fundamental (albeit unarticulated) objective using blacks to sustain the status quo. With this goal in mind the cognitive input of language remediation programs has of necessity to be educationally patronizing and linguistically stultifying. Since it ain bout the acquisition of real knowledge at all—which gives people power, both to change themselves and their society (1977, 209).

The textbooks currently in use help maintain the status quo. Richard Ohmann, in *English in America: A Radical View of the Profession*, took an informal survey of fourteen texts currently in use in English classrooms. He concluded that:

158   *Janis Epps*

These authors make relatively explicit what almost all assume: composition helps students get ahead in society and also helps preserve society itself in its American form. The authors see their craft functioning within the status quo. They see the users of that craft as pursuing mainly individual goals against an unchanging social backdrop. And they see students (future people, one could say) as undifferentiated, except by personality and personal goals. In short, the textbooks operate without a stated analysis of literacy in technological society and without a politics (1976, 146–47).

Striated and segmented, the composition classroom functions in much the same way. As teachers, we have successfully taken the life-blood out of our teaching of composition and made it a course which punishes and literally kills off those who have the greatest needs to change the status quo.

"Teaching strategies which seek only to put white middle-class English into the mouths of black speakers ain did nothin to inculcate the black perspective necessary to address the crisis in the black community" (Smitherman 1977, 209). They are not killing us anymore by lynching us from oak trees, but we're dying nonetheless in English classrooms nationwide.

References

Freire, Paulo. *Education for Critical Consciousness.* New York: Seabury, 1974.

Ohmann, Richard. *English in America: A Radical View of the Profession.* New York: Oxford University Press, 1976.

Smitherman, Geneva. *Talkin and Testifyin: The Language of Black America.* Boston: Houghton Mifflin, 1977.

Woodson, Carter G. *The Mis-Education of the Negro.* New York: AMS Press, 1933.

Youdelman, Jeffrey. "Limiting Students: Remedial Writing and the Death of Open Admissions." *College English* 39 (January 1978): 562–72.

A New Lease on Writing

Jacqueline Royster
Spelman College, Atlanta, Georgia

The achievement levels of black students in writing, like those of students in general, are inadequate. The students are not demonstrating the quality of skills which we would like. They do not seem to be consistent in their abilities to judge a writing task, to formulate appropriate strategies for carrying out the task, or to produce written products which are representative of clear and effective thought and clear and fluent usage of language. Generations of inequities—political, economic, educational, and social—certainly have to be held accountable in large part for this dilemma. However, we cannot spend our time bemoaning past injustices. We are most obligated now to keep them from being ongoing injustices. As professional educators, our task is to move students, despite inequities, from where they are to where we would like them to be.

Such has always been the unnegotiated mandate of the black colleges. Their records demonstrate that their historical missions have had to be the positive redirection of the inequities of the past into the achievements of the present and future. Their tasks have been to take their students, usually with excellent potential but sometimes weak academic preparation, and to make sure that they are competent and competitive in the modern work force and in their present-day communities.

One important example which these colleges offer the rest of higher education is their tendency to view black students in a more positive light. The students are not continuously categorized as the "minority" population or the "nontraditional" population, or by some other classification which places stress on separateness from the "normal" group of students. Quite the contrary. On the campuses of historically black institutions these students are the tradition and have been for over a century. They are accepted as typical rather than atypical students, and the concentration of effort is on the development and enhancement of them as students from diverse backgrounds and with various goals and aspirations. There seems to be a need for other educational institutions to move toward a similar perspective. The black colleges have been successful in producing graduates who can go on to high levels of achievement from a general perspective. The implication is that their approaches might also have potential for positive gains in the specific area of writing achievement as well, especially if our view of the general problem of writing skill development is clarified.

As educators, we are no longer concerned with looking at blacks and other minorities as our special problem-ridden students. We now know that students in general are (as we have heard so much recently) "at risk," and black students are no exception. They have always been at risk. Now we find, though, that they are not alone. The inadequacy of students' writing skills nationwide has dictated an acknowledgment of our basic responsibility: providing academic excellence for everyone. There is obviously a need for a broadly based change, but for black students in particular the question we must ask is: How can we redefine the problem so that realistic solutions can be formulated which will address current students, problems, and needs in meaningful and productive ways? Clearly, what we need is a new lease on writing.

The Beginnings of the New Lease

In the 1960s and 1970s we saw the generation of many data on the language and language uses of black people. Much of how teachers operate today is based on these data. Having isolated, analyzed, and synthesized various bits of linguistic information, we have become more conscious of occasions when grammatical errors are not errors but the problems of one system interfacing with another. We know more than we have ever known before. Our sensitivities have been heightened, and we have learned to address, as stated earlier, the "nontraditional" student. However, the hypotheses and theories which have grown out of this data base have been inadequate to address the challenges which we face in the classroom. We still cannot realistically claim that there has been any significant impact on the improvement of writing skills. Logically, then, one must assume that either the hypotheses and theories are inadequate, or the data base is inadequate, or both. Since the latter is likely to be the case, then the first effort toward meaningful change is to expand and clarify the data base.

There are many questions to be raised in this arena, but two basic ones are evident. First, who are the students and how do they use language, written and otherwise? Second, what processes do effective writers follow in the creation of their products and, by the same token, what happens when good readers read? The need for more information about the individuals whom we face is a crucial one. We need to know the specific features and conditions which may separate black students from others in the academic environment. We need also to understand better the features and conditions which are similar for all students regardless of individual backgrounds. Further, we must be particularly sensitive to the impact of changes economically, socially, or politically which might also impact upon the academic environment.

For example, twenty years ago we typically taught black students who had grown up in black communities and who had been educated with other black students by black teachers; those teachers, in turn, had also grown up with and been educated by black people. Do we know the impact of these circumstances on the education of those students? Today the changing levels of participation by blacks in society indicates that the circumstances have changed somewhat. We must consider, then, whether the changes (whatever they are and for whomever they are) make any difference in terms of the nature of the individuals we now face and the kinds of writing strengths and weaknesses these students are likely to exhibit. We must continually assess and reassess our data base to assure ourselves that our field of vision is not just clear, but finely tuned.

The same is true of our explorations of the writing-reading process. We need to know the dynamics of our actions as writers and readers. We know that there are features, values, and relationships to account for in both writing and reading. We know, in addition, that there is an interrelationship between the two processes that we must also fathom. What we don't know is enough about these processes to formulate clear conclusions about how we do either or how we should teach others to do either. Our understanding is simply incomplete.

Presently, there is tremendous activity in this area. Many researchers are on the move and their efforts should yield much needed information. Examples abound. There are Janet Emig (1982) and Janice Lauer (1982) with the process of inquiry; Sondra E. Perl (1980), Carol Berkenkotter (1981), and Ann Matsushashi (1981) with the composing process; Linda Flower and John R. Hayes (1977; 1980) with problem solving and the composing process; Lester Faigley and Stephen Witte (1981), Michael C. Flanigan and Diane S. Menendez (1980) with revision; Mimi Schwartz with revision (1983b) and word processing (1983a); Jerrie C. Scott, Lynn Q. Troyka (1983), and Charles Bazerman (1980) with reading and writing relationships; Sheridan Blau (1983) and Ann Brown (1980) with cognitive and metacognitive processes. Even so, we are fundamentally still in need of much focusing and fine tuning, and there is obviously much work ahead.

Moving Ahead

With the recognition of the need to expand and clarify the data base, we still cannot allow ourselves to get stuck in this clarifying mode. The information is important and needed, but we must move beyond the continuous maintenance and operation of data to the formulation and implementation of new theories based on the upgraded data.

In this effort, we have to be more concerned with not being limited by setting our own parameters too narrowly. We cannot be restricted by previously established perspectives of black students or of previous expectations for their academic achievement. These views just may not be capable of highlighting objectives and strategies that are adequate or productive in developing skills. Since solutions are dictated by the point of view one has of the problems, then we must make sure that our points of view can yield productivity. If problems have not been adequately addressed by the perspectives of the last twenty years, i.e., if students are not able to write effectively, then perhaps it's time to change the perspectives. Perhaps it's time to redefine the parameters, to take a close look at our discipline and a closer look at ourselves to see if perhaps some of the coordinates which have been programmed into current mechanisms might not be wrong.

We have spent time classifying black students into atypical categories, for instance, using minority, nontraditional, and other "sidestream" categories as opposed to "mainstream" ones. Perhaps doing so has not been productive. Even the more positive views based on such categories tend to picture black students as capable of normalcy rather than as normal. What benefits in skill development have been derived from doing so? The students are still not writing as effectively as we would like. If there have been any benefits at all, they obviously are not enough for us to continue along this path.

A more productive approach might be to take a more comprehensive view by categorizing black students, in keeping with Mina Shaughnessy's insights (1977), as inexperienced communicators who need to increase their flexibility, broaden their horizons, and expand their skill ranges. In the past we identified differences between traditional and nontraditional students. Perhaps these distinctions may now be subsumed if we can identify differences between experienced and inexperienced readers and writers as a broader category. If we can find out who these particular students are, where they are in our conceptualization of the writing process, and what strategies they have developed already for their communication tasks, then perhaps we can determine a direction and a mechanism for their expansion and further development. If we can set our sights more broadly so that we can include the previously nontraditional, separately classified exceptions, perhaps our barriers to success will not seem so impenetrable. Perhaps we can begin to formulate theories and develop strategies which will prove to be more productive in the actual improvement of writing skills. Actually, though, if the writing problems of black students can be recategorized as the problems of inexperienced communicators, then there are areas already identified which seem to have tremendous potential. The current trend toward process-oriented teaching seems to be a key asset.

In selecting a process-oriented approach, we must still be mindful that it implies a dynamic interactive relationship. The problem in focusing on process is that even though we are making marvelous discoveries, we still do not know enough about what constitutes the process and how those constituents interact, such that in operation our process sometimes seems to get sidetracked by the touchable, tangible product. We start out wanting to concentrate on improving the process so that the yield will be better, but sometimes we run out of vocabulary, techniques, energy, and time, and end up focused once again on our more comfortable, customized product where our old habits were formed. Despite these periodic inconsistencies, however, there is still the potential for great rewards, especially in the areas of inquiry, problem solving, and revision.

The potential for these strategies seems apparent when instructors are confronted by some students' inability to formulate questions. They have apparently learned to ask for clarification or to respond from likes and dislikes, but their questioning strategies may not include, to an acceptable degree, how to respond critically and with insight. They can generalize about feelings, but they may have more difficulty formulating questions with regard to the hows, whys, and wherefores of the values imposed by the feelings. They can react when questioned, but they seem not to have learned the significance of examining for themselves the quality of the idea as well as the idea itself. Consequently, they sometimes have difficulty producing pieces of writing which have life and substance, as well as structure, development, and organization.

In a confrontation of this sort, focusing on process provides some comfort. Discussions, papers, and other classroom activities can by this mechanism be viewed as dynamic parts of our overall experience as life-long learners, critical thinkers, problem solvers, and active participants in our communities. One example from my own experiences of how this focus can be manifested is in the use of brainstorming to get the students to see the importance of using their imaginations and letting their thoughts give birth to other thoughts. I have sometimes used a dramatic visual aid as a springboard to class discussion and then used the discussion as the basis for an individual follow-up writing assignment. For example, I have presented to a class a photograph of a middle-aged black man whose face shows the wear of the years (Bigby and Hill 1972). He is looking through a broken window, but there is little evidence in the picture of where the man is or what he is looking at. My first question is usually, "Who is this man?" and then perhaps "What can you say about him?" With little effort, the students can formulate various scenarios and assign various values. They can be spurred on by each other to greater and greater detail so that by the end of the discussion they have an information base from which they can develop a paper. I find that once the students engage in a few activities of this nature, I can use aids that are less dramatic and still get from them evidence of imaginative use of detail.

I also find that a rather simple questioning base such as this one can be extended to include basic problem-solving techniques and self-analysis and peer review. Problem solving can be translated as strategy-building, i.e., the clarification of the task, the exploration of values and choices, the selection of specific strategies, and the manifestation of those strategies into action. The students sometimes need to know just where to start in fulfilling a writing task and how to proceed with the task in a systematic manner in producing a draft (Flower and Hayes 1977). If they can start sometimes with questions to ask themselves, they are able to bring their ideas into focus and have some sense of writing as a process of decision making. The questions might include:

1. What is your specific *topic*? Include all significant limitations, e.g., descriptive, chronological, and spatial.

2. What is the particular question which you seek to answer about the specific topic?

3. What is your dominant purpose in this exploration?

4. What do you expect to achieve through the communication? How do you expect your reader to be affected?

5. Why is achieving this end significant?

6. Who is your audience—general characteristics, educational levels, general values, etc.?

7. What is your point of view?

8. With what tone of voice do you expect your paper to be read?

9. How will you determine length?

With a general exploration such as this one, the students are able to consider the values in engaging in the particular task and begin to see some of the choices which might be available and the decision which might need to be made in the process of solving the writing problem and producing a first draft.

The concept of drafting, i.e., the process of revision, then becomes increasingly important with the students' acceptance of the notion that they are involved in the act of creating, shaping and re-shaping, finishing and refinishing, viewing and reviewing, all with the specific intention of trying to elicit a particular response or set of responses from the potential readers of the ideas which they are framing. The task, then, is not to concentrate on surface modifications but to re-assess quality, impact, and overall effectiveness as determined by goals and objectives specifiable by the writer as part of the fundamental process of composing.

This act of reassessment ties directly into the process of self-analysis and peer review, that is, the formulation of specific questions to provoke thought about the written product. The questions are raised to get the students thinking about whether the ideas as framed will have the impact the writers anticipate. Sometimes the initial questions, in a peer review for example, can be very general.

1. What do you like best about this draft? Why?

2. What do you think the writer wants to do through this draft?

3. How do you think the writer wants the reader to be affected by the draft?

4. What do you think is the most fundamental point of this draft?

5. What parts of the draft do you think need further attention?

In fact, given the group of students and given their level of experience with responding as peers, sometimes just one question is sufficient to get the writers to consider substantive rather than surface changes.

The fundamental point to be made is that a process-oriented approach to the development of the writing skills of black students has the same potential that it has for the skill development of other students. If we do ineed move in this direction, what we will have to acknowledge first is that even though black students may be different from other students in a variety of ways, the process for educating them may be essentially the same as the process for students in general. We, then, might be in a position to stop identifying black students as forever atypical and to start concentrating our attention on the pressing battle to determine how children with all of their individual differences learn—and how and when we as educators can intervene positively in the learning process.

Secondly, as educators concerned with academic excellence for all, if we can stretch beyond customary limits (which by our own experiences have proven themselves to be inadequate), if we can find ways of looking which nurture and sustain the minds placed in our charge, if we can reorder priorities, readjust perspectives, broaden concepts and definitions of the who, what, how, where, and why of skill development, maybe our theoretical frameworks can serve us better so that the strategies which grow out of them can be more productive in eliciting from any student the types of writing behaviors which we find more acceptable.

References

Bazerman, Charles. "A Relationship between Reading and Writing: The Conversational Model." *College English* 41 (February 1980): 656–61.

Berkenkotter, Carol. "Understanding a Writer's Awareness of Audience." *College Composition and Communication* 32 (December 1981): 388–99.

Bigby, John, and Russell Hill. *Options: A Program for English.* New York: Houghton Mifflin, 1972.

Blau, Sheridan. "Invisible Writing: Investigating Cognitive Processes in Composition." *College Composition and Communication* 34 (October 1983): 297–312.

Brown, Ann L. "Metacognitive Development and Reading." In *Theoretical Issues in Reading Comprehension,* edited by R. J. Spiro, et al. Hillsdale, N.J.: Lawrence Erlbaum Associates, 1980.

Emig, Janet. "Inquiry Paradigms and Writing." *College Composition and Communication* 33 (February 1982): 64–75.

Faigley, Lester, and Stephen Witte. "Analyzing Revision." *College Composition and Communication* 32 (December 1981): 400–14.

Flanigan, Michael C., and Diane S. Menendez. "Perception and Change: Teaching Revision." *College English* 42 (November 1980): 256–66.

Flower, Linda, and John R. Hayes. "Problem-Solving Strategies and the Writing Process." *College English* 39 (December 1977): 449–61.

_____. "The Cognition of Discovery: Defining a Rhetorical Problem." *College Composition and Communication* 32 (February 1980): 21–32.

Lauer, Janice M. "Writing as Inquiry: Some Questions for Teachers." *College Composition and Communication* 33 (February 1982): 89–93.

Matsuhashi, Ann. "Pausing and Planning: The Tempo of Written Discourse Production." *Research in the Teaching of English* 15 (May 1981): 113–35.

Perl, Sondra. "The Composing Processes of Unskilled College Writers." *Research in the Teaching of English* 13 (December 1979): 317–36.

_____. "Understanding Composing." *College Composition and Communication* 31 (December 1980): 188–201.

Schwartz, Mimi. "Two Journeys through the Writing Process." *College Composition and Communication* 34 (May 1983): 188–201.

_____. "Revision Profiles: Patterns and Implications." *College English* 45 (October 1983): 549–58.

Scott, Jerrie C. "Reading-Writing Relations: From Theory to Pedagogy." Manuscript, n.d.

Shaughnessy, Mina P. *Errors and Expectations: A Guide for the Teacher of Basic Writing.* New York: Oxford University Press, 1977.

Troyka, Lynn Q. "The Writer as Conscious Reader." In *Selected Papers from the 1982 New York Writers Conference.* New York: Instructional Resource Center, City University of New York, 1983.

Hard Words and Clear Songs: The Writing of Black Poetry

Haki R. Madhubuti (Don L. Lee)
Institute of Positive Education

Prologue

Writers write. What they write about tells the reader to what extent they are involved with the real world.

Writing for me is a difficult process. I write best under pressure, under a deadline set for me by someone or one that I set for myself. I am not a professional or leisure writer. I do not earn my livelihood from writing, nor do I allot special time in the day just to write. Much of my writing is notetaking. I take an abundance of notes and these notes, at a later time, are developed into poems, essays and occasional fiction. Writing for me is also a form of life-therapy, but it is not my life. My life is too complex to be limited to one stimulus.

Writers are questioners of the world and doers within the world. They question everything and are not satisfied with quick surface answers. Richard Wright was a questioner. We can see it in his works—the fiction and nonfiction. W. E. B. Du Bois was a questioner—his output was triple that of the "average" writer, but he always maintained a high level of quality and content. Both men were of the world, but in their own way refused to be subordinated to the world. They were fighters, always aware of the war, and writing was a war weapon. And writing at its best for them was a tool, a vocation, a hammer to be used for the survival and development of the Race.

Aims

The writer is also the lively but lonely investigator, the seeker of unknowns, the wanderer along back alleys, through power corridors, and into the far reaches of her or his own mind and that of his or her people. Essentially, the loneliness comes from the demands of the writing form; although there are exceptions, one usually does not write in a group. Writing is a personal occupation, one man or woman, one pen or typewriter. Once the writer leaves the research, the study, she or he does battle with the blank sheet of paper. The writer is alone. It is a lonely vocation that is bound to affect the writer and those closest to him or her. When the writer begins to work, the most important concern is the relationship between the writer and the subject. The central question becomes: How to bring life to the subject?

This process, above all, requires discipline. The creative process is a disciplined process which most writers have had to teach themselves. In most cases, as soon as the writing begins, the interruptions seem to multiply—these interruptions are both real and unreal. Each phone call is attacked or ignored because the writer is more, or less, sensitive to the uses of his or her time. Family relationships are altered during this period. Also, the book that could have been read easily two months ago becomes a *priority* now—not because the book is essential to the writer's subject, but because it becomes a part of the writer's internal interruptions. These types of interference are often rationalized as direct contributions to the writing. Nonsense. Writers waste time, as do most people; this is why discipline is so important.

In many ways all writers are re-creators. They take in the world and retell it, reinterpret it for others in a form and style that should be unique for them, the readers, and the times. These times are space age times, and words come and go like Chicago's weather. The way the writer uses the words tells as much about him or her as a word-user as anything else can. The major distinction that can be made between writers (other than forms they work in) is their ability to say the same thing differently, originally using and "misusing" the language at will. The language is the tool, the weapon, and writers must train themselves to use it as a carpenter trains to use wood and nails, or as a farmer trains to use the earth.

Writer and Teacher

Just as I am a writer, I am also a teacher, and one of the most important tasks that I have as a teacher is to demystify the act of writing, particularly as it applies to the writing of poetry. I have discovered through years of experience that one of the best ways to teach young people how to develop their interests in poetry is to use music and recorded poems as they engage in the writing act. Both of these approaches I find personally rewarding, and as a result, I am able to heighten the students' interests not only in content but in the poet's craft as well. By increasing their awareness of the form and structure of poetry through a rigorous examination and discussion of poems students are better able to understand that the poet—like other writers—does more than record first impressions. The students also come to recognize that the writing of poetry is a complicated process requiring all the skills needed by writers of other forms, plus additional ones as well. Most important, these students begin to perceive that the poet, just as other writers, must develop—or rather possess—a keen eye, catching and questioning everything, the largest and the smallest detail, and reproducing it in a condensed form that challenges the readers' minds and emotions.

I have found that many poems written by Afro-American poets can be used to serve this purpose. I find that as a teacher, I can take the best of these writers and use their works as examples of how young people can begin to fashion language into a memorable experience, a form that challenges the reader on several levels. After all, that is what poetry does.

The writers who provide the best examples are not necessarily the best. Yet most do have something to say and say it in a way that people can understand and relate to. Langston Hughes's work is an excellent example of style and content that black people can relate to. His jazz poetry and "simple" folk tales not only established him as a "professional" writer of the very best order, but earned him the title "Dean" of black writers from his own people. Sterling Brown also comes to mind in terms of original style and content; his poetry and essays exemplify the highest tradition of black oral communication combined with scholarly research. For me, the content is as important as the style. Beautiful writing that does not say anything is only that—beautiful writing. Yet, bad writing containing the most revolutionary ideas is equally—first and last—bad writing. A standard must be met if the writer is to communicate effectively. The ability to develop a style that is clear, original, and communicative is what separates writers from nonwriters.

There are many ways to make a poem "a memorable experience," Gwendolyn Brooks says. One can use images, that is pictures, visible pictures, which carry the characteristics of the subject or which suggest the meaning and mood the writer is trying to create. One of the strengths of using images and metaphors is that often they carry the weight of symbols; that is they suggest multiple levels of meaning to the reader as well as allow the reading of his or her own experience into the image or metaphor. Another important technique for making the poem a "memorable experience" is to create characters, real people with whom the reader can feel and empathize. In poetry, however, when creating characters, the poet should search for only those crucial characteristics which symbolize what the character is most essentially about. Images, metaphors, characters take on visibility and become memorable by the use of concrete details. The following are examples of what I mean.

> . . . Prophet Williams, young beyond St. Julia,
> and rich with Bible; pimples, pout; who reeks
> with lust for his disciple, is an engine
> or candid steel hugging combustibles.

Gwendolyn Brooks created this character in the poem *In the Mecca*. She is able to establish through suggestion the real character of Prophet Williams. She does this in part through concrete choice of metaphor. When she compares the prophet's passion (for his disciples) to an "engine of candid steel hugging combustibles," she is able to suggest, on the one hand, the great power, probably physical power, of the prophet, and on the other, the coldness and real dispassion or lack of passion of the prophet. In this case, then, the metaphor allows her to make several statements at the same time, using very few words (simple words).

In the long poem *In the Mecca*, Ms. Brooks chooses those select, concrete details which are crucial to an intimate understanding of that character. She says of Briggs, a young brother intimate with the neighborhood gang, "Briggs is adult as a stone." The stone as an image or metaphor for Briggs's development is most appropriate as it allows her to make several profound statements with only six simple words. A stone is hard as Briggs is hard. A stone does not grow as organic matter as human beings grow, thus suggesting Briggs has reached a point beyond which he cannot go. It also suggests a certain one-dimensional aspect of Briggs's character.

The Use of Words

The raw materials of the poet are the words and sounds. The right, most appropriate, most exact choice of words is part of what makes the experience of the poem memorable. The following examples from Ms. Brooks illustrate how the right word is specific and concrete in nature, yet often carries the massive power of the symbol (allowing each reader to be consciously directed into a myriad of experiences, emotions, and meanings). We see also from Sister Brooks (again, *In the Mecca*) that this appropriate choice of the exact word need not be a long, multisyllabic, "difficult" word.

Conduct your blooming in the noise and whip of whirlwind

Blooming and *whirlwind* are concrete, visible, physical realities, and because of their concreteness, we immediately recognize that each belongs to opposite categories of reality; in fact, the nature and purpose of the whirlwind is to destroy all blooming. Thus Sister Brooks is able to make a very strong political comment without resorting to trite political cliches. The use of words which have physical, visible existence is often more powerful, more clear than abstractions like "the universe" and "the cosmos."

St. Julia, a character described by Sister Brooks in the poem *In the Mecca*, is a "good" church-going sister who dearly loves Jesus. Ms. Brooks has St. Julia cry out:

> He's the comfort and wine
> and piccalilli for my soul

Piccalilli here is another extremely concrete word, a simple word that reveals Sister Brooks's intimate knowledge of the black community's eating habits (piccalilli being just the right topping for black-eyed peas and rice, she didn't say "relish"). Through this word, we can make some very concrete deductions about where and how St. Julia grew up as well as how she feels about Jesus.

Sometimes the beginning poet will use complete grammatical sentences (using connectives like "and," etc.) when often just an elliptical phrase will do. It is just as important for the poet to know what to take out as to know what to put in. The following example from Johari Amini ("Let's Go Somewhere") shows how effective the use of only those words (carefully chosen) necessary to create the intense moment of message and mood can be.

> I am too past youth
> too strong
> too black
> to cry
>   still. . . .
> need
> comes: a steadied
> profuseness; insensitive
> spreading
> spreading

The problem of triteness—that of using words and phrases which have been used over and over again and are no longer fresh and vivid—usually falls into the category of street rap or in the form of imitating nineteenth-century European phrases (personifying the sun and moon, "thou," etc.). The problem with the rap is that it is a potentially very powerful form. To exert its power, the writer who uses it must do more than copy or imitate the vocabulary of the rap. He or she must create an originality and a tension on the printed page; using the words of the rap alone on a piece of paper cannot of itself carry the nuance and rhythm of a brother on the corner rapping out his mouth. In the same way, for example, Langston Hughes in his blues poems—because he only "copied" the superficial form of the blues lyric—could not really reach the power of a Blind Lemon or a Muddy Waters. The printed page imposes limitations that sound does not.

A Sense of Direction

Actually, a sense of direction comes from the world that students are involved in every day. If a student's work is putting comic books together or is being a professional student, he or she will see the world differently than a person working on the line at Ford Motor Company. If students question what they see, a whole new world opens up.

If what young people write about is to be meaningful, it must have some relationship to reality. And reality is not the same to the doer as it is to the sayer. There are four areas in which students should concentrate much of their efforts if they are to develop as a person and a writer:

1. Study and Research: This is of the utmost importance for writers of nonfiction and certain kinds of fiction such as historical fiction. Margaret Walker's research for her novel, *Jubilee*, took almost a lifetime, and Chancellor William's research for his monumental study, *The Destruction of Black Civilization*, took eighteen years. The two books mentioned will live because they are packed with life-giving and stimulating information written in a readable style.

2. Writing: The major endeavor for the beginning writer must be writing. The writer should at first put him or herself on a schedule in order to acquire discipline. Discipline in doing anything that is important is a must for the writer. The writer is his or her own whip. Self-discipline is the hardest to achieve but if achieved is the writer's most important asset. He or she should keep a small notebook in which to jot down all ideas. Writers should never rely solely on memory. They should not

throw any of the notes away but keep the unused ones for late⁻ Though students may want to concentrate in one area of writing, they should gain knowledge of all kinds of writing—fiction, nonfiction, children's, radio and television, magazine-journalism, poetry, and drama.

3. Revision: Writers never accept a first draft of their work. The art of writing is frequent revising. Writers must be their own worst critics. Writers must be their own editors.

4. Workshop: For the beginning and the inexperienced writer, workshops are good mostly for the associations that are formed with other writers. Also, workshops are probably one of the few places a young writer can get competent and truthful direct criticism. Many good writers have been involved in workshop experiences.

Final Words

Writing is a form of self-definition and communication through which writers basically define themselves and their relationship to the world. The writer is essentially always searching for the core of the definition, looking for the gut—the truth. There are few good writers who lie; there are a lot of liars who try to write, and unfortunately, they are in the majority. But they come and go, passing through like a European wind penetrating the African heat only to be eliminated by the warmth of reality.

A writer is a questioner, always asking, always seeking the bottom line, always looking for the essences within the essence—always looking for the enemies of the world. When writers stop questioning, they stop having anything to say. When writers question, they are doing more than admitting that they don't know everything, they're assuming a posture, a relationship with the world that is conducive to creativity. Writers who humble themselves before knowledge of any kind generally end up wiser and as voices with something meaningful to say.

References

Amini, Johari. *Let's Go Somewhere*. Chicago: Third World, 1973.
Brooks, Gwendolyn. *In the Mecca*. New York: Harper & Row, 1968.
———. *Riot*. Detroit: Broadside, 1969.

———. *Report from Part I*. Detroit: Broadside, 1970.

———. *To Disembark*. Chicago: Third World, 1981.

Brown, Sterling A. *Southern Road*. New York: Harcourt Brace Jovanovich, 1932.

Hughes, Langston. *Montage of a Dream Deferred*. New York: Holt, Rinehart & Winston, 1951.

———. *Selected Poems*. New York: Alfred A. Knopf, 1959.

———. *The Best of Simple*. New York: Hill & Wang, 1961.

Lee, Don L. (Haki R. Madhubuti). *Book of Life*. Detroit: Broadside, 1975.

———. *Earthquakes and Sunrise Missions*. Chicago: Third World, 1983.

Teaching the Teachers to Teach Black-Dialect Writers

Paul A. Ramsey
Educational Testing Service, Princeton, New Jersey

Last spring I volunteered to teach an English graduate course entitled "The Teaching of Writing to Speakers of Dialect." Of course everyone speaks a dialect, but the graduate students were no fools. They knew that this verbose title was a euphemism for teaching black students in remedial courses to write. After consenting to do the course, I panicked. I am black and therefore thought by my department to know something about "these dialect problems." Of course I felt just about as much in the dark (forgive the racist imagery) on this matter as most of my colleagues, though I regularly taught the remedial, freshman English course which enrolls mostly Black and Spanish-speaking students. Now I was going to be unmasked as being as unenlightened and unexotic as my white colleagues. Heaven forbid! I scurried around to the graduate students who might take such a course and made them promise that they would not pre-register, hoping that the course would fold for lack of enrollment. But, alas, it didn't. So on the first day of class, I went to the assigned room, met my ten white English graduate students, confessed my ignorance, and began to teach what proved to be a fairly useful course, that is, I learned a lot by teaching it.

We began the course as all good graduate courses begin and end, with the students doing most of the work. We tried to make a complete annotated bibliography from 1964–77 on "black dialect and writing" from four journals which publish in this area: *English Journal, College English, College Composition and Communication,* and *Florida Foreign Language Reporter.* We dittoed our bibliographical finds each week and also starred and commented on the most interesting articles. The students murmured about the amount of time our comments took each week, but I found the practical ideas for teaching writing which came from these articles and the students' comments most helpful.

The articles were also helpful, especially when compared with the readings in our three texts, in eradicating the naiveté with which some of the students began the course: they wanted me as a black teacher of remedial composition to tell them how to teach black dialect writers in twenty-five words or less, and if not in so few words, in no more than fifteen weeks. The readings proved, in a way my words never could, that the specialists, black and white, have answers to the questions—different answers: "Bidialectalism is the goal"; "Students should be encouraged to use their dialect"; "Speaking in dialect is fine, but writing in it isn't"; "The problem is that blacks and other indigents are so impoverished that they can't understand certain concepts, not even simple concepts like 'next to,' since poor people don't have two things to put 'next to' each other" (Kaplan 1969). My students quickly saw that there were many theories, some of them foolish, most of them untried, few of them proven. In short, there were no pat answers or foolproof methods for teaching black dialect writers.

At the beginning of the semester, I emphasized that the class would be practically—rather than theoretically—oriented. Neither I nor the students wanted a course which simply discussed the teaching of writing. We wanted a course that would help us teach dialect writers more effectively. For homework each week we graded and commented on a dialect-writer's paper, then in class we analyzed and criticized the comments we had made on the paper. In addition, by pretending that they were a remedial composition class, my graduate students permitted me to show them how I teach my developmental classes.

Each student also made a presentation which reflected his or her particular dialect interest, and here I use "dialect" in the broadest sense of the word. One student's interest was in TESOL, so she presented useful materials and methods for teaching foreign students to speak and write standard English. Of course, much of what she said could be applied to teaching dialect speakers and writers if one adheres to the bidialectal school. Another presentation—one which I at first thought was pressing the limits of the word "dialect"—was given by a student interested in teaching deaf students. Her presentation, however, proved to be most relevant when she explained that nonstandard "signing" is being discouraged by school officials at educational institutions for deaf people.

Even before we began the presentations, the course began to break out of the boundaries of teaching dialect writers and moved to the larger question of how to teach writing. The non-dialect articles students chose for their bibliographies showed that they had an innate sense that a course on how to teach dialect writers must really be a course on how to teach writing. Our discussions of "the teaching of writing to dialect speakers" always ended up on "the teaching of writing." When the two other remedial composition instructors came to our class, they dutifully began discussing their minority students' writing problems, but at the end of the hour they found that they were discussing the problems in teaching any college student to write. I found that I was giving lectures titled (or mistitled) "Organization and the Dialect Writer" or "Paragraphing and the Dialect Writer," but somehow after my opening comments, I dropped the "Dialect Writer" and discussed the how's of teaching, or trying to teach, organization or paragraphing.

How to Teach—Not How to Teach Blacks

What I learned from our inability to stay on the topic of the course was that maybe we did not really need the course. The real problem was not how to teach black dialect speakers to write, but how to teach any student to write. The basics of writing—how to organize, how to develop a paragraph, how to write with specificity rather than in generalities—are not racial. Of course there are special nuisances when teaching dialect writers: how to get that "s" on the third person present tense singular and the "ed" on the past tense. But these grammatical irregularities, though they grate on the ears and eyes of almost every English teacher, are minor when compared to the problems of teaching that essays must proceed logically and clearly and be about one, and only one, "thesis idea" (Smitherman 1972; Sternglass 1974).

What I saw for the first time was that this obsession with black dialect was really a new form of racism at work in the field of writing. (Well, I guess racism is never new, it simply masquerades in new terminology.) Ironically, the unintending culprits are the linguists who have recently given us a plethora of literature on black dialect. The very volume of material on black dialect has sanctioned a type of racism which masquerades as "the English professor's excuse." It goes something like this: "We've admitted these ['unqualified minority' understood] students, and ah, I don't know how to teach them to write. They, ah, have dialect problems, and ah, I don't know what to do with them." Does this sound familiar? It does to me: "They," "them," "the blacks," "those exotic primitives over there are so different/dumb/dark, I don't know what to do with them. They're nothing like me." The very quantity of literature on dialect speakers and writers supports the they're-so-different-therefore-I-can't-teach-them attitude. If teachers feel they cannot teach until they have read Sledd, Labov, Dillard, Steward, Shuy, Feigenbaum, Smitherman, to name a few—few of whom agree—then they will never teach these students. Again, I admit that there are unique problems in a dialect student's paper (Fasold and Wolfram 1975), but I am absolutely certain that there is no positive correlation between the difficulties in teaching dialect speakers and the number of articles and books on the subject (he says as he writes yet another article on the subject).

What I found was that my graduate students were afraid to teach minority students to write because the graduate students felt they did not know enough. When I thought about conversations I had had with my colleagues, I found the same to be true of most of them. No wonder I kept getting the remedial composition course. I was one of the few who did not believe that my black students were too exotic to teach (I hope "exotic" in the mind of enlightened English professors does not read "dumb"). If enough college teachers assume this humble I-don't-know-how posture, the effect will not be unlike that of the slave laws which forbade "them" to learn to read and write.

As is always the case with racism, no matter how altruistically motivated, when we accept its premises we stop seeing people as people and see them instead as racial globs. I saw the seeds of this attitude in some of my graduate students and see its fruition in some of my colleagues. Not a semester goes by that someone does not come to me with a paper in hand, face in contortion, and say, "I have a black student who doesn't know how to write. Dialect problems. What should I do?" When we sit down to look at the paper, I ask my concerned friend to point to the dialect features: a double negative here, a nonstandard "be" there, but, all in all, few real dialectal problems. Most of the time the paper is indeed poorly written, but the problem is usually that the student simply does not know how to write a paper. He or she does not know that a paper is about one thing which we call a "thesis" and that a paper is constructed in paragraph units which are about one specific "topic." I suspect that if a white student had come with a similar paper, my colleagues might have thrown up their hands in dismay that such a student should get into college, but at least they would have been able to see the student's paper and not just the student's pigmentation. If my colleagues really had seen the student's paper, they would have at least been able to judge correctly that the writing problems were more basic and severe than the problem of dialect. And ideally, with this more accurate assessment, they would have begun to help this student or found someone else who could.

In my graduate course, we spent relatively little time on whether black students should be taught standard English. The fact is that most black college students want to learn it. Whether these students should want to learn standard English, I will leave to James Sledd, moral theologians, and the black students themselves. If they do want to learn to speak and write in standard English, I want to teach them as effectively, sensitively, and painlessly as possible. If there are students who do not feel they need to write and speak in standard English to survive in college, fine. They may not need to learn it if they choose their classes carefully enough. And none of us need to worry about imposing an unwanted education on a student. I have yet to teach a student standard English or anything else she or he does not want to learn. As to preserving black culture, I assure all the liberals of the English profession an "s" or "ed" here and there will not destroy the culture. It has endured more than a singular verb-ending or past tense.

Undoubtedly, the most interesting class of the semester was when the students in my remedial composition course came to a graduate class and told their prospective teachers what they hoped to gain from a composition course: they wanted to learn to write effectively in standard English. Most of them, unfortunately, valued standard English more than their own dialect. Such conservatism appalled my liberal graduate students. They tried to explain to my composition students that one dialect was not better or more correct than another. Dialects are simply different! Of course, this is true and black students must be reminded of it, but the fact of the matter is that most minority students are too practical and smart to pay much attention to these liberal platitudes, even if they are true. Pragmatically, some dialects are better than others. Some open doors and create positive impressions, while others lose jobs by creating negative impressions. Whether this should be the case is another matter; unfortunately, it is the case.

What I ventured to share with my graduate students was that I was not nearly as worried about the attitudes of my black students toward their own dialects as I was about the attitudes of my white colleagues, the attitudes of the graduate students themselves, and the attitudes of the white students they would someday teach. If we want to change attitudes towards dialects, the place to begin is with white students not black ones. White students are the ones who will one day most likely be in the power positions. They are the ones whom the dialect speaker will need to speak and write for. How truly revolutionary it would be if white students were taught to respect nonstandard dialects.

With these final words of wisdom I ended the course. I don't know what, if anything, my graduate students learned—does anyone know this about students? They were kind enough to make positive comments about the course in their well-written, standard English evaluations. Needless to say, I learned a great deal, for I learned that one of the worst things that can happen to either students or teachers is to be too blind or too afraid to teach what they know.

References

Bentley, Robert H., and Samuel D. Crawford, eds. *Black Language Reader.* Glenview, Ill.: Scott, Foresman & Co., 1973.

Dillard, J. L. *Black English: Its History and Usage.* New York: Vintage, 1973.

Fasold, Ralph W., and Walt Wolfram. "Some Linguistic Features of Negro Dialect." In *Black American English,* edited by Paul Stoller. New York: Dell, 1975.

Kaplan, Robert B. "On a Note of Protest (in a Minor Key): Biadialectism vs. Bidialectism." *College English* 30 (1969): 387–88.

Smitherman, Geneva. "English teacher, why you be doing the thangs you don't do?" *English Journal* 61 (January 1972): 59–65.

Sternglass, Marilyn S. "Dialect Features in the Compositions of Black and White College Students: The Same or Different?" *College Composition and Communication* 25 (October 1974): 259–63.

Stoller, Paul, ed. *Black American English.* New York: Dell, 1975.

The Composing Process of Black Student Writers

Robert J. Fowler
Allegheny Community College, Pittsburgh, Pennsylvania

A review of the literature which deals with the composing process and nonstandard dialects shows that the merger of the two is quite a feasible undertaking. If writing as a process is to take into account the dynamics of the individual writer, then it would be quite beneficial to consider the strategies employed in the composing processes of black dialect speakers. Fowler (1980) describes a case study investigation of the writing processes of three degrees of dialect users ("Degree" refers to the number of predetermined black dialect features present in a diagnostic composition. The students were classified as follows: 1-2 features present—low; 3-5 features present—moderate; 6-above features present—high.): a low, a moderate, and a high user of nonstandard English composing in the transactional, expressive, and poetic modes as outlined by Britton et al. (1975). The student's writing processes were analyzed in two ways: by observing them during the stages of incubation/conceptionalization, production, and revision, and according to their use of the intellectual processes of change, contrast, classification, physical context, focus, and sequence. The subjects were assigned six compositions to write and were requested to use the talk/write and the nontalk/write methods in the three modes of discourse. The writing processes of these students were observed in terms of these specific writing factors: time, revision, translation, fluency, omission, and production.

The study revealed that generally, the low nonstandard dialect user needed the least amount of time to write the most (actual number of words) and the high nonstandard dialect user utilized the most amount of time to write the least. The low and moderate dialect users generally thought of mental outlines prior to writing, but the high nonstandard dialect user was more concerned with putting the thoughts on paper the "right" way. Also, the low nonstandard dialect user made the fewest pauses during the writing process, and the high nonstandard dialect user made the most. All three of the students' writing patterns were continuously progressive and additive in nature. The student who was classified as the high nonstandard dialect user made the greatest number of translations from black dialect to standard English during the writing process, while the low nonstandard dialect user made the fewest translations. Also, all three of the students placed a great deal of emphasis upon grammatical revisions.

This study demonstrated that by examining the writing process of dialect speakers researchers can focus on what these students actually do when they write rather than scrutinizing what they have written. By observing specific writing factors: time, revision, translation, fluency, omission, and production, employed during the writing process, certain implications for teaching can be drawn. In the following section each of these factors will be briefly discussed and specific suggestions about teaching composition to these students will be made.

Time Factors

The greater the degree of black dialect utilized by an individual, the more time is required for that individual to start and complete a writing assignment, generally. ("Time" here refers to either prewriting time, actual writing [production] time, or complete writing time [a combination of the first two times].) Therefore, the teacher of composition should make allowances. In cases where writing tasks are timed, or time limits are imposed by class periods, the composition teacher should be aware that the extent to which the student is a black dialect user will, generally, determine the amount of time it will take for the individual to start and complete a writing assignment. Much of this time is spent on thinking about how to put thoughts in writing the "right" way.

The following activities are suggested.

1. Encourage "freewriting," in which the student writes continuously for a period.
2. Encourage drama activities in which the students' role-play is a good prewriting activity.

Both of the activities above will help students to put their ideas on paper. Freewriting might help to lower writing anxieties, since the student will write nonstop, disregarding all rules of grammar and mechanics. Drama activities provide ideas for writing. Using either one or a combination of these activities may reduce the amount of time spent on a writing assignment.

Revision Factors

It appears that black dialect speakers concentrate heavily upon having a grammatically correct composition. The composition assignment should attempt to get the student to write for meaning first, then work on the minor errors of transcription. In essence, the teacher should make every effort to get the student to put ideas on paper first, then work on correcting structural elements and grammatical features.

The following activities are suggested.

1. Employ the freewriting activity in order to get the student to get thoughts on paper before beginning to revise.
2. Design writing assignments which will encourage the more subjective elements of composition (e.g., tone, style, audience). For instance, the teacher can give a composition assignment with the directions, "Write this assignment for your peers," or "Write this assignment for a group of elementary students." This will help the student establish a sense of audience.
3. Employ sentence-combining exercises to enhance style and syntactic maturity.

The first activity might help the student to give ideas priority over grammatical elements. Activities two and three will help students to examine elements of composition—other than the grammatical. They may develop a need to make changes other than grammatical revisions during the writing process.

Translation Factors

The extent to which black dialect speakers make translations from their dialect to standard English is dependent upon the extent to which the individual is a black dialect speaker. "Translate" denotes the act of vocalizing in black dialect and converting this dialect into standard dialect before transcribing these thoughts to paper.) Generally, the greater the degree of black dialect spoken, the greater the number of translations made. Considering the fact that these translations do require time, this evidence can partially account for the differences in writing times for students who speak varying degrees of black dialect.

The following activities are suggested.

1. Employ the nonstop (freewriting) exercises again.
2. Design role-playing exercises in which the student must talk in standard English.

The nonstop writing exercises might discourage the time-consuming behavior of attempting to translate from black dialect to standard dialect during the writing process, since the student must concentrate on getting *ideas* on paper. The role-playing exercises will give the student practice in using standard dialect orally. Theoretically, a proficiency in oral standard English will have some influence on the written form, thereby decreasing the number of translations needed. The student who is proficient in oral standard English will write better—not having to "translate" before writing.

Fluency Factors

Writing fluency appears to be influenced by the extent to which an individual is a black dialect speaker. ("Fluency" here refers to the extent to which the writer is able to write without pause—either silent or writing pauses.) Generally, the higher the degree of black dialect used by the individual, the less fluent (more pauses) will be the writing behavior; conversely, the lower the degree of black dialect utilized by the individual, the more fluent (fewer pauses) will be the writing behavior.

The following activity is suggested. Develop exercises which will help the student think in "thought groups." Marking off thought groups in written passages may help.

The concept of "thought groups" means a group of words which convey an idea. This activity draws parallels between the reading and the writing process. If the student is able to observe units of thought in written form, then maybe the student will be able to understand better the concept of writing in "units of thought," thereby decreasing the number of writing pauses.

Omission Factors

Several studies reveal that nonstandard dialect speakers tend to omit (sometimes referred to as "miscue") words, phrases, etc. while writing, even upon rereading (Shaughnessy 1979; Perl 1979; Fowler 1980). Consequently, these omissions are still present when the final paper is presented to the teacher. ("Omission" refers to the exclusion of certain inflections, words, phrases, etc. in the written form.)

The following activity is suggested. Design peer evaluation exercises to help the student to view critically the writing of other students, as well as her or his own writing. Perhaps this will decrease the number of these omissions.

Production Factors

Generally, the number of written words produced by a black dialect speaker will vary according to his or her use of black dialect. The higher the degree of black dialect utilized, the fewer words will be produced; and the lower the degree of black dialect utilized, the greater the number of words will be produced.

An investigation into the writing processes of black student writers has revealed that the degree to which the speaker is a dialect user influences the amount of time spent on writing assignments, the number of words produced and the amount of translations from black dialect to standard English. Freewriting (and many of its variations) has been suggested as one of the major techniques for building writing fluency.

References

Bailey, Richard W. "Dialects and the Teaching of Composition." In *Varieties of Present-Day English*, edited by Richard W. Bailey and J. L. Robinson. New York: Macmillan, 1973.

Britton, James, Tony Burgess, Nancy Martin, Alex McLeod, and Harold Rosen. *The Development of Writing Abilities (11–18)*. London: Macmillan Educational, 1975.

Fowler, R. J. "An Analysis of the Composing Process of Three Black Adolescents" (Ph.D. diss., University of Pittsburgh, 1979), *Dissertation Abstracts International* 40 (1980): 4934A.

Labov, William. *The Study of Nonstandard English*. Champaign, Ill.: National Council of Teachers of English, 1970.

Perl, Sondra. "The Composing Processes of Unskilled College Writers." *Research in the Teaching of English* 13 (December 1979): 317–36.

Shaughnessy, Mina P. *Errors and Expectations: A Guide for the Teacher of Basic Writing*. New York: Oxford University Press, 1979.

Teachers as Editors:
The Student Conference

Vivian I. Davis
Tarrant County Junior College, Fort Worth, Texas

A few years ago I asked my high school students to keep a record of the kinds of mistakes they made on their papers. I hoped that keeping their own records would call the students' attention to the "mistakes" they were making in usage, punctuation, spelling, etc. "If they are aware of their errors," I reasoned, "they will correct them and thereby improve their writing." Much to my surprise and their disgust, the students found that they were making the same mistakes repeatedly. It made no difference that I marked each infraction on every paper and tried to teach the class what their mistakes were and how to correct them. My plan served only to focus on what the students were doing "wrong" to the disregard of the good writing they did. Rather than helping them to improve their writing, I succeeded in discouraging them and convincing them that indeed, they would never be writers.

Many English teachers have had similar experiences. They usually respond with one or two commonly accepted rationalizations: "Writing cannot be taught," "These kids will never learn how to write well because they don't speak standard English," "They need to learn grammar," "The high school teacher can't be expected to make up for all those lost years in the early grades." The list goes on. The real problem, however, is that teachers need a more effective approach to the teaching of writing. Professor Wallace Douglas suggests that the English teacher should be an editor for the student writer. English teachers do not disagree; and if they understood Professor Douglas's theory more clearly, I believe more of them would put it into practice. I do not mean to imply that Professor Douglas's explanation of theory is unclear, but English teachers, having themselves gone through traditional composition courses, have a very narrow concept of what an editor does. The English teacher's own teachers did not take the role of editor, and the educators who trained English teachers did not teach them a single course in editing.

English teachers would like to try a different approach to the teaching of writing. Most of us agree that doing business as usual is not effective even for our best writers. The remainder of this paper consists of a sample lesson in which the English teacher acts as an editor. I should point out here that I am not saying anything that Professor Douglas has not already said. My purpose here, in lieu of the kinds of editing courses we English teachers need, is to attempt to develop the role of editor in *bas-relief*. I believe once teachers understand that role, they will go on to develop the skills necessary to become good editors for their students.

The First Conference

The editor/teacher begins to work with the student writer before a single word goes on the paper. There should be communication, written or spoken, between student and teacher which leads to an agreed-upon proposal about what the student will write. Though this process sounds very formal, it need not be. It takes the place of the traditional writing assignment in which the teacher tells students to write a certain type of essay on a specific subject in a predetermined number of paragraphs or words. As editor, the teacher needs to be aware of what kind of writing would interest the different audiences a student writer could address. Suppose that a class has just read the play, *The Amen Corner*, and the teacher wants to encourage them to write essays as a response to the play.

> Teacher: You seemed to enjoy reading this play. I wonder now that you've read it if you may want to pass on anything to others in writing.
>
> Student: Yes, I'd like to say that just because a person's parents hate each other, doesn't mean the kid hates them.
>
> Teacher: A good insight. Is there anyone or any group in particular to whom you want to get that message across?
>
> Student: To everybody sort of, but mostly to the parent that the kids stay with when they get separated. That's usually their mother.
>
> Teacher: Fine. Will your paper be a long one or short or what?
>
> Student: I'd say about a page, or a page and a half. I want them to get the idea that they should not try to turn the kids against their father because he left. That could have some kind of com-

plex on them, and they don't want to hurt their mother's feelings either.

Teacher: Let's see if I have it right. You are going to write a paper, about one or one and a half pages long, mostly to mothers who keep their children after separating from their children's fathers.

Student: Or else the father left 'em.

Teacher: Okay. The mothers who keep the children though the father is not there—separated, divorced, or gone away.

Student: Mostly just gone away and left them there.

Teacher: Okay. The paper is for mothers whose husbands just left them by themselves to rear the children.

Student: Yeah.

Teacher: Now you want to tell the mothers what?

Student: The kids don't hate their father even though he went away and left them. They don't like it, but they want to be a part of him too.

Teacher: Didn't you say the mothers should not try to make the kids hate their father because. . . .

Student: Yes, because the kids will be frustrated. They like their mother and their father, but they don't want to hurt their mother's feelings.

Teacher: I think you have a good plan. Why don't you just write it down now. Just write it the way it comes to you then we can go from there.

The teacher and the student here agreed on a proposal for the paper. The teacher gives the student credit for getting some idea from the play. She does not tell the student what ideas to write about. She asks the student what audience he wants to address and continues to stay with that question until the student clarifies for her (and for himself) exactly what audience he wants to address. The teacher also accepts the student's judgment about the length of paper to which he can commit himself. Exactly what he wants to tell his audience is the student's decision to make. Through this process, the teacher/editor and the writer have come to an agreeable contract.

The process is, of course, not always as easy as the one provided in my example. To get started identifying audiences, and ideas to write about, students may work together in small brainstorming groups. When it is apparent that the students have exchanged information and ideas, the teacher may ask the students to write down the audiences they wish to address and the ideas they want to present. The proposals may then be refined in a conference with those writers whose plans demonstrate that they need to talk further. Proposals that show the students are ready to write should be accepted—with comments if necessary.

The teacher/editor is involved in the student's production of a first draft only if the student wants help. In other words the teacher should not walk around the room, look over the writers' shoulders, and point out misspellings or fragments or other usage infractions. The teacher/editor should make available such references as dictionaries, thesauruses, and copies of the primary work from which the students got their writing ideas. (For example, to help the student with writing this paper, the teacher should make available copies of *The Amen Corner*.) When students ask questions, the teacher should answer as simply and briefly as possible. Students who need music to write by should be allowed to bring their radios with earphones. Within the limitations of the classroom itself and the daily time schedule, the teacher should allow the writers to get their first drafts on paper as quickly as possible.

The first draft is what I call the modeing clay. Students should understand that their papers are not yet finished. They are ready to begin the process of revision. Revision is what must be done to the first draft to make the paper do what the writer intended for it to do at the time the proposal was made. I should honestly say that sometimes the rough draft shows that the writer's mind changed after the time the proposal was made. Sometimes the change is all for the better. In such a case, it is necessary to determine what audience the rough draft is actually addressed to, and what ideas are actually presented to the audience. Then it must be decided if the ways the draft differs from the original proposal will make it a better paper. The teacher/editor and the writer must go with the plan for the better paper.

The Second Conference

Because the revision process is a matter of making many decisions about what to leave in the paper, what to take out, what to change, what to reorder, I have chosen to use the following episode as an illustration.

The play, *The Amen Corner* gives a very important point if you have to keep your child by yourself. Sometimes fathers goes away wrong, but the child does not hate them. He still love his father and wants to understand. But he still will love you too. But he don't want you to say alot of bad things if you are made. Because you are the one have to keep the child and take care of them.
The best thing to say something good, or if the mother can't she should just not say nothing. The child feels you are angry at him and then he is not happy, he doesn't want you to be hurt, but he can't help it. He loves you and his father too.

This essay is certainly not a finished product, but it has some very sophisticated ideas. There are numerous *errors* that traditionally the English teacher would mark with appropriate symbols for correction. The better approach, however, is to help the student understand how to revise the paper himself. In this case, a conference with the student would be the most meaningful. Following is an example of a conference on this essay:

Teacher: I read your essay and I think you have some important insights. You covered the point you planned to cover in it. As I read it, I did feel there are some things you could do to improve it. Will you read your paper aloud for me?

(Having the student read the paper aloud should make clear any points of confusion about what the student meant to say and also make the paper fresh in the student's mind.)

Teacher: Now that you have read the paper, do you think it is clear who you were writing to in the paper?

Student: I was talking to the mother.

Teacher: Is there anything in the paper to let the mother know that you were writing to her?

Student: Well, I think so. It says, "If you have to keep your child by yourself."

Teacher: What lets the mother know you were talking to her?

Student: The mother has to keep her child.

Teacher: But you wrote "if *you* have to keep your child." Could *you* be a father as well as a mother?

Student: Um, yes.

Teacher: How could you write it so the mother would know you are writing directly to her?

Student: Well, I could say, "if the mother have to keep her child just her alone."

Teacher: See if you can write it that way. Start at the beginning.

Student: (writes) "The play, *The Amen Corner* gives a very important point if the mother have to keep her child by herself."

Teacher: Why does the mother have to keep her child by herself?

Student: Cause the father gone away.

Teacher: Do you think you should put that in the sentence so the reader will know why?

Student: Yes. I can put it on the end "the father went away."

Teacher: Try it.

Student: (adds to the sentence) "cause the father went away."

Teacher: Good, now read the sentence.

Student: "The play, *The Amen Corner* gives a very important point to the mother that have to keep her child by herself because the father went away."

Teacher: Good. Now I think the mother knows you are talking to her—to the mother who has to keep her child by herself because the father went away. Are you satisfied with your next sentence?

Student: Yes. It tells the father maybe was wrong when he went away.

Teacher: Does it tell anything else?

Student: Hum, about the child don't hate them.

Teacher: I think that sentence explains something important to the mother. It is a good sentence. I am a little confused by your next sentence. Will you read it to yourself?

Student: (reads to himself) Hum, it's not good, but. . . .

Teacher: I think it is good. There is just one thing I'm not sure about. The first word says "he"; I think "he" means the child. Is that right?

Student: Yeah, he loves the father.

Teacher: Could you write it so I would be sure that "he" means the child?

Student: It says so—"He loves his father."

Teacher: Suppose I change "he" and wrote "the child still loves his father"? Would that keep me from not being sure who "he" is?

Student: Yeah, but I know who it is.

Teacher: Of course you do, but remember when you write something, you know exactly what you mean, but the person who reads it might not be sure.

Student: Okay, let's see, you can write it "The child" and take "he" out.

Teacher: (writes) "The child still loves his father and wants to understand." I think that helps clear it up for the reader.

Student: It's okay. Means the same. Okay.

The teacher does not ask a technical question such as "What is the antecedent for the pronoun 'he' at the beginning of this sentence?" She helps the student to understand why it is a good idea to change "He" to "The child." The teacher is also sensitive to the writer's resistance to changing *his* sentence; therefore, she does not force him to write the change, but rather rewrites the sentence herself so that the writer can read it and compare it with his own sentence.

Since the teacher has made clear the need for the change and did not change the meaning of the sentence when she revised it, the student is able to accept her change. Subtly, however, the teacher has made another change. She changed the student's word "love" to "loves," adding the *s* to agree with the subject, "child." The student does not question the change; therefore, it may be assumed that it is agreeable to him. The teacher has a clue that the student may accept such a change. Note that when he talks he usually makes subject and verb agree. Furthermore in this very sentence he writes "wants." It may be that he inadvertently omitted the *s* on the word "love," or that he uses love and loves interchangeably. Rather than jump to the conclusion that this child speaks black dialect and therefore should be allowed to write as he speaks, the teacher takes the chance and makes the change. If the student had questioned, she may simply have answered, "'Loves' goes with 'The child,'" and not have gone into any "grammatical" discussion.

Teacher: Now, let's look at the next sentence. Are you satisfied with it?

Student: (reads aloud) I'll change "he" to "the child" again?

Teacher: Well, you could do that. Do you think it would help the reader?

Student: Yeah, I think so. (Changes "he" to "the child").

Teacher: Is there anything else you want to change to help the reader know who you are writing about?

Student: Not unless . . . No.

Teacher: Who is it that the child will still love?

Student: Still love? Oh, his mother. Yes, I will change it. (Talks to himself) But, he, I mean, the child, will still love the mother too. I'm taking "you" out. Is that okay? for "the mother"?

Teacher: I think it's a good idea. Maybe you can change it now so you won't forget. It's shaping up nicely. Do you like it?

Student: Yeah, it's nice. Should I make "he" "the child" in the next sentence too?

Teacher: I don't think you have to this time because you said "the child" in the two sentences before this one. I think the reader will know you mean "the child" if you say "he" in this sentence.

Student: I think he will.

Teacher: Well, let me read the sentence aloud now. (Reads)

Student: I said "mad," not "made." You said "made."

Teacher: Well you wrote "m-a-d-e" on your paper. How can you write "mad"?

Student: (Erases the *e* with a chuckle.)

Teacher: "A lot" is two words "*a l-o-t.*" Now let me read the next sentence to you.

(The teacher reads so that it is obvious the next group of words does not complete an idea.)

Student: Let me see. You didn't read it right. It sounds funny on the end.

Teacher: Okay, you read it for me.

Student: But he don't want you to say a lot of bad things if you are mad because you have to keep the child and take care of them, I mean, of him.

Teacher: Well I thought you started a new sentence at "Because," but you read both parts together.

Student: That's the way it belongs together with this first part (pointing).

Teacher: Well can you change it so that anybody reading it will know that all of this (gestures with finger) goes together? Try writing it as one sentence.

Student: (Revises—takes away period and writes a small letter to begin the word "because.")

Teacher: Okay now let's read it again. (Reads) I got it that time. Do you see why a little period and a capital letter make a difference?

Here the teacher does not ask the student to explain why it was necessary to revise the fragment. It is not necessary to ask. Whether the student can explain the "rule" or not is irrelevant. He knew how to make the change. Note also that the teacher does not, at this point, mention pronoun-antecedent agreement, or that the word "don't" does not agree with the pronoun "he." Everything cannot be taught in one short essay; furthermore, the teacher wants to let the student know that he *can* write his ideas. There will be other opportunities to discuss the rules about what verbs go with what pronouns or what pronouns with what antecedents. Since disagreements are common in the writing of many students, the subject may be discussed with the entire class or with those students who are affected.

Teacher: I want to suggest something here. Your next sentence gives a bit of advice to the mother. You're telling her what?

Student: It's best for her to say something good or not say nothing at all.

Teacher: Exactly! The way you said it is better than the way you wrote it. Write down what you just said.

Student: (Writes) Yeah, it's shorter, but I got my idea all in. I left a word out of it the first time, but this one is better. (Writes) "It's best for the mother to say something good or not say nothing at all!"

Teacher: I had a suggestion. You started a new paragraph with this sentence, but it seems to belong in the first paragraph. Would you agree?

Student: Let's see. No, no. It could be. Why did you suggest it?

Teacher: It seems to me that this sentence advises the mother how to talk with the child without saying bad things just because she is angry about the situation.

Student: It could, but that's what makes the child unhappy. He knows she is mad, but he loves his father too.

Teacher: Yes, it could go there, but the way you have the last part written, I don't get the connection between this sentence and the rest of the paper. Explain to me what message you want to get across in this part.

Student: Well, ah, just what I said. To the mother, not to say these bad things. This just gets the kid upset. He thinks his mother don't like him then. You see?

Teacher: I think I'm beginning to see how that first sentence relates Let's see if we can get the relationships between the sentences in there for the reader.

Student: I don't see what'cha talking about now—it's got a relationship between the kid and the mother. Explain how you mean.

Teacher: Well, you want that new first sentence, (reads) "It's best for the mother to say something good or not say nothing at all." The next sentence actually explains why. Can you see that? Let me ask you this. Look at this paragraph; find the sentence in the paragraph that tells why the mother should say something good or nothing at all. (Waits while the student reads to himself.)

Student: Well, why? It's really two sentences that tell "why." The child will be upset because the mother is mad because she has to keep him without no father, but he don't want to hurt. . . . No, I guess it's just one sentence that tells why.

Teacher: Read the sentence word-for-word out loud.

Student: Okay. The second one because "The child feels you are angry at him and then he is not happy." I'd say that does tell why.

Teacher: I agree with you, but I'm not sure the way you have it now is exactly clear. You said a very important word, "because," just before you read the second sentence. Let me write your first sentence, the word, "because," and then your second sentence. I think you will see what I mean. (Teacher writes) Now read it.

Student: Well, now let's see that. You got the two sentences put in one. Okay. (Reads) "It's best for the mother to say something good or not say nothing at all because the child feels you are angry at him and then he is not happy." Still ain't right though. Something sounds wrong.

Teacher: Let me put in a two-letter word, right there, right after "because." Now you read it.

Student: Yeah, that's it. Sounds right now. (Reads to himself) No, take out the "and" now. (Reads the sentence to himself again.) Okay now.

Teacher: All right, how about the last two sentences? Satisfied with them?

Student: Okay, except maybe in the last sentence. I'm gon' fix that one up—rewrite the "you." Make it, "He loves his mother and his father too." They're both still okay with him—his mother and his father also. Okay? (Teacher gestures, okay.) I'm gonna rewrite it all over now. Thanks a lot. You helped me a lot.

Teacher: But you did the first writing with no help from me at all. I just helped you edit your paper. There's more we could do with it, but if you're satisfied for now, you can copy it into your notebook. You may want to choose this paper for the class volume. If you do, we'll have to work on it more. Put it in standard type English.

Student: (Moving away.) Okay. This'll be three papers. I'll choose my best one. This one is pretty good.

A few comments should be made about the part of the conference related to the last paragraph of the paper. This teacher does not harp at the student about "transitional sentences" or "topic sentences." She tries to get the student to understand why the first sentence could belong at the end of the last paragraph. She tries to make sure that her work with the student does not damage his self-esteem as a writer. Rather than merely accept the teacher's suggestion, the student argues his point—the teacher listens and takes direction from the student. Fortunately, as often happens when students talk out what they meant to write, the student revises his own first sentence of the paragraph. The teacher wisely hears the revision and has the student write it down. This helps the student realize another technique he has available within himself.

As the interview progresses, the teacher skillfully enables the student to intuit, perhaps only vaguely at this point, another meaning for the term "relationship." At first the student perceives "relationship" as "kinship," but the teacher does not pounce on that as an opportunity to teach a vocabulary lesson. As an editor, her job is to help the student/writer revise the essay. The relationship between the two sentences in question is obviously one of cause and effect. Teacher/editor never says so. Assuming the student can reason, and can perceive the relationship, the teacher uses the student's own sentences to help him intuit the relationship. Not only is the student able to perceive the relationship, but he retains the feeling that he is capable of writing.

The teacher/editor demands a great deal from the student in this essay—something different from changing spelling, bandaging sentence fragments, changing dialect, or writing topic sentences. The teacher is aware of the demands she is making and has a sense of how much is enough for this time. As the interview comes to a close, the student decides on a last revision which reveals he is already aware of such a stylistic abstract as tone. He realizes that the tone of his paper is conciliatory. He wants to end the paper on that note.

Rewriting his paper is no longer punishment for making mistakes. The student wants to rewrite the paper because he is happy about the way the revisions change it. He can still recognize it as his own work.

> The play, *Amen Corner*, gives a very important point if the mother have to keep her child by herself because the father went away. Sometimes fathers goes away wrong, but the child does not hate them. The child still loves his father and wants to understand. But the child still will love the mother too. But he don't want you to say a lot of bad things if you are mad because you are the one who have to keep the child and take care of him.
>
> It is best for the mother to say something good or not say nothing at all because if the child feels the mother is angry, at him, then he is not happy. He doesn't want you to be hurt, but he can't help it. He loves his mother and his father too.

This paper is not a polished version either. There are subject-verb disagreements, pronoun disagreements, unnecessary uses of the definite article, unnecessary repetition of the conjunctions "but" and "because," to mention some considerations for further revision. The interview shows that the teacher/editor does not leave the student/

writer with the notion that the revised paper is yet ready for publication.

The teacher/editor should be guided by at least the following basic understandings:

1. Student/writers must be in control of their own writing.

2. Compositions must *not* be perceived as tests of spelling, vocabulary, punctuation, usage, etc.

3. Editors must help writers to make their own decisions about what to change in their writing. Editors must not simply become rewriters for writers.

4. The focus in the composition class must be on helping the student learn how to become a more confident, more mature writer. Focusing on "errors" does not teach the writer what to do or what not to do.

5. Revision, a most critical step in the writing process, must be structured into the teaching of composition. If professional writers need editors, why should student/writers be expected to develop without them?

Using the Laboratory Approach to Enhance Writing Skills

Carolyn Drakeford
Benedict College, Columbia, South Carolina

Rationale

The teaching of writing continues to be the subject of a whirlwind of contradictory articles, studies, proposals, and information. Yet rarely in this storm about the teaching of writing are we offered glimpses of the simple truth—that writing is basically a self-taught skill produced mainly by rewriting, and that the teacher's primary role must be to guide the youngster through this difficult act of self-teaching (Murray 1968). A major problem facing teachers of writing is that, as professionals, we have the responsibility to help students gain skills which will help them learn how to think, to organize, to be clear, and to be precise. We have the responsibility to help students want to write as much for themselves as for their audience (Laque and Sherwood 1977).

We need a process through which students can enhance their communication skills on an individual basis and, at the same time, receive positive reinforcement of expression of ideas. Having worked for the past ten years in an environment which caters to minority students whose language skills are extremely diverse, I found that once provisions are made to address the individual needs of each student, considerable progress is made in acquiring and retaining the skills needed for the flexible use of language.

The best method I have found to meet the needs of all my students is the use of audio-visuals designed to present and reinforce concepts pertinent to the development of writing skills. These materials should begin at the level of the students' achievements, and a variety of media should be used in instructional presentations (Fagan 1971).

The potential for teaching and learning is unlimited and the results can be deeply rewarding (Brandon 1971). Audio-visual instructional materials have several distinct advantages: (1) providing immediate feedback for concepts introduced in class, (2) allowing students to respond to the information that is presented, (3) keeping students aware of the objectives of the lesson, (4) continuing self-evaluation to help students know if they are grasping the content, (5) permitting students to work at their own pace, (6) reinforcing each new point, (7) requiring no elaborate settings, (8) repeating a lesson as many times as the students feel they need to understand the material, and (9) allowing teachers to design further assignments based on students' individual needs. For these reasons it seems highly likely that the materials will enable writers to feel much more comfortable about the task of writing because the materials are given at their performance level. I have devised an annotated list (reproduced at the end of this article) of materials that I have found to be quite successful in getting a student to feel more at ease when asked to put ideas on paper. This list by no means represents all aids that are available to improve writing skills; however, I have tried to indicate the kinds of materials as well as the specific areas that they address.

Engaging students in the writing process goes a long way toward solving traditional concerns about skill instruction, for if students are truly involved, they simply write better than they do when the writing process consists solely of an exercise in grammar or rhetoric (Judy and Judy 1979). Therefore, the classroom needs to be transformed into a laboratory, or at least the laboratory method of instruction should be used. The major emphasis of this approach is to address the individual differences of the learners. The ideal lab-class setting (Figure 1) should contain tables arranged so that the student can work individually; a place, perhaps in the corner of the room, where the teacher can hold conferences; a library of books on writing; a bulletin board to display writing samples; provisions for overhead projectors, tape recorders, and other audio-visuals (Murray 1968). Many teachers think that using the laboratory approach is an arduous task, but with enough effort, support, and creativity, it can be done with a minimal amount of time.

The Laboratory Method

Once provisions have been made to use the classroom as a lab the next step is to determine a strategy. The first concern should be the needs of the writers. Consequently, an assessment of their skills needs to be made. The best method is to require students to write a timed essay *and* to take a grammar test. These evaluations must be used together because each one separately may not provide the

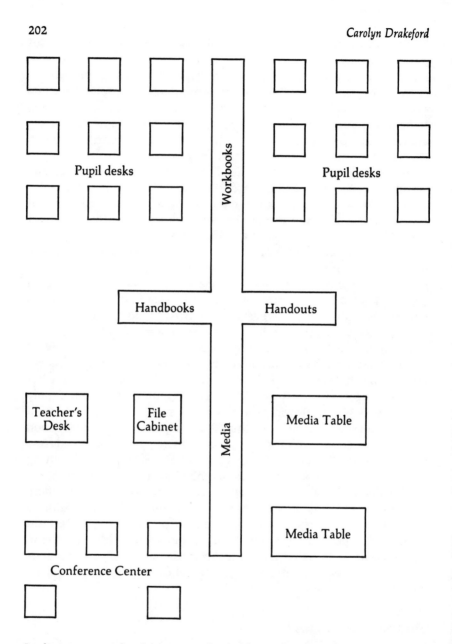

In this situation, the classroom is divided by shelves which store the work-books, handouts, handbooks, and media. One corner is used for individual conferences while students are still able to do individual or group work at their desks. Displays, charts, and posters about writing should be placed on the walls.

Figure 1. Model Classroom-Laboratory.

teacher with enough information. Depending upon the circumstances or the students' levels, standardized tests such as the College English Placement Test, the College Placement Test in English Composition, or the California Achievement Test in Language may assist teachers tremendously. After these assessment measures have been administered, individualization must take place.

A folder is set up for each student to keep an accurate record of his or her progress. A chart (Figure 2) should be established for the benefit of each student as well as the teacher. Next, the student is introduced to suitable books, media, and other materials and guided through the necessary chapters, filmstrips, or workbooks. For example, if a student is having a problem with fragments, there are several filmstrip-cassette series which a student may hear and see to obtain a better understanding of the concepts of a sentence and its structure.

Each student works on the areas identified on his or her pretests during the semester or the year. When students finish the audiovisual materials or workbook exercise or the chapter in a handbook, they then are tested in two ways: they are administered an exercise to evaluate their performance, or they are asked to write several sentences or a paragraph. After these are checked, the teacher decides if the student's performance warrants additional practice on that skill or if the student is capable of moving on to one of his or her other weak areas.

This approach requires time and must happen in a step-by-step manner (Schlawin 1975). The list of materials that follows is composed of items that I have found beneficial for writers from many levels. Exercises, laboratory periods, textual lessons, and conferences should occupy the students' time between themes (Marsh 1956). Students need to compose in as many forms of discourse as possible. They then can experiment with personal writing (journal, autobiography, sensory writing, feelings, sketches); popular forms (ads, commercials, concert reviews, songs); imaginative writing (fiction, stories, science fiction, fantasy); informative-persuasive writing (essays, editorials, reviews, news, reports); and media writing (TV scripts, tapes, montages, collages, radio programs).

The Task of the English Teacher

Each of us has to incorporate new ideas or methods into our own teaching and learning cycle. Using the laboratory approach in the English classroom requires that teachers be willing to develop new pedagogy and try more flexible methods of classroom organization

STUDENT'S NAME _____ CLASS PERIOD _____

DATE	AREA TO BE ADDRESSED	MATERIALS USED	LEVEL	ADDITIONAL INFORMATION

Figure 2. Progress Chart.

(Burgess 1973). Teachers must use their own initiative in learning how to use media and in developing individualized programs for learners. The students we teach are used to receiving information through and learning from multimedia sources (Thompson 1977). Today English teachers need more than ever to exhaust all means in order to make certain that students master the art of composing effective sentences, paragraphs, and essays. The laboratory approach permits students to work on their own in a setting that is conducive to learning and enables them to become better writers and communicators of the English language.

Audio-Visual Instructional Materials

I.   Filmstrip House
     432 Park Avenue, South
     New York, New York 10016
     A. Advanced English Composition
        (Four filmstrips)
        The aim of this series is to help students who have already mastered the basic skill of composing a theme to write better papers; for instance, emphasis is placed on organizational support and the editing process.
     B. Sentence Structure with Diagrams
        (Four filmstrips)
        Basic writers will benefit greatly from this series which will aid students in understanding the basic grammatical unit—the sentence, thus enabling them to write as well as recognize completely expressed ideas.

II. Encyclopaedia Britannica Education Corporation
     425 North Michigan Avenue
     Chicago, Illinois 60611
     A. Beginning Grammar
        (Eight filmstrips)
        Students will become familiar with the parts of speech and how each is used effectively in English grammar. The function of each part is discussed with exercises to show its use in sentences.
     B. Parts of Speech
        (Eight filmstrips)
        In this series students are told that grammar is the study of the features of a language. The series introduces parts of speech as words which establish and show certain relation-

ships in the English system. Students learn about the introduction, body, and conclusion of an essay as well as appropriate methods of developing certain types of paragraphs such as comparison, contrast, and classification. Revision is also stressed.

C. Understanding the Sentence
(Eight filmstrips)
Examples are given of the relationship and differences between words, phrases, and clauses. The parts of a sentence or clause are discussed to aid in understanding the framework of a well-expressed idea. Other items such as the verb and the sentence, agreement problems, and kinds of sentences are presented.

D. Organizing Your Writing
(Five filmstrips)
A very good series for students who have difficulty organizing the whole theme. Writing is compared to climbing stairs in that steps must be followed sequentially. Thus, students view the process as one which involves completing tasks such as the beginning, middle, and end of a paper as less difficult.

III.   The Center for Humanities
Communications Park, Box 1000
Mount Kisco, New York 10549
NOTE: All slides, filmstrips and pictures used in these sets are based on the background and everyday experiences of students.

A. Grammar—"I Found a Dollar Walking Home"—Solving Common Sentence Problems
(One record, one cassette, one set of slides)
Extensive drills are given to aid students in recognizing and avoiding such mistakes as run-on sentences, fragments, subject-verb agreement, pronoun-antecedent agreement, ambiguous reference, misplaced and dangling modifiers, and parallel structure. All these concepts are emphasized as being necessary for clear, effective writing.
Additional exercises are given at the end of each lesson. Instructor's guide is also provided.

B. Communication Skills: Expository Writing
(Six records, six cassettes, six filmstrips)
A remarkable program which reinforces the basic five-paragraph expository paper, with emphasis on the major components of an essay—paragraphs. Specifically, students are

instructed on the introduction, body, and conclusion of an essay as well as appropriate methods of developing each type of paragraph, such as comparison, contrast, and classification. Revision is also stressed.

C. The Research Paper Made Easy: From Assignment to Completion
(Six records, six cassettes, six filmstrips)
The research process is divided into nine parts with exercises before and after each step, from choosing a subject to writing the final draft. Such skills as organizing, notetaking, and documentation are presented in a lively fashion to ease many fears students have about completing the research paper.

D. Creative Writing: Imagination and Self-Expression
(Three part set: records, tapes, slides)
Models of writing done by Steinbeck, Woolf, Joyce, Thurber, Tennyson, Eliot, and others provide a basis for students to use their imagination to express their ideas. The glossary of creative writing focuses on such terms as plot, metaphor, imagery, and symbol, giving students a better command of how other writers master this task.

IV. Eyegate House
Jamaica, New York 11435

A. Techniques of Paragraph Writing
(Four filmstrips, two cassettes)
Students who have not mastered writing a good paragraph will benefit greatly by learning the parts of a paragraph, planning a paragraph and topic sentence, and exploring various methods of development such as comparison, examples, and cause-effect.

B. Techniques of Theme Writing
(Two cassettes, four filmstrips)
The whole theme is presented in a fashion that allows students to move from one step to another with greater flexibility. Methods are indicated to assist in beginning and ending a theme, with additional exercises on transitional devices and methods of arranging paragraphs.

C. How to Write Reports
(Five filmstrips with cassettes)
This series enables students to have less fear about completing a longer piece of writing such as a report. Information is presented to help students proceed through organizing the

paper, collecting data, and using courses, resources, and tables. Finally, students are exposed to synthesizing these concepts into an acceptable well-written form.

V.   The Continental Press, Inc.
     Elizabethtown, Pennsylvania 17022
     Language Skills Tests, LST 1–24
     (Twenty-four filmstrips with written pre- and posttests on mechanics, vocabulary skills, language usage, sentence structure, and paragraphs)
     Specifically designed for high school students, a built-in system allows students to take a pretest, use the appropriate filmstrip with exercises, and then take a posttest to assess their mastery of the content. This system gives teachers a very good indication of any additional work students may need in the areas listed above.

VI. Charles E. Merrill Publishing Company
     1300 Alum Creek Drive
     Columbus, Ohio 43216
     Process One: A Multimedia Writing Program (Fifteen filmstrips, text, fifteen cassettes)
     As the name suggests, this program presents writing as a process. The program is composed of a series of skills that can be mastered by all students. Major emphasis is placed on discovering ideas through experiences, organization, diction, sentence structure, paragraphs, and grammar and usage as they relate to effective writing. Students' interest level is usually high as they proceed through the tapes and filmstrips of *Process One*. A text is provided to make the lessons easy to follow.

VII. Guidance Associates, Inc.
     Communications Park, Box 3000
     Mount Kisco, New York 10549
     A. Speaking of Grammar
        (Two filmstrips, two cassettes, two records)
        A teacher's manual contains the script, operational instructions, and introductory and follow-up exercises. The best feature of this program is the incorporation of three systems of grammar—traditional, structural, and transformational-generative—into exercises pertaining to the parts of speech as they function in the English grammatical system.
     B. Speaking of Spelling
        (Two filmstrips, text, two cassettes)
        The approach here is to introduce spelling from a historical

standpoint. The program looks at the structure of English and delves into spelling patterns, syllabification, word roots, mnemonic devices, and spelling demons. A must for any student who feels he or she cannot spell.

C. Language Basics: Verbs

(Two filmstrips, text, two cassettes)

The program is presented as a story and is not drill-oriented. Exercises are geared toward identifying action and linking verbs, complements, verb phrases, inflections, and principal parts.

D. Language Basics: Nouns

(Two filmstrips, two cassettes)

Worksheets and exercises accompany the tapes and filmstrips and provide students with an opportunity to see nouns as important words in English grammar. Students are shown the kinds and uses of nouns as well as how to identify them.

E. Language Basics: Adjectives and Adverbs

(Two filmstrips, two cassettes)

Understanding the function of modifiers is the key concept of this series. Given in the form of a folktale, these two types are explained in reference to how they make writing clearer through providing additional specific information.

F. Writing: From Imagination to Expression

(Four filmstrips, four cassettes, four records, and manual)

Through drawing upon their experiences, students are encouraged to use their perceptions of these experiences to produce writing which reflects the use of the five senses.

G. Writing: From Assignment to Completion

(Two filmstrips, two cassettes, two records, and manual)

Approached as a difficult task, the writing process is introduced through using a student, David, to show how he begins and accomplishes each objective until the finished product has been written. The major emphasis is to show all students that, once begun, writing is not difficult if logical steps are followed. Organization is the key factor, but the program includes lessons on unity, coherence, diction, and paragraph development.

VIII. Educulture

3184 "J" Avenue

Costa Mesa, California 92626

(These programs are self-tutorial, self-motivated mini-courses in a module format.)

A. Rhetoric and Critical Thinking
(Twenty-five audio-tutorial mini-courses, twenty-five cassettes and manuals)
Containing five sections, this program answers many teachers' prayers. First, parts one and two deal with methods of expository development giving clear details about thesis and support in writing an expository essay. Part three focuses on logic in writing or reasoning. Students learn how to use evidence to develop an argument and how to avoid fallacious reasoning. Part four concentrates on style and diction, and enables students to make proper choices in words to get their messages across to their readers. Finally, students learn how to do special kinds of writing such as literary critical papers, research papers, reports, and technical writing. Each module is self-contained with a cassette and a manual designed to aid each student with his or her specific weak area. Concepts are introduced and students are tested to see if they understand before moving to another section.

B. Mini-Grammar
(Cassettes with manuals)
The self-paced audio-tutorial program gives students an individualized approach to grammatical errors common to most of their writing. The main topics that are covered deal with such concerns as the simple sentence, parts of speech, independent and dependent clauses, phrases, agreement, common sentence errors, and misplaced modifiers. Students work at their own pace on whatever problem they are experiencing in writing classroom assignments.

References

Brandon, Liane. "Using Media Creatively in the English Classroom." *English Journal* 60 (December 1971): 1231–33.

Burgess, Anthony. "The Case for Diversity." In *New Movements in the Study and Teaching of English*, edited by Nicholas Bagnall. London: Temple Smith, 1973.

Fagan, Edward R. "Individualizing the Study of English." *English Journal* 60 (February 1971): 236–41.

Johnson, Nancy W. "A Successful Placement Test for Basic Writing." In *Basic Writing: Essays for Teachers, Researchers and Administrators*, edited by Lawrence N. Kasden and Daniel R. Hoeber, Urbana, Ill.: National Council of Teachers of English, 1980.

Judy [Tchudi], Stephen N., and Susan Judy [Tchudi]. *The English Teacher's Handbook: Ideas and Resources for Teaching English.* Cambridge: Winthrop, 1979.

Laque, Carol F., and Phyllis A. Sherwood. *A Laboratory Approach to Writing.* Urbana, Ill.: National Council of Teachers of English, 1977.

Marsh, Philip M. *How to Teach English in High School and College.* New York: Bookman Associates, 1956.

Murray, Donald M. *A Writer Teaches Writing: A Practical Method of Teaching Composition.* Boston: Houghton Mifflin, 1968.

Schlawin, Sheila A. "Instant Individualization Takes Time." *English Journal* 64 (November 1975): 57–58.

Thompson, Nancy Cromer. "Multi Media: Some Ideas on How English Teachers Can Develop an Expertise in Multi-Media." *English Journal* 66 (April 1977): 92–95.

Structuring the College Composition Class around the Black Basic Writer

Barbara Hunt
Washtenaw Community College, Ann Arbor, Michigan

After a conference, my students hand in their final drafts for evaluation. Sometimes, though, students are encouraged to evaluate their own papers. They break into groups and each student in the group is given a theme to read and a list of criteria from which to evaluate the paper being read. Within a group each student is requested to read a colleague's theme, and then hand it to the student on her or his right for additional reading and evaluating. This process is repeated until all of the papers in the group are read and evaluated. They are then given to me for a final appraisal. When the themes are returned to the student-authors, the students are not only able to benefit from my assessment of their writing, but they also are able to benefit from their peers' critiques, which often have more impact than my evaluation.

In the process of these peer critiques the students apply questions that determine the writing ability of the student author. A group consists of five people—the initiator (responsible for asking the questions and eliciting answers from the group), the recorder (responsible for writing down the responses of the group), and the respondents (the rest of the group).

The peer critiques are very effective because my students are taught to use questions such as the ones below to evaluate their themes.

1. Is there a thesis sentence? If so, what is it?

2. Does the thesis follow an introductory paragraph? Explain.

3. Are the paragraphs well developed and unified? Explain in detail.

4. What specific examples are used to develop the paragraphs? Explain.

5. Do the paragraphs follow each other in a logical progression? Explain.

6. Is there a conclusion? Explain.

7. Are there any mechanical problems in the paper, e.g., spelling, punctuation, capitalization, grammar, omissions? Explain.

8. How can this theme be improved? Explain.

During peer criticism, my basic students learn some specific behavior necessary for effective writing. These students feel more comfortable with one another than with a teacher hovering over them. Students are also reading and analyzing, probably for the first time, the writing of other students who commit similar, if not more grievous, writing errors than they. A dialogue such as the one below for the question, "Are the pararaphs well developed and unified?" is typical.

"Where is the topic sentence?"
"He doesn't have one."
"All of the sentences are run together."
"No, I think they don't say anything."

In this kind of discussion, the students are discovering that writing is an act of communication and that the better the writer, the better the communication.

Peer criticism as well as student/teacher conferences have proved successful as a component of my writing programs. Since students are not only asked to take writing out of an abstract form and give it some concreteness, they are also given an opportunity to focus on writing in an analytical way and to examine their behavior as writers. Both peer criticism and the student/teacher conference involve small-group or individual instruction in a nonthreatening atmosphere. Essentially, basic writers benefit from peer criticism and student/teacher conferences because they become active participants in the act of learning to compose.

References

Collignon, Joseph. "Why Leroy Can't Write." *College English* 39 (March 1978): 852–59.

Fassler, Barbara. "The Red Pen Revisited: Teaching Composition Through Student Conferences." *College English* 40 (October 1978): 186–90.

Murray, Donald M. "Write before Writing." *College Composition and Communication* 29 (December 1978): 375–81.

Shaughnessy, Mina P. *Errors and Expectations: A Guide for the Teacher of Basic Writing.* New York: Oxford University Press, 1977.

Using the Oral History Approach to Teach Freshman Writing

Ethel Taylor and Ernest Bradford
North Carolina A&T State University, Greensboro

The desire to help students to develop the necessary skills for effective written communication has sparked an unprecedented effort among English teachers to experiment with new methods and materials.

The teachers at the university with which we are affiliated are no exception. In a body of more than five thousand students drawn from some thirty-six states and several foreign countries, there is much diversity of culture and academic preparation. All of these students, however, regardless of their major fields, must take the two-semester freshman composition course. Intimidated on one side by the complaints of other departments of the university and sparked on the other by our own perceptions, a selected group of English teachers developed a proposal for action. The purpose of this proposal was to develop a curriculum which would provide experiences which would build writing skills, extend limited experiential backgrounds, and relate to the student's planned area of specialization.

The present writing program at our school is both remedial and developmental. It focuses on the "how" and "what" of writing, using literature as the core. In addition, some attention is given to students' chronic writing deficiencies through individual and group tutoring. Aware that much research has indicated the importance and complexity of the writing process, the experimenters studied the literature for possible ideas and procedures with the idea of change in mind. Studies by E. Bates (1976), Miller and Gordon (1974), and E. T. Higgins (1977) on the conceptual link between social development/ awareness and effectiveness in communication were helpful. So also were studies by Fantini and Weinstein (1968) and Tinto and Sherman (1974) on the importance of some kind of awareness component in basic skills programs. Fantini and Weinstein's study suggests that a student's self-image is enhanced by personal identity, cultural enrichment, and multi-cultural experiences. In fact, Fantini's study stresses the fact that relevant education must be based on the students' learning styles, must utilize material within their realm of experience, must take their feelings into consideration, and must recognize the student's legitimate concerns.

All of these studies encouraged the experimenters to establish a section within the freshman composition program using the oral history approach. Specifically, our colleagues wanted to use this method to explore the history and culture of the university and the surrounding area as a relevant means for developing basic skills such as reading, writing, thinking, listening, and research. They hoped also that this approach would establish a degree of continuity between the freshman composition course and the sophomore courses in humanities, history, literature, and political science.

The Oral History Approach

In the approach frequently used in the freshman composition courses, a skill is taught and the student is asked to demonstrate acquisition of this skill through a designated writing experience. The teacher grades the writing exercise and asks the student to make revisions. This process continues until the skill is satisfactorily acquired. This technique was not abandoned, but the skill which in the usual approach is an end in itself, became, in the experimental approach, the means to an immediate end. For example, in the regular course based on the process-centered approach, the students are taught to write a paragraph with a topic sentence and supporting sentences using examples. They are given or choose a topic, and then they write, and rewrite until they have mastered this skill to the instructor's satisfaction. In the experimental course, using the experiential approach, the procedure was the same, but the students were responding to an actual situation. They were involved in an experience and were asked to respond to that experience, incorporating previously learned skills into this written response.

The experimenters assumed that the composing process is complex and sequential. Initially, the focus was on the students' personal experiences; it then moved gradually to the more formal transactional modes and to research. The experimenters realized that they could not "go in all directions at once," that is, "tackle immediately all of the writing deficiencies of students." Consequently, they established priorities. The following mechanical problems were considered of first importance: (1) errors in subject/verb agreement and sentence sense, (2) sentence fragments, (3) run-on sentences, (4) errors in tense, and

Ethel Taylor and Ernest Bradford

(5) obvious misspellings. The basic paragraph pattern of topic sentence, supporting sentences, concluding sentence, and the basic theme pattern of topic paragraph, supporting paragraphs, and concluding paragraph were established as minimal competencies for paragraph and theme writing.

The experimenters intended to focus upon values orientation and the development of experiential background as they relate to the composing process using the oral history approach. The oral history approach is not new, but as Ann Shockley (1978) has noted, it has gained enormous popularity as a research technique as a result of the use of this method in Alex Haley's book, *Roots*. Margaret Walker used this same technique in her epic portrayal of the trials and triumphs of her grandmother in the novel *Jubilee*. Shockley points out that what gives this approach added impetus is the tape recorder, which gives a sense of immediacy to the eyewitness account. She points out further that at this time, historians, scholars, and anthropologists acknowledge that Afro-American history is chiefly oral. The tradition extends from the 1870s, when the Fisk Jubilee Singers traveled throughout the United States and Europe giving renditions of spirituals which they had learned from their slave parents, to the 1900s, when black scholars such as John Cade of Southern University, Ophelia Settle of Fisk University, and Lawrence Reddick of Kentucky State elicited personal narratives from ex-slaves in Louisiana, Tennessee, Kentucky, and Indiana (Schockley 1978). The experimenters believe that they are among the first to use the oral history approach in the teaching of freshman writing.

The oral history approach was appropriate to use in this university setting because the university is rich in cultural history and was the fountainhead of the sit-in movement of the 1960s. On February 1, 1960, four university freshmen challenged the segregated eating custom of a local five-and-dime store downtown, thereby spurring the acceleration of sit-ins throughout the nation (Wolff 1980). Many of the participants in this social drama were still in the university community. In addition, there were individuals available who were "living libraries" for the university and surrounding community.

Following is a description of the experimenters' procedures. A unit of four to six weeks duration was developed around a central experience, for example, the sit-ins at the university. This experience was retold through interviews with persons who participated in it, for example, a president emeritus of the university who functions as a griot having watched the university develop for over a half century.

Other persons, such as the trained oral historian employed by the local library, were also interviewed and served as valuable sources of information.

The Program

The students' responsibilities were (1) to do as much reading as possible on the sit-in movement in general, the Civil Rights Struggle of the 1960s, the history of the South, and the concept of a democracy; (2) to write a summary essay and a précis dealing with either an in-class presentation or outside reading/personal interview; (3) to write letters of invitation, requests for information, and thanks and (4) to prepare questions for the interview.

Typical questions prepared for one interview were: How did the students of that period compare with the present ones? and did the students' tendency to question established customs have a precedent among the student body? Questions like these initiated class discussion dealing with the larger issues of citizenship responsibilities, the abuses of power, freedom and responsibility, and justice.

The teachers' responsibilities were (1) to put pertinent materials on reserve; (2) to serve as catalysts through lectures, discussions, and audio demonstrations to keep the students on target; (3) to teach the essential characteristics of an effective interview, for example, being a good listener and being objective; (4) to review for students the formalities of letter writing; (5) to teach the appropriate footnote form for documenting information from books, newspapers, magazines, and interviews; and (6) to teach or review the structural design to be followed for all paragraphs and themes; that is, topic sentence, supporting sentences, concluding sentence previously mentioned.

The expected student outcomes were practice in use of the library, practice in empirical thinking—making judgments, developing a greater sense of personal worth—and seeing themselves as part of a larger tradition—the university, the South, the nation, the world.

The expected skills to be mastered were the proper form for footnotes, the designated structural design for paragraphs and themes, the formalities of the formal letter, written and oral work free from the mechanical errors (e.g. subject/verb agreement) previously outlined.

The extent to which students had achieved these outcomes was most evident in their oral participation in class and in their written assignments. Generally, the oral history approach sections showed a greater familiarity with library sources such as encyclopedias, yearbooks, and indexes; and they were more adept at seeing the relationship between contemporary events and past history as evidenced in the content of their papers and in their chosen topics.

A selected number of papers of the students in the oral history sections were compared with those in the regular sections in terms of the primary traits stipulated for the structural design of paragraphs and themes. Using the primary trait evaluation procedure, the experimenters found that the oral history sections mastered the structural design scheme by the third written assignment, as compared to the fifth written assignment for the regular sections. At the end of the third written assignment, over 90 percent of the students in the oral history sections had mastered the structural design, compared to 40 percent for the regular sections. The oral history sections also had fewer errors of the kind specified for top priority.

The experimenters felt that this oral history approach was commendable, because of the enthusiasm of the students. In comments to the experimenters, most students said that they enjoyed the course, because they were less apprehensive as to whether they could achieve well enough. Students were not led to believe that they were better writers than they actually were; however, through this approach, they were made aware of the strengths that were already evident in their own writing. In addition, this approach through initial emphasis on students' immediate concerns helped them to assume more readily the responsibility for their own writing growth.

References

Bates, Elizabeth. *Language and Context: The Acquisition of Pragmatics.* New York: Academic Press, 1976.

Higgins, E. T. "Communication as Related to Channel Incentive, and Social Class." *Genetic Psychology Monographs* (1977): 75–141.

Fantini, Mario, and Gerald Weinstein. *The Disadvantaged: Challenge to Education.* New York: Holt, Rinehart & Winston, 1968.

Miller, LaMar P., and Edmund Gordon. *Equality of Educational Opportunity: A Handbook of Research.* New York: AMS Press, 1974.

Shockley, Ann Allen. "Oral History: A Research Tool for Black History." *Negro History Bulletin* 41 (1978): 787–91.

Tinto, V., and R. H. Sherman. *The Effectiveness of Secondary and Higher Education Intervention Programs: A Critical Review of Research.* New York: Columbia University Press, 1974.

Wolff, Miles. "How It All Began." In *Civilities and Civil Rights,* edited by William H. Chafe. New York: Oxford University Press, 1980.

Using Folk Literature in Teaching Composition

Edward Anderson
John Tyler Community College, Chester, Virginia

When black people were first brought from the West Coast of Africa to American soil, they were brought from different localities, but they shared common cultural patterns which were rich in tradition and folklore. Much of the transplanted African culture found expression in oral literature, music, and dance.

Literary and rhetorical types of African oral tradition show direct expression of the black American experience from colonial days to the present. They show many aspects of the human condition and many elements of universal appeal, though they express these aspects in different and unique ways. The black oral tradition gives evidence of what it means to be "black" in America.

Making use of this black American folk tradition in the classroom can do much to change negative attitudes about its producers and about personalities who are presented in the literature. More importantly, these can serve as wholesome instructional materials and aids in the teaching of English composition. It is important that teachers be aware of certain facts about the black folk tradition and the variety of curriculum materials that treat the tradition, so that they may adequately use these materials in their English composition classes.

What Is the Black Folk Tradition?

Stylistically, the black American folk tradition can be classified into sacred and secular types of oral expression. The sacred style is rural and southern. It is fixed in the black religious experience (i.e., spirituals) and church tradition. The secular style is urban and northern, but it has roots in the South and is rural in nature (i.e., blues, folktales, and the street culture styles of the rapper, the sounder, and the signifier).

The call and response pattern, found in the speech and musical forms, appears in both the sacred and the secular styles of the black

oral tradition. The call occurs when the speaker makes a statement
or the leader sings either the first line or the first word of a song.
The response takes place when, true to the speaker's expectations,
the listener answers back, or when the chorus of singers finishes the
line of the song or repeats what the leader has sung. The interplay
between the two continues throughout the production of the work—
with a statement and then with a reaction to the statement.

Black folktales sprang from an oral tradition and are usually
animal tales. Some of these tales were written later by authors who
used the same features found in the original folktales. These features
are a particularly characteristic use of irony, boasting, symbolism,
and hyperbole with the unique treatment of storytelling and narrative
elements.

Sermons delivered in dialect were first developed in the seventeenth century. These are rich in Biblical images, poetic language (i.e.,
metaphor and similes), rhythmical patterns, emotional appeal, often
skillful narrative development, and the use of idiomatic expressions
drawn from the language of the Bible. They blend the commonplace
experiences with historical events and are characterized by allusions
and symbolism.

As a type of black folk oral literature, ballads are narrative poems
which sprang from the life of Afro-American people and were
adapted for recitation and singing. The subjects of the ballads are
heroes who performed unusual acts and were presented as epic figures (i.e., "Frankie and Johnny," "Railroad Bill," "John Henry," "Casey
Jones," and "Stackolee"). These ballads were and still are being transmitted and changed by word of mouth and they most often record
tragedies in the lives of black people.

The anonymous spirituals (e.g., "Steal Away to Jesus," "Deep
River," "Go Down Moses," and "Nobody Knows De Trouble I See")
comprise one of the most realistic and beautiful forms in oral tradition. The themes of these spirituals, which were developed during
slavery and on plantations, voice a note of protest and deep religious
conviction. They bring the Christian Bible alive through vivid symbolism, images, and figurative language, as well as black dialect and
rhythm. These spirituals also revealed the slaves' thoughts on planta-
tion life, their faith in their religion, their desire for freedom from
sin, and their desire to fly to freedom.

The blues were also an anonymous type of black folk poetry and
might be considered a unique form of the secular song. Although
they have been refined since the days of slavery, these songs origi-
nated in that era and deal with universal themes such as grief, self-

pity, hard times, varieties of bad luck, often unrequited love and despair. In contrast to the spirituals which were intended for group singing, the blues are sung solo. They are mocking, ironic, and tragic-comic.

Afro-American jokes are not quite as unique a literary representation of cultural ancestry as are the other forms of the black folk tradition. These jokes are terse but witty tales which depend upon a punchline conclusion for comical effect. In the story (or joke) a represented verse or song usually provides humorous conclusions to produce an emotional effect. Black dialect is used as the mode of expression of Afro-American jokes.

The Rhetoric of Black Literature

In "The Logic of Non-Standard English" William Labov (1969) recognizes elements of verbality, grammaticality, and logic in the language of black users of nonstandard dialects. Afro-American culture and lifestyles encourage and almost demand the use of fluency and verbal strategies that are not the same kinds of rhetorical strategies and dialect that the mainstream culture uses and thrives upon. The verbal and rhetorical strategies that have been produced and used by blacks are rapping, running it down, jiving, shucking, copping a plea, sounding, and signifying. These strategies emphasize rhetoric and the art of persuasion through the skillful use of language.

The following (mainly urban) ghetto verbal strategies used by Afro-Americans are parts of their oral tradition and culture that demand the use of the street culture's secret code as well as an exclusive type of ghetto idiom:

Rapping is one of the most widely used of all the black verbal strategies. It is often referred to as a form of conversation that is lively, interesting, and fluent. Rapping may also describe a narrative or a colorful rundown of a past event. Most of the time rapping is a sales-type of persuasion with a lively personal style that thrives upon control and manipulation of someone in order to make that person do or give up something.

Running it down is a verbal instrument which involves giving (or requesting) information, advice, clarification, or addition to some information already presented. It is a way of giving explanation or repetition, and it comes as a request that hinges upon surprise or disbelief on the part of the listener in understanding what has already been said. Style and personality are at the center of this strategy.

Jiving often refers to communication (used by the audience or the listener) which "puts someone on" or which is difficult for someone to believe (i.e., the listener gives the impression that the speaker might not be reliable or honest).

Shucking has a particular meaning when used by black Americans, especially when referring to whites. Roger Abrahams and Geneva Gay (1972) believe that many shuckers are "Uncle Toms" and "Aunt Janes" or those who "when confronted with a compromising and dangerous situation (whether the danger is physical or emotional)" very often do "what is expected of (them)" by portraying "simple-mindedness, pleading and submission, and even confession of guilt along with oaths and penance." Shucking is a defensive verbal strategy, but when one is shucking in order to "whup the Game," he or she is using the offensive strategy as a guise designed to manipulate someone to make him or her give up something or feel or act a desired way. Many Afro-Americans desire to use strategies that to non-Afro-American blacks are offensive strategies to express their feelings of pride and self-assertion. When blacks use shucking on other blacks, they use appropriate folk talk and gestures that "play overtones in which the person being 'put on' is aware of the attempts being made and goes along with it for enjoyment or in appreciation of the style" (Kochman 1969).

Copping a plea, like shucking and jiving, emphasizes the ability to get out of a situation through compromise. However, copping a plea is a more direct verbal strategy in which one recognizes the superiority of someone else and, hence, asks or begs for mercy, pity, or sympathy, which Thomas Kochman calls "total loss of face" or "loss of status among one's peers."

Sounding aims to insult someone in varying ways and degrees ranging from word games used to test attitude and disposition, to friendly and petulant quarreling, and to words used to start a physical fight. The sound may be a simple challenge. The effectiveness of the sound is measured by the quickness of the answer or response that is received in reply to it, or by its unexpected or quick-willed nature. If it takes the contender a long time to respond to the sound, then the sound is said to be good or effective. Other terms that refer to sounding are "coming down hard" or being "foul" or "cold." The aim of sounding is to take status from an opponent through the use of verbal power by making the opponents feel they must gain their status by sounding back—either on the speaker or the group members they encounter. Group presence is important to the game (very often helpful in preventing a physical fight).

Signifying is a verbal strategy that is referred to in some places as sounding or insulting someone. It involves boasting, implying, begging, or inciting someone through the use of gestures or verbal play.

Signifying refers to the use of verbal innuendo; to carp, needle and lie, and cajole and it means to talk around the subject while never quite coming to the point. It also means making fun of a person or a situation. To stir up fights between friends by telling stories is an example of signifying.

These verbal and rhetorical strategies serve definite needs and functions in the black American community—needs that teachers and other educators should become aware of and familiar with if they are to do adequate jobs in the classroom. When properly applied, these same black verbal and rhetorical strategies can be used effectively in the English literature and composition classrooms for both motivational and instructional purposes.

In the Classroom

Rhetoric, the art of oral and written persuasion, and the elements of written composition, may be presented in the English composition classroom by use of the elements of the black oral folk tradition. Ballads, folktales, blues, spirituals, and other types, that are especially narrative in nature, may be used to teach narration. Those elements in this tradition that create an image or paint a picture are useful in teaching descriptions. Others may equally be examined for the manner in which cause-effect, comparison or contrast, and other expository forms are used. Students may also examine the rhetorical styles and structures of church sermons and use them as ethical, rational, and emotional appeals for their argumentative essays. Similarly, the styles and messages of many of these sermons may be used as models for persuasive speeches or essays.

Different oral traditions and verbal and rhetorical strategies may be analyzed or compared in terms of their effective use in certain situations. Tales and sermons may be summarized or paraphrased to provide students with practice in restating ideas in their own words and using their own style.

Students may examine their own daily lives for elements of the folk tradition and for contemporary verbal strategies which are frequently found in television and radio shows, and in concerts, books, conversations, and church services. A journal of these contacts may be kept and used later as primary data for research and reportage assignments.

In addition, the examination of different oral types can be helpful in the teaching of introductory literature. Many of these tales and songs not only contain literary elements, but also treat universal human conditions. Ballads, spirituals, and blues may be used to teach some aspects of poetry, as can the poetry of black American writers who use elements of oral tradition in their works, in their short stories and in their novels.

Black folktales may be read and then retold in standard English. The lessons or the themes gained from the telling of them may be discussed and used as sources for topics of oral and written assignments. Much of this type of literature lends itself very easily to dramatic readings. Many of the verbal strategies that rhyme can be chanted in unison. This activity is very pleasant for young children who may clap their hands or use a simple musical instrument. Readers theatre may be enjoyable for older children who may deliver the folktales from memory or read them aloud using pitch and tone to convey various emotional qualities. Material from ballads and tales may be adapted to the stage as a drama, or the ideas may be acted out in improvisations or from memorized scripts. Numerous topics for discussions and writing assignments may be drawn from these dramatizations.

Finally, students may examine and discuss the black American dialect found in folk songs, sermons, and jokes and use these forms as material for code-switching or shifting exercises.

To conclude, the black American oral tradition of literature and verbal rhetorical strategies expresses the Afro-Americans' reality. These forms contain many literary and rhetorical techniques and linguistic expressions that make them effective tools for motivating and instructing students in English literature and composition classes.

References

Abrahams, Roger D. *Deep Down in the Jungle.* Chicago: Aldine Publishing, 1970.

Abrahams, Roger D., and Rudolph C. Troike, eds. *Language and Cultural Diversity in American Education.* Englewood Cliffs, N.J.: Prentice-Hall, 1972.

Baker, Houston A., Jr. *Black Literature in America.* New York: McGraw-Hill, 1971.

————. *Long Black Song: Essays in Black American Literature and Culture.* Charlottesville, Vir.: The University Press of Virginia, 1972.

Bowdre, Paul Hull, Jr. "Eye Dialect as a Literary Device." In *A Various Language,* edited by Juanita V. Williamson and Virginia M. Burke. New York: Holt, Rinehart & Winston, 1971.

Brewer, J. Mason. *American Negro Folklore.* Chicago: Quadrangle, 1968.

Brown, Claude. "The Language of Soul." In *Aspects of American English,* edited by Elizabeth M. Derr and Ralph M. Aderman. New York: Harcourt Brace Jovanovich, 1971.

Brown, Harry Matthew, and John Milstead. *Patterns in Poetry—An Introductory Anthology.* Glenview, Ill.: Scott, Foresman & Co., 1968.

Brown, Sterling A. *Negro Poetry and Drama, and the Negro in American Fiction.* New York: Atheneum, 1969.

Brunvand, J. Harold. *The Study of American Folklore.* New York: W. W. Norton & Co., 1968.

Butcher, Margaret Just. *The Negro in American Culture.* New York: New American Library of World Literature, 1956.

Chesnutt, Charles Waddell. *The Conjure Woman.* Ann Arbor, Mich.: University of Michigan Press, 1969.

Courlander, Harold. *A Treasury of Afro-American Folklore.* New York: Crown, 1976.

Dorson, Richard M. *American Folklore.* Chicago: University of Chicago Press, 1969.

———. *American Negro Folktales.* Greenwich, Conn.: Fawcett, 1967.

———. *Negro Folktales in Michigan.* Cambridge: Harvard University Press, 1956.

Du Bois, W. E. B. *The Souls of Black Folk.* Chicago: A. C. McClurg, 1903.

Dundes, Alan, ed. *Mother Wit from the Laughing Barrel.* Englewood Cliffs, N.J.: Prentice-Hall, 1973.

Fasold, Ralph, and Walt Wolfram. "Some Linguistic Features of Negro Dialect." In *Teaching Standard English in the Inner City,* edited by Ralph Fasold and Roger Shuy. Washington, D.C.: Center for Applied Linguistics, 1969.

Gayle, Addison, Jr., ed. *The Black Aesthetic.* Garden City, N.Y.: Doubleday, 1972.

Genovese, Eugene D. *Roll, Jordan, Roll.* New York: Vintage Books, 1974.

Grier, William H. and Price M. Cobb. *Black Rage.* New York: Bantam, 1968.

Hughes, Langston, and Arna Bontemps, eds. *The Book of Negro Folklore.* New York: Dodd, Mead & Co., 1958.

King, Woodie, Jr., "The Game." *Liberator* (August 1965).

Kochman, Thomas. "'Rappin' in the Black Ghetto." *Trans-action* (February 1969): 31.

Labov, William. "The Logic of Non-Standard English." *Florida FL Reporter* (Spring-Summer 1969).

———. *The Study of Nonstandard English.* Champaign, Ill.: National Council of Teachers of English, 1970.

Lester, Julius. *Black Folktales.* New York: Grove, 1969.

Major, Clarence. *Dictionary of Afro-American Slang.* New York: International Publishers, 1970.

Robinson, William H., Jr., ed. *Early Black American Poets.* Dubuque, Iowa: William C. Brown, 1969.

Slim, Iceburg. "Pimp: The Story of My Life." Manuscript.

Southern, Eileen. *The Music of Black Americans: A History.* New York: W. W. Norton & Co., 1971.

Turner, Lorenzo Dow. *Africanisms in the Gullah Dialect.* Chicago: University of Chicago Press, 1949.

Teaching Writing to Gifted Black Students

Delores Lipscomb
Chicago State University, Illinois

Last year, I was requested by the Bureau of Language Arts of the Chicago Board of Education to develop a course in expository writing for fifteen gifted eighth graders. These were students who had scored in the ninety-fifth percentile in verbal ability on the Iowa Tests of Basic Skills, and between 200 and 600 in verbal ability on the Scholastic Aptitude Test. The average high school junior or senior usually scores about 368 on the verbal section. More than half of these students scored at least 360.

I reasoned that although these twelve- and thirteen-year-olds had actual verbal abilities of high school juniors and seniors, their writing abilities might not be as advanced. Both the Iowa Test of Basic Skills and the Scholastic Aptitude Test measure recognition of usage, grammar and syntactic structures. These tests do not measure actual writing behavior. Furthermore, while most of these students had been engaged in prior writing tasks, these tasks had been grounded in narration, description and other forms that focused on subject matter that the students experienced directly.

By nature, expository writing entails a gathering and probing of data that demands some degree of distance between the subject matter and the writer. In expository writing, writers work with intangible objects and ideas. They must objectify their feelings and thoughts, draw inferences from them, and finally explain them in some logical manner. In this process, the writer becomes increasingly anonymous as the subject matter becomes central (Moffett 1968).

James Moffett maintains that children's writing is grounded in narration because their abstractive powers are unable "to conceptualize and interrelate intangible things." Objects and ideas that are not a part of their direct experiences are difficult for them to conceptualize. A final reason that Moffett offers for children having more difficulty with exposition is that they are frequently unable to objectify their feelings and discuss them.

Certainly, the curriculum had to be adjusted to account for all of these elements, including the potential disparity between verbal ability and writing practice. To bring these diverse yet related elements together, the curriculum had to reflect the naturalness of the writing process and the inherent language ability that these children possessed. Hence, clear objectives had to be set, and writing tasks had to be carefully planned and sequenced. The tasks had to lead from simple to complex and from personal commentaries and observations about oneself to short investigative reports. These tasks, though they were imposed, also had to follow a natural sequence that led children naturally from one assignment to the next as they speculated about issues and problems in their daily lives. The objectives were threefold: (1) to provide the students with writing tasks that have real world applications; (2) to give them an expanding repertory of writing strategies that will enable them to analyze their experiences whatever they are; and (3) to help them to explain these experiences in some objective, logical manner.

Three basic threads of writing permeated the course: (1) writing about literature, (2) writing about oneself and the community, and (3) research and reportage. In the writing about literature sequence, the students write essays and short pieces about nonfiction. Reading assignments are always followed by a lively but thorough discussion of the universal themes and issues found in literature. Also, short nonfiction prose pieces introduce students to rhetorical techniques that they later practice themselves. Engaging students in this continuous recycling of reading and writing helps them to internalize ways of thinking about written language. As the students become critically conscious of written language, they learn the subtle techniques that authors use to convey a message.

The writing-about-oneself-and-others sequence consists of units that move students naturally and logically from simple to complex thinking tasks. The students write an opinion essay that requires them to generalize about their experience, a problem/solution essay that raises critical questions about their observation, a casual analysis essay that involves analyzing some aspect of their behavior, and a persuasive essay that requires them to develop and present a proposal for an improvement in their school or community.

Research and reportage, the third component of the course, is a natural outgrowth of the work that the students have been doing in examining and analyzing their experiences and observations. Though library work is encouraged, the emphasis here is on research, not necessarily library research. Students work with both primary and secondary sources.

On the first day of class, the students are given an informal diagnostic test which consists of writing two short essays which utilize the skills that I intend to teach in the course. The first essay asks the students to describe an experience and to explain its importance. The second requires them to form an opinion regarding one of their beliefs and to explain the opinion.

I evaluate the papers using an instrument developed by the faculty of the English department of Chicago State University. This instrument is used to evaluate essays written by students in freshmen composition classes. The essays are not formally scored, but I do use the results in the following ways: (1) to evaluate the students' abilities in order to determine the nature and sequence of assignments; (2) to diagnose specific strengths and weaknesses of individual students; (3) to determine the effectiveness of a particular writing assignment; and (4) to report progress to students, parents, and administrators. The diagnostic instrument examines the papers in the areas of organization and development, meaning and style, and usage and punctuation.

Generally, the students are very capable writers who master the different tasks and srategies rather quickly. Their content is fresh and imaginative, and the lack of focus and poor organization that existed in initial papers are easily remedied.

But in spite of their verbal fluency and ability to analyze and synthesize information, a large number of these students have problems with basic skills such as spelling, punctuation, and usage. Because knowledge of mechanics is important, occasional short drills are used. However, the major thrust of the course is to allow them to experiment with more complicated linguistic and rhetorical forms. As they do so, they naturally make errors from time to time. These errors are a part of the growth and learning process. Feedback from the instructor or another student, and extensive use of revision, helps them to correct these mistakes. In this respect, many of the errors are easily corrected as the students master the different writing tasks.

The sequence that I have described has been successful in my class. The students tell me that the writing is challenging and difficult in the beginning, but that they learn a great deal about writing. This response is heartwarming, but equally important is the progress that I observe. I see the students gain mastery of the composing act, develop as thinkers, become critically conscious of their experiences, and learn something about themselves and the world around them. It is this type of education that Carter G. Woodson (1958) calls for in *The Mis-Education of the Negro*, where he states that "Real education means to inspire people to live more abundantly, to learn to begin with life as they find it and make it better." These courses should provide these naturally talented students with tools to help make the world better.

References

Freire, Paulo. *Pedagogy of the Oppressed*. New York: Herder & Herder, 1970.

Moffett, James. *Teaching the Universe of Discourse*. Boston: Houghton Mifflin, 1968.

Woodson, Carter G. *The Mis-Education of the Negro*. New York: AMS Press, 1933. Reprint. Washington, D.C.: Associated Press, 1958.

Development of a Sight Vocabulary into a Reading and Writing Vocabulary

Arthuree McCoy, retired
Linda M. Kumi, A.L. Williams Co.

Learning to read and becoming a proficient reader demand the development of language concepts based on prior knowledge and experience. The development of proficiency in reading moves from understanding that written language is oral language in written form to the point when one must also understand that the written form carries information to the reader. Children have always brought considerable experience to school in hearing and speaking. With the advent of television into the home, a first grader's vocabulary ranges from an estimated 10,000 to 40,000 words. It is obvious that a system of teaching that makes use of this child's existing vocabulary can tap a great many of the natural resources in a child's preschool learning (Thomas 1963).

Whole Word Perception

A student's oral vocabulary consists of the words used in spoken communication of any kind, while the sight vocabulary consists of words that the student has learned to recognize on sight as a whole word. The student recognizes his or her name and words found in the community and in the classroom with a little encouragement from elders or peers. The teacher must take what the child knows and make that a part of the listening and speaking vocabulary, and help the student to read and write fluently.

As the teacher works with the reading program, there is a steady accumulation of new words, first in lists and then in stories. Students should recognize the word as a whole and the letter elements that spell it.

This procedure avoids the dangers inherent in labored sounding-out, and also, from the beginning, teaches children to see words as wholes. The whole sound-spelling pattern and the whole meaning pattern are joined into a single unit of perception. This is another way of saying that every word children learn becomes a sight word. This goal of whole word perception is simplified and expedited if children also know the letters that make a word, and know why those particular letters make it. This method relies on the child's own language knowledge, making it quite easy to combine the systems.

Writing from dictation is introduced as soon as correct letter formation is taught. This process begins simply: The teacher pronounces a sound that has already been presented; the child listens to that sound, and writes the letter that spells it.

After many exercises in correct letter formation, writing expands to include punctuation, and spelling. The skills gained as a result of this discipline will enable children to express themselves confidently through their creative writing talents.

We will show how to use the pupils' oral language and words taken from a basal reading program to develop a sight vocabulary for the purpose of developing reading and writing fluency. Each lesson in this series took approximately thirty minutes to present. Because of the varied activities involved in presenting it, students rarely became bored.

This program was developed with a class of twenty-five pupils, a teacher, and a paraprofessional. The class was heterogeneously grouped; however, they were separated into ability groups to share their experiences with each other. Their experiences were recorded by the teacher, who was careful in selecting students for each experiential group.

The children lived in an inner-city urban community. They entered the first grade with many experiences which they had acquired from their homes, families, community activities, television, the playground, and guided learning in kindergarten. The teacher used this knowledge of her class to set up her program of building a sight vocabulary from the oral language they brought to the first-grade class.

This program developed in four stages: (1) implementing oral language, (2) using early recorded oral language, (3) individualizing thoughts into sentences, and (4) individualizing thoughts into paragraphs.

Implementing Oral Language Experiences

During the first stage, the teacher develops confidence and growth by accepting pupils' oral language and by observing these general rules. The teacher

1. Guides students in the rules of sharing, knowing when to talk and how to listen,
2. Is careful not to talk down to the children,
3. Helps the pupils to clarify words and meaning already a part of their vocabuaries,
4. Encourages expansion of their ocabularies.

An effective way of developing children's oral language is to use games that focus their attention on words and events in their environment. By forcing the children to concentrate on a particular subject or situation, the games hold their interests and allow them to discover and learn new words to handle ideas. This learning process occurs in a variety of contexts much like the normal manner in which the children acquire vocabulary. The directions for several of these games follow:

A Memory Game

Make a series of flash cards using familiar words seen in the children's environment, such as: STOP, DANGER, NOTICE, EXIT, NO ADMITTANCE, or DO NOT ENTER. When a card is shown, players are asked to name a place were they have seen the word or phrases on the card. Players give answers such as "I saw the word 'STOP' at my street corner."

The player who remembers the most places where the words or phrases are seen is declared the winner. Try to use words that you are sure the children see in their surroundings. Success is important at this stage.

What Did You See?

Tell the children to close their eyes for a moment and think about something they saw on their way to school that morning. . . . After a minute say, "Now, open your eyes. What did you see, Sammy?" Sammy may say, "I saw a car." The game continues until all the children in the group have had a chance to respond.

Another game that can be used to help prepare the group for independent thinking is:

Because: Cause and Effect

The first player describes an event in his own way, e.g., "The dog barked." The second player is required to give a reason, e.g., "The children were playing with the dog." The third player must give a probable effect, e.g., "The children stopped playing with the dog, and he went to sleep."

Players are encouraged to state their causes and effects promptly. Answers can be challenged by other players. The player who gives the answer must be able to defend his answer.

Yes, No, Maybe, Blue

Explain to the children that you are going to ask them questions in turn. Their reply must be prompt; however, they are not allowed to use the words, "yes," "no," "maybe," or "blue," in their answers. (The words are written on a chart as a reminder of the words they cannot use.) Proceed around the semicircle asking such questions as: "Are you five years old?" "Do you like ice cream?" Play quickly; your purpose is to stimulate thinking among the group. The winner is the pupil who successfully avoids the use of, "Yes," "No," "Maybe," and "Blue."

Let's See What You Can Do

The use of the children's names in song is an excellent way to include the shy pupil in the sharing activity.

Tune: "London Bridge"
I know a little girl named AKO-SU-A KU-MI, AKO-SU-A KU-MI, AKO-SU-A KUMI.
I know a little girl named AKO-SU-A KU-MI; let's see what she can do. (Akosua starts to scratch her arm because she could not think of anything to do. The teacher leads the children in the remainder of the song.)

She can scratch her arm, and we can too; we can too; we can too.
She can scratch her arm, and we can too.
And have fun doing it.
Akosua smiles; her classmates can hardly wait to hear their names sung by the group.

Art Activities

Sharing is also an activity that provides students with a wide range of skills. Children love to share things that give them pleasure. One way of creating a sharing environment is to create a classroom rich in art activities.

The teacher places a tray in the center of a table with supplies such as string, yarn, colored circles, colored squares, colored crayons, glue, scissors, and construction paper. Pupils are encouraged to take material from the tray to make original art designs. If the pupil wants to write a story about the art work, the teacher or the paraprofessional assists. When a pupil does not want a story written about his or her picture, the teacher and the assistant respect this wish. The pleasure of expressing one's self through art is a worthwhile experience. Also, using the material from a single tray reinforces sharing.

Using Early Recorded Oral Language

In preparation for this early stage of writing, the class is divided into three groups: Group "A" is directed to work with the teacher; Group "B" is given independent word games; Group "C" is assigned to the paraprofessional for a language arts activity. Group "A" assembles in a semicircle around a large chart tablet with the teacher in position to act as a recorder.

The teacher says, "Tell me one thing about yourself. Think about what you want to say, then raise your hand when you are ready. I will write your words. You will learn to read your words; later you will learn to write what you want to say for all of us to read."

A pupil's raised hand indicates readiness to speak. The teacher writes the pupil's name on the chart. Everyone waits as Glenn, the first speaker, makes his comments for the teacher to record. The teacher forms each letter with great care to show the students examples of what their words look like in print and the correct way to form their letters. Everyone listens as Glenn speaks; the teacher writes his statement verbatim as he dictates.

Glenn: I am going over to my cousins' house.

Matthew: I am going to my aunt's house when school is over.

Olivia: Yesterday, I went over to my cousins' house.

Mark: I went to my cousins' party.

It is common for young children to repeat the same words used by their peers. Because children learn from each other, repetition is a form of reinforcement that is necessary in the early stages of pupils' development. The script above contains examples of this type of repetition in which the pupils repeat some of the words that their peers have used before them. However, each statement is slightly different and original.

After the students have composed their sentences and the sentences are written on the tablet, pupils read them to the group. When the whole group has finished giving their contributions, the children take turns reading the chart aloud to the other members of the group. The experience chart is left on a chart stand within easy reach so that the children can read their statements whenever time permits. Each week a word list is taken from the class's new experience chart, and the reading program's word list. The words are taught to the children through memory games and activities.

Individualizing Thoughts into a Sentence

The teacher uses the sentences of three of the children who contributed the items before. The items are recorded with the same teaching methods used to develop the items in Figure 1. The teacher acts as recorder. As mentioned earlier, the members of the group are asked to think about what they will say as well as how they will say it.

Glenn: I saw, "The Haunted House on a Hill." It was a movie on T.V.

Matthew: I saw Adonis coming to school.

Mark: My mother bought me a white shirt.

Now each pupil's contribution is clearly his own. Each child's contribution is composed of new words, and few of the words used by their peers are repeated.

Additional work with the sight vocabulary and the increased use of responses will lead to greater confidence. This increases each child's willingness to try new words and different sentence patterns.

With training, children use more individual expressions. The oral language develops into a larger sight vocabulary, which helps to develop a writing vocabulary. Each pupil keeps a word book to record the new words for the week. There are never more than twenty new words. There are charts and other words in the classroom decorations. During this development, the pupils are drawing pictures and dictating stories to the teacher or to the paraprofessional. All of these words act as aids when the children are ready to write their own stories. When pupils feel that they can record their own stories, they are encouraged to do so. Pupils are invited to share their stories with the group or with the whole class.

When their sight vocabularies are large enough that the teacher knows that they can write their own sentences, pupils are given assignments to write sentences such as, "I went to the lunchroom. . . ." They are told to write the reason in their own words. A typical assignment required students to write a story about one of their drawings using words that they know, or can find. Throughout these recordings, the teacher and the assistant are always available to help if needed.

Individualizing Thoughts into a Paragraph

Although the children are writing their stories at this stage, the sharing in a group is necessary in a classroom with individualized instruction. It gives pupils practice in respecting the rights of others. By this time, the pupils have learned how to tell a story in sequence, and they enjoy sharing the stories with the contributor. During this stage, the teacher continues to act as a recorder.

This list contains examples of stories dictated to the teacher.

> Glenn: My aunt is coming to my house to spend the night. My mother and father are going out. They are going to put the bird cage in our room.

> Matthew: My mother took me to Jamaica Avenue to buy me Easter clothes. And my cousin took me over to his house to spend the night.

> Mark: I went to the park with my father and sister and brother. We had fun.

These stories contain the pupils' own sight vocabularies, now expanded into sentences. When the pupils read their words aloud, they know how their stories should sound. If the teacher has not recorded the stories just as they wanted them to, they make corrections, often deleting words, rearranging material, and adding new words. Thus, editing is a natural process whereby the students learn to make their recordings approximate their ideas and thoughts. As they read their stories aloud, they begin to see how written language works. They also begin to see how what they say looks in writing.

This procedure is a satisfying way to build a sight vocabulary and to develop early writing skills. Each part of this series of lessons contributes the necessary learning skills of listening, reading, and writing, and, most of all, a feeling that each person in the class has something worth saying and can say it.

Summary

What are the important aspects of this developmental process?

1. Pupils use their own vocabularies.
2. Pupils learn how to listen to their classmates.
3. Pupils learn to think about what they want to say.
4. Pupils are encouraged to initiate their responses when they are ready.
5. Pupils learn how to express their own ideas.
6. It is easy for pupils to read what they have just said.
7. Pupils' oral vocabularies become a part of their sight vocabularies.
8. The words give pupils expanded knowledge that enables them to read books from the library.
9. This heterogeneously grouped class works on an individualized basis. The children write their own stories when they are ready.
10. Pupils are able to edit their stories, with the assistance of the teacher or the paraprofessional.

As a result of this process, the class develops into fluent readers with good comprehension skills. The children also become fluent storytellers and at an early age learn to share their ideas in writing.

References

Arnold, Arnold. *The World Book of Children's Games.* New York: Thomas Y. Crowell, 1972.

Freeman, Lois, M. *Betty Crocker's Parties for Children.* New York: Golden Press, 1965.

Gale, Leah. *Nursery Songs, Fourteen Childhood Favorites.* New York: Golden Press, 1959.

Handbook for Language Arts, Pre-K, Kindergarten, Grades One and Two. Board of Education of the City of New York, Curriculum Bulletin, 1965–66. Series No. 8.

J. B. Lippincott Company, Basic Curriculum Series—*Basic Reading A.* New York: McCracken Walcott, 1975.

Naumann, Nancy. "Beginning Reading at All Grade Levels." *Learning* (November 1980): 32–34.

Shane, Harold G., June Grant Murlry, Mary E. Reddin, and Margaret C. Gillespie. *Improving Language Arts Instructions in the Elementary School.* Columbus, Ohio: Charles E. Merrill Books, 1962.

Thomas, Rachel. *Young Children's Library.* Parents Magazine Enterprises, 1963.

Wynne, Edward A. "Team Learning: Bringing Virtue to the Classroom." *American Educator* (Summer 1981): 29.

Teaching Tip: Giving Students Feedback

Thomas Clifford Bibb
Alabama State University, Montgomery

Teachers often discover that students lack the endurance to deal with long or complex writing assignments. But strategies can be devised to eliminate hostility toward these assignments. This particular strategy works successfully ninety-five percent of the time, but students must be willing to cooperate with it. Further, the teacher must be willing to sacrifice precious time to follow through the strategy.

The strategy requires several forms: written comments in two parts on mechanics and content, student-written responses to my comments, verbal comments in individual sessions, and verbal comments to the entire class.

At the beginning of the quarter, I ask the students to write sample paragraphs or short themes—one page minimum. Students may select one of the following:

1. You are trapped on an uninhabited island, and there is no hope of rescue.

2. You are in a time machine that can take you to any year, past, present, or future. Where would you stop, and what would you see?

3. What is the most important quality that you require in a potential mate and why?

Writing exercises like these usually elicit copious pennings from the students. I collect these, and write comments on the back page, leaving space for the writers to respond to my comments. I then take excerpts from their sample paragraphs and short themes and duplicate them. I return the sample paragraphs and short themes to the students along with a list of standard comments and the meanings of the comments. I give the students five to ten minutes to look over their papers; then I open the floor for questions about my comments and vice versa.

When I no longer have questions, and questions no longer come from the floor, I distribute to the students the mimeographed sheets of excerpts from their writing samples. I criticize these excerpts, giving both positive and negative feedback, and encourage the students to ask questions about my comments. Frequently, I receive both negative and positive feedback from them. Afterwards, the students come to my office for private conferences about their papers and the comments thereon. The private conference is a must.

With the exception of the first step which is group interaction about what my abbreviations and symbols mean, I continue this process throughout the quarter. Verbal feedback in the group progresses from teacher-oriented to student-oriented interaction. The students begin to learn principles, anticipate what I would say about a particular excerpt, and contribute insights of their own.

This strategy sparks class interaction and sometimes disagreement over particular issues, and demonstrates to the students the flexibility of the language. When the students are willing to participate in the strategy, a combination of these kinds of feedback works quite successfully. Moreover, this combination clarifies my comments, helps me to understand the students via their comments, increases the students' awareness of how language operates, and increases the rapport between us for the sake of learning and thinking critically.

IV Literature

Introduction: The Literature of Black America—The Noise of Reading

William W. Cook
Dartmouth College, Hanover, New Hampshire

H. "Rap" Brown, in his autobiographical work *Die, Nigger, Die!*, observes that school and the language of schooling are irrelevant to his life, are destructive of that life, and are impediments to acquiring a true education.

> If you leave school hating yourself, then it doesn't matter how much you know. . . . I was in constant conflict with my teachers in high school. I would interpret the thing one way and they would say it's wrong. . . . The street is where young bloods get their education. I learned how to talk in the street, not from reading Dick and Jane (1969, 21).

The absence of a language which he considered legitimate, the presence of lives and life styles which condemned the life he knew and cherished, in combination with the rejection of his attempts to bring his own experiences and values to bear on the literature which he read, were the sources of the self-hatred which he saw as one result of attending school.

Joan Baratz (1974), in "A Cultural Model for Understanding Black Americans," offers one explanation for this gap between that which is lived outside the school and that which occurs inside. Baratz draws a clear distinction between education—the transmission of culture—and schooling—that part of culture taught by professionals in organized institutions. In societies in which there are few major differences between the cultural values of groups of individuals, schooling, and education are not sharply divided or at odds with one another. In more heterogeneous or more complex societies, the gap between the two may be great.

> In a heterogeneous society . . . if the schooling that was originally generated by one segment of the society is foisted onto other elements of that society, there may be a discontinuity between the expectations, attitudes, and values taught in the

home culture and the ones that are implicit or explicit in the
school culture, the school culture having been imposed onto the
children from diverse backgrounds (1974, 112-13).

The world which Brown saw in school was a world which denied the
existence of the language he had learned. He did not see the expressive forms of that language, the dozens, signifying, or sounding
in the literature which he was required to read. His response with
minor variations is echoed in both the fiction and nonfiction written
by a widely diverse group of writers.

> They (blacks) view their language as part of them, not to be
> demeaned—a linguist would go farther, and say that all dialects
> are equal, that black speech is as good as any other. If it is not as
> fashionable as Back Bay Bostonese, it preserves what the fa-
> shionable dialects never had and would have been lost except
> for the so-called dialect speakers (Laird 1973, 134).

The preceding statement is taken not from a black linguist, but from
Charlton Laird. Frantz Fanon (1967), in *Black Skin, White Masks,* makes
a case for the relationship between language and culture and between
language and power. To abandon one's language is to abandon one's
way of thinking and to abandon one's culture. "A man who has a
language, consequently possesses the world expressed and implied by
that language. . . . To speak a language is to take on a world, a
culture" (1967, 16, 38). By the same token, to abandon one's home
language is to reject the culture which is directly linked to that
language.

If language is more than mere word, gesture, tonal variation, and
so on, literature is more than the sum of the words and events which
it includes. Literature, employing language as one of its components,
offers readers an image of the world, a culture. It reflects not only
the world of the readers, but connects that world to other possible
worlds. At its best, it gives the readers a clearer understanding of
themselves and the culture in which they live. The individual who is
unable to read—and "reading" is always something more than the
process of decoding symbols—is deprived of just those liberating and
consciousness-expanding experiences that literature affords. The
book is for that person "a universal blank."

How do we exploit the power of literature to clarify and expand
the world of the reader? We would want to be sure that we arrange
for a reading experience that reflects the way we apprehend ourselves
and our relationships. If awareness and maturity develop in such a
way that we first expand our consciousness beyond the self to the
closest others and thence to more distant others, one method of

organizing reading experiences would be to assure that they follow a similar pattern: a movement from the more to the less familiar. David Dorsey, in "Minority Literature in the Service of Cultural Pluralism," puts it this way:

> Because literature expresses the most cogent propositions by implication, it relies directly on the primal perceptions. When the reader's experience and perceptions do not correspond with those of the text, "noise" is immediate and conscious . . . Only literature can objectify one's own value system from the communal. Only by defining cultural differences can one consciously identify one's own culture in oneself (1977, 17–18).

Literature forces us to know who we are by knowing the "other" of the literature which we experience. The difference between our own world and the other world of literature is the source of the "noise" referred to by Dorsey. If the "noise" is too great, if we can see nothing of our world or our home language in the literature, we may—like H. "Rap" Brown—not be able to hear the voices which speak to us through the works which we read. "Noise" is to be desired; too much "noise" is to be avoided.

How do we, as teachers, prepare ourselves to make the fullest use of our students' experiences in making our selections? in presenting these works to students? It would seem that early in our planning we would want to know as much about the home language of our students as possible; that we would want to grant that language a dignity equal to that of other languages; and that we would admit that language to the classroom. Equally important would be our knowledge of the experiences which our students bring to the classroom and to our selection of literature which recognizes those experiences and which attempts to give them coherence and aesthetic form. We need to know, in short, the relationships among literature, language, and life; in particular, we need to know the relationships among black literature, black life, and so-called mainstream literature. J. Lee Greene, in "Black Literature and the American Literary Mainstream," offers one way of approaching the latter task.

> To assess properly and to appreciate fully the literary achievements of black writers in America, one must focus on the ways in which the two literatures (black literature and "Mainstream" literature) differ. The literary devices in black American literature—imagery, symbolism, language, structure—have been molded by the cultural experiences of its writers. And while those experiences are distinctly American, the critical tools used in the study and appraisal of traditional American literature cannot always be strictly applied when determining the literary

achievements of black American writers. And it is technical artistry, rather than sociological import, that distinguishes black
American literature as literature of merit (1977, 28).

This is not to say that the critical tools possessed by the literature
teacher who has no training in the teaching of black literature are
useless. Rather, Greene would argue that application of these critical
tools will be similar whether we are dealing with black or mainstream
literature—similar, but not identical!

Much of the discussion above assumes a comparative approach to
black literature, an assessment of its conformity to and its divergence
from the "mainstream." The teacher must ask the following: What
are the dominant themes? Are they the same as, different from, or
slight variations on traditional themes? What is the function of language in the work? Do we hear a single language/dialect or has the
artist used a combination of speech patterns? What is the relationship
of literary allusions to the culture out of which the work comes? If
modern literature is encyclopedic—that is, it subsumes much of the
tradition which precedes it—what must the intelligent reader know
of that tradition if he or she plans to read modern works?

We need to understand the cultural tradition out of which literature rises because literature reflects culture. It helps us to discover
where we stand in relationship to our culture and where that culture
stands in relationship to others. It is not an accident that Langston
Hughes (1974) symbolizes his beginning to study life by throwing
away his books. The books he discarded in *The Big Sea* did not tell him
what he wanted to know about life. He had to plunge into that sea
and discover it for himself before he could write. Other writers
followed a different path. For Richard Wright in *Black Boy*, books were
a source of liberation.

> I concluded the book with the conviction that I had somehow
> overlooked something terribly important in life. I had once tried
> to write, had once reveled in feeling, had let my crude imagina-
> tion roam, but the impulse to dream had been beaten out of me
> by experience. Now it surged up again, and I hungered for
> books, new ways of looking and seeing. It was not a matter of
> believing or disbelieving what I read, but of feeling something
> new, of being affected by something that made the look of the
> world different (1966, 272–73).

Books were the source of "new ways of looking and seeing." What
was life like for that individual who did not have the gift of reading?
for whom books were dead? We find such a person in *American Hunger*.

> "Can't you really read?" I asked.
> "Naw," she giggled. "You know I can't read."

"You can read *some*," I said.
"Naw," she said.
I stared at her and wondered what a life like hers meant in the scheme of things, and I came to the conclusion that it meant absolutely nothing (1977, 32).

This focus on the liberating and life-giving power of books is not limited to Wright; it is repeated in numerous slave narratives, novels, poems, and plays by black Americans. For those who were able to enter the world of books, reading represented an expansion of life, a raising of the low ceiling of expectation which James Baldwin saw as limiting the growth of black people. The presence of books was important, but more important than that was the presence of books which spoke to the needs of the reader, which told him or her something important and which generated a minimum of "noise."

Cora, in Alice Childress's recent novel *A Short Walk*, experienced interfering "noise" from books early in life. At the Onward and Upward School for Colored Children, a black-run preschool experience, she is struck by the characters in the reader used in class. She asks if Ned, the central character in the story, is white. Miss Emily answers.

Sho, Ned is white. What else he gon be in a white folks' book? You ain't write a book, is you? Ned gotta be white and his hair yaller and his eye gon be blue ... Even the blind see that. (1979, 54)

Miss Emily's blindness is not limited to her sightless eyes, but Cora is a different kind of person. She sets about shaping a life different from the world of Ned. She is determined to see black and to see it dignified. She is a writer, a new black writer.

The experience of literature often leads to writing. The number of writers who are determined to do something about the gaps they experience in reading are legion. The number who want to emulate an admired model are just as numerous. Others, realizing from their reading experience that the life they experience can and ought to be the subject of literature, join the ranks with as much enthusiasm as the first groups listed above. Readers frequently write! Reading provides both inspiration and subject matter for writing. It shows us that we can use writing to give shape to our experience, to share that experience and, as was true of Wright, to fight.

It had been my accidental reading of fiction and literary criticism that had evoked in me vague glimpses of life's possibility ... It was out of those novels and stories, out of the emotional impact of imaginative constructions of heroic and tragic deeds, that I

felt touching my face a tinge of warmth from an unseen light,
and in my leaving I was groping toward that invisible light (1966,
283).

Literature gave him a life and a possible future. It also gave him a
method for dealing with that life and that future. "Could words be
weapons? Well, yes, for here they were. Then, maybe, perhaps, I
could use them as a weapon?" (1966, 272). He learned that words
could say and do what he wanted them to say and do. He learned
that they could be a defense against a life which threatened to crush
him, and he learned that they could be shaped into a weapon to be
used in his struggle against his enemies. He could shape a literature
from these words that would include him, his needs, and his
experiences.

Langston Hughes, like Wright, knew the power of literature. He
also knew the importance of a literature that reflected the world of
his black readers. He was aware of the limitations which American
society had placed upon black writers. One of those limitations had
to do with invisibility.

They were not taught. Julian Mayfield was asked to name the black
writers who influenced him. His response to this question is indicative of the invisibility suffered by those writers who attempt to get
on paper the life of black Americans. "In the early years there were
no black writers who influenced me because I don't recall that I knew
of any (other than the poet Paul Laurence Dunbar). I don't believe a
single black writer was ever mentioned in any of my classes" (O'Brien
1973, 143). They were discouraged from making full use of their
materials. John O'Brien, who reported the interview with Mayfield,
also records the following comment by Arna Bontemps.

> The white aesthetic eliminates folk sources and sociological
> topics; it says that these are not legitimate material for art. If
> you accept that, you really eliminate the black writer's whole
> range of experience from serious literature, because a third of
> all he knows is folk and about another third is classified—rather
> arbitrarily—as "sociological," and only one-third comes out of
> the traditions of the English language which he is using. He is
> so inhibited that he's left out (1973, 5-6).

They were misread. According to John O'Brien, critics have failed to
read black literature *as* literature, as art.

> The black writer is rarely talked about as an artist. Such matters
> as style, form, structure, symbols, and characterization are usu-
> ally ignored by critics. Most criticism of black literature is de-
> voted to a discussion of the "message." This indifference to form
> has led to the great misunderstanding about themes (1973, xiii).

Hughes was determined to correct this situation; he was joined by a number of other artists. His "The Negro Artist and the Racial Mountain" (1974, 190) was a kind of literary Declaration of Independence, an announcement that he would place black faces and black life on the printed page and on the stage.

> But someday, somebody'll
> Stand up and talk about me,
> And write about me—
> Black and beautiful—
> And sing about me,
> And put on plays about me!
> I reckon it'll be
> Me myself!
> Yes, it'll be me.

Our task, as the following selections will show, is to bring that world into our classes, to deal with it as art, to explore its language and its people, and to provide for our students the liberating of the mind and spirit that is the result of close contact with great art. What follows are a few suggestions as to how this might be done.

References

Baratz, Joan. "A Cultural Model for Understanding Black Americans." In *Black Dialects and Reading*, edited by Bernice E. Cullinan. Urbana, Ill.: National Council of Teachers of English, 1974.

Brown, H. Rap. *Die, Nigger, Die!* New York: Dial, 1969.

Childress, Alice. *A Short Walk.* New York: Coward, McCann & Geoghegan, 1979.

Dorsey, David. "Minority Literature in the Service of Cultural Pluralism." In *Minority Language and Literature*, edited by Dexter Fisher. New York: Modern Language Association of America, 1977.

Fanon, Frantz. *Black Skin, White Mask.* New York: Grove, 1967.

Greene, Lee. "Black Literature and the American Literary Mainstream." In *Minority Language and Literature*, edited by Dexter Fisher. New York: Modern Language Association of America, 1977.

Hughes, Langston. *Selected Poems.* New York: Vintage Books, 1974.

Laird, Charlton Grant. *You and Your Language.* Englewood Cliffs, N.J.: Prentice-Hall, 1973.

O'Brien, John. *Interviews with Black Writers.* New York: Liveright, 1973.

Wright, Richard. *American Hunger.* New York: Harper & Row, 1977.

———. *Black Boy: A Record of Childhood and Youth.* New York: Harper & Row, 1966.

From Oral to Written: Origins of a Black Literary Tradition

Martha K. Cobb
Howard University, Washington, D.C.

In the year 1919, author and scholar W. E. B. Du Bois called a meeting of black people in Paris; a Pan African Congress in concept as well as in name. Those who attended included African students in European universities, blacks then on the European continent, and those from the Caribbean and the United States. They met February 19, through February 21, of that year, establishing among themselves relationships and guidelines, however tenuous, for future communication. If this early Pan African Congress meant new solidarity of black peoples around the world, then its immediate fruits were disappointing. Yet it furnished for the intellectuals and the politically oriented delegates who came looking for answers to questions concerning the black man's future a symbolic step toward collective consciousness that overrode language, geography, and national status.

The Congress prefigured the emergence, in the United States, of what Alain Locke in less than ten years was to call the "New Negro" in a book by that title published in 1925. In Haiti it anticipated Dr. Jean Price-Mars's book, *Ainsi parla l'oncle* (Thus Spoke the Elder), published in 1928, which advised young Haitian writers to seek their materials in history, the folklore, and the arts of their own race. In Cuba, Fernando Ortiz in 1923 would publish *Glosario de afronegrismos* (Glossary of Black Speech), which was to become a valuable source of African references and of Cuban folk language and customs for the poets who initiated Afro-Cubanism in their writing. And for Africans, whose continent was still largely under the rule of European states, the Congress produced a consciousness of political presence and power that would later direct the African drive for liberation.

Black Literature in the Twentieth Century

Langston Hughes, born in 1902 in the United States; Jacques Roumain, born in Haiti in 1907; and Nicolás Guillén, born in 1904 in

Cuba, were subsequently to be affected by this new consciousness and were to contribute to it through their poetry and prose. All three poets matured in the first half of the twentieth century and wrote at a time when racial awareness of a group socio-cultural consciousness was beginning to articulate its values in the arts, particularly in music, dance, and literature. They illustrate the scope of black literature, the very concept of which poses a problem in terminology. Janheinz Jahn (1968) attempts to resolve it by defining as "Neo-African" that literature written by black writers in a European language during and since the era of colonization and slavery. Such writers are either Africans or the descendants of Africans, and they write in the language of the European countries which controlled their homelands or in the language of the country where history has situated them. Chronologically, Neo-African literature extends from the medieval epoch in Europe to the present century in the Americas. Geographically, it is found in Africa, where literary works are being produced in English and French primarily; and in those countries of the Caribbean, North, and South America where the slave exile carried Africans.

For Hughes, Guillén, and Roumain, Neo-Africanism offers an approach to their works which takes into account the totality of black literature: its racial orientation, modes of expression related to African sources, historical experiences of African peoples, and its sense of a common social experience whose human significance was carried into the Americas and sustained in Africa despite the dismemberment of that continent.

The Shared Experience

Introducing a comparative approach to black literature suggests a vision of the whole, a dimension of literary research and teaching that not only includes the African background and New World modifications, but also seeks correspondences and cultural analogies which appear in the thought, the expression, and the cultural artifacts of literature, from the Caribbean, the United States, and South American countries. Writers other than Hughes, Guillén, and Roumain can be selected from an English-speaking, a Spanish-speaking, and a French-speaking country, but these particular literary artists best exemplify the first significant stage of black literary development at a time when the overflow of artistic ferment ensuing from the period of the 1920s to the 1940s carried black creativity onto a world stage.

The concept of a shared black experience emerges conjointly in the islands of the Caribbean and in North and South America. Variances in cultural development can be mainly attributed to language differences and religious affiliations which are predominantly Protestant in North America and in the English-speaking islands of the Caribbean, but are Catholic in French-speaking, Spanish-speaking, and Portuguese-speaking countries. Another differentiating factor which has contributed to the social stratification within black communities during and after slavery involves those European racial attitudes which led to what we can call an Anglo-Saxon stance with respect to social relationships in English-speaking countries that was distinctive from the Spanish, French, and Portuguese colonial master-slave, male-female relationships, where a more openly acknowledged mixing of the races took place. And undoubtedly, but to a lesser extent, different forms of government played a role in developing distinctive aspects of black culture, but it is certain that to most black people there was little difference to be found in the governments they lived under so long as they were enslaved, exploited, and suffering under the daily reality of racism.

It is evident from my approach here that I do not see literature developing in a void unrelated to the cultural climate that directly or indirectly governs people's lives. For black people, as for any other people, literature projects the communal wisdom of a culture, the survival strategies, hero-images, woman-images, social ordering, and authority symbols that ultimately determine values. First, then, come formal and thematic roots which thread their way through song, story, poetry, and drama in patterns that reveal common elements and bonds among the variant experiences of black people. One such experience, for instance, is the particularity of black suffering which will range in expression from the poignant to the polemic, and, as a relief from the human situation, will as often as not include a measure of humor to throw in the face of life's paradoxes.

Hence in establishing a literary identity as one aspect of black studies, investigators need to take into serious account black writers in other parts of the Americas who express a racially oriented vision of reality. What, we might ask, do we in the United States have in common with them? What themes and images appear in the writing of the Caribbean that we recognize as part of our own reality? And what constitutes the underlying form of black writing across disparate languages, geographic landscapes, and national affiliations?

In seeking cultural continuities and corresponding literary patterns that link a black aesthetic, I propose two approaches. The first focuses on oral cultures in the African tradition that survived the rupture of transplantation and reappeared in slave communities as diverse as those of eighteenth- and nineteenth-century Uruguay, Cuba, Haiti, Colombia, Santo Domingo, as well as in the United States. The second is to link these residuals of African oral traditions to written literature, taking into account those writers of the twentieth century who have consciously sought to reflect and interpret a racial ethos in their presentation of themes and images and in the forms and styles created by black communities.

Stephen Henderson in his critique and anthology, *Understanding the New Black Poetry* (1973), rightly draws attention to the *continuity* and *wholeness* (his italics) of the black poetic tradition in the United States, suggesting its interaction on two levels, the oral and the written. I would simply add that this oral/written tradition has also maintained itself outside the United States, in other countries of the slave diaspora. Henderson's call for a critical frame based on black speech and black music as poetic reference further emphasizes the totality of a black experience which literature communicates in a wide range of countries outside the United States. However, to music and speech I would add black religious expression as a creative source from which all forms of the black aesthetic have drawn.

Elements of the Oral Tradition

When Africans arrived in the Americas, one of the first and most carefully regulated interdictions was that which prohibited their learning to read or write. Looking back from the vantage point of the twentieth century, I suggest a two-fold outcome not totally inhospitable to black men and women from Africa as they recalled and handed down stories and proverbs, some of which retained traditional African characters in African tales. Moreover, they were forced to depend on the ear as they acquired English, French, or Spanish. Thus as they grasped and transmitted the vocal sonority of Old Testament stories in the United States, they improvised their own versions of what they heard, they took possession of the new languages they were compelled to learn unassisted, and they gave to French, English, and Spanish their own cadences, embellishments, and a style which writers like James Weldon Johnson, Langston Hughes, and Sterling Brown captured on the printed page in the United States and, which, in non-English speaking countries, Nicolás Guillén (Cuba), Adalberto Ortiz (Ecuador), Nicomedes Santa-Cruz (Peru), Jacques Roumain and Philippe Thoby-Marcelin (Haiti) transformed into modern poetry. In

Spanish and Francophone cultures, slave societies began to blend that which was African with the pageantry and color of Catholic liturgy and church processions. Furthermore, in these countries, drums, less stringently prohibited than in the United States, were reconstructed by slaves with materials at hand, and used in a blend of African rhythms with New World expression. The sounds and rhythms of these drums will reappear in literature. In the United States, rhythmic hand-clapping, foot-tapping, and instrumental effects such as that of the banjo served as substitutes for the drums.

Clearly, history, social reality, and expressive style converge. Their interweaving signals a process of transculturation leading to related literary traditions. These traditions in their first stage then were based upon an oral culture whose circle of creativity embraced religion, music and dance, folk wisdom, and mother wit as responses to the immediate needs of enslaved peoples. Given the ethnic origins and the common historical base of the slave diaspora, correspondences in forms and subject matter held together despite geographic and language differences. Here we can direct our attention to samplings from early oral poetic expression recorded in diverse countries. Later analogous stylistic devices and thematic concepts will appear in written literature.

For instance, in the United States, auditory and visual imagery combined with elements of selective improvisation to make statements, to depict a concrete racial reality, to fashion out of the chaos of slavery hero-figures and concepts of freedom, to protest social conditions, and to express aspirations for a better future. Invariably, a sense of "voice," of speaker-audience relationship, of the performing power of the word come through clearly. Moreover, religious aspirations became metaphors for freedom as in this example:

> This ole ship is a reelin' an' a rockin'
> This ole ship is a reelin' an' a rockin', rockin', rockin',
> Makin' fer de promise lan'

Alliteration and repetition not only assist memory, but also achieve a sense of motion and rhythm which make the word and event whose key idea is finding freedom, whether spiritual or physical. In the next excerpt, again drawn from a religious context, sound imagery enables listeners to "visualize" the event, while the use of the vocative, calling directly upon God, establishes the dignity of the slave in relation to the cosmogony that includes both the supernatural and the natural. Thus,

> Oh, the lightnin' flashin' an' the thunder rollin', rollin', rollin'
>   (three times)
> Lawd, I know my time aint long; Lawd, I know my time aint
>   long.

Similar devices of combined style appear in the following passage.
(With stress on sound imagery with a variation of thematic concept
that describes divine intervention on Judgment Day):

> Don' yo' see de chariot ridin' on de clouds?
> De wheels in de fire how dey roll, how dey roll!
> O dat mornin' you'll hyar a mighty roarin',
> When de Heabens fly away.

In contrasting oral context, themes revolving around women anticipate to a great extent the later blues songs, and ultimately the
poetry of Langston Hughes or Sterling Brown. Thus,

> I hate to hear my honey call my name,
> Call me so lonesome an' sad . . .

or

> Brown skin woman, she chocolate to de bone . . .

while in a somewhat different vein, the knowing lines,

> No need babe, tryin' to throw me down,
> Cause I'm po' boys jus' come to town . . .

and again,

> I got a little black woman, honey, name is Mary Lu
> Treats me better honey, heap better'n you.

The images employed in social statements describe poetically the
conditions of black people, their responses to those conditions, and
their desire to escape them. For example,

> Captain, captain, how can it be.
> Whistles keep blowin', you keep a-workin' me?

And

> Git up in mornin' when ding-dong rings,
> Look on table, same ole things.

Unmistakably a comic element slides in, a self-mocking humor in the
two selections above, which the reader, though distanced from the
speaker's voice by time, geography, and expressive media, can still
hear, or even "visualize" from a printed text.

In the following selection, theme and verbal art are integrated more militantly:

> Me'n my pahdner an' two'r three mo',
> Goin' raise hell 'round pay car do'

Again, as in the religious expression, the need to break free evokes sriking images.

> Some o' dese mornin's bright an' fair,
> Gwine to hitch my wings an' try de air.

The transplanted African had to organize his apprehension of a new and alien world from the immediacy of his own circumscribed situation. It became a double vision of reality, created out of tensions that easily recognized the differences between the life of the slave and that of the master, as in these lines from the slave secular that Frederick Douglass remembered hearing and which he placed in his autobiography, *My Bondage and My Freedom* (1853):

> "We raise de wheat
> Dey gib us de corn
> We bake de bread
> Dey gib us de crust
> We sif de meal
> Dey gib us de huss . . ."

Every line indicates how clearly the slave perceived the irony of his position.

The call-and-response, so much a part of Negro spirituals, work songs, and seculars, demonstrates the circularity of human relationships that binds each to the other. Hence the members of the audience, touching one another in the circle, face the leader-speaker and confirm their relationship by response to his words. Each is a dynamic and unbroken part of the whole.

Thomas Wentworth Higginson recorded this example in *Army Life in a Black Regiment* . . . which begins with a call and a response:

> In de mornin'
> In de mornin'
> Chille'n? Yes, my Lord!

There is no set pattern for call-and-response, although when the leader forms a question the auditors respond, most often with a "shout." Work songs, road songs, prison songs, as Sterling Brown points out, invite rhythmic shouts in time to bodily movement:

If I'd had—hunh—
My weight in lime—hunh
I'd a-whupped my captain—
Till he went stone-blind.

The Black Oral Tradition in Other Languages

Transplanted Africans in the Spanish and French Americas have voiced their themes in oral patterns reflecting their cultures and their African heritage. From Argentina, a declaration of love,

Morenita, morenita	Colored girl, colored girl
tu amor me mata	Your love is killing me
quéreme, morenita	Love me, colored girl,
no seas ingrata.	Don't be so mean.

In Venezuela, religion is the subject,

Negra fue Santa Efigenia	Black was Saint Ephigenia
la madre de San Benito	The Mother of Saint Benito
Negros fueron los tres clavos	Black were the three nails
con que clavaron a Cristo.	With which they nailed Christ.

A more militant theme that connects religion with freedom appears in nineteenth-century oral expression from Uruguay,

Quiero ser libre	I want to be free
pues libre nací	Since I was born free
y no conocí	And I knew
mas amo que Díos.	No other master than God.

and it ends with the chorus that discloses a wry sense of humor:

Cállate moreno	Keep quiet, colored man
te digo	I tell you
déjate de hablar	Stop your talking
si el amo te oye	If the master hears you,
¡caramba!	The devil!
te va a castigar	He's going to punish you.

From Haiti, the theme of fighting for freedom appears in a poetic call to battle:

Grenadiers à l'assaut!	Grenadiers to battle!
Ça qui mourri affaire à yo!	Whoever dies it's your own affair.
Nan point maman, nan point papa!	Not your mama's, not your
Grenadiers à l'assaut!	papa's!
Ça qui mourri zaffaire à yo!	Grenadiers to battle!
	It's your own business, who dies!

Early political songs illustrate the theme of black vis-à-vis mulatto that will concern Haitian writers in the twentieth century, containing lines like the following:

Eh bien, ces mulâtres	Oho! these mulattos
Dis lâches autrefois	You call coward before
Savent-ils se battre	Do they know how to fight
Campés dans les bois?	Camped in the woods?
Ces nègres à leur suite,	And the blacks, now
Vous font prendre la fuite?	Are they making you take flight?
Vive l'indépendance!	Long live independence!

In addition to patriotic content, early Haitian poetry contained tributes to women, sung and recited in the Creole idiom. These themes later migrated into the written forms of standard French and were expressed in a wide range of poetry by Francophone writers of the twentieth century.

In other parts of the French- and Spanish-speaking Americas, collectors of folk expression have recorded call-and-response arrangements, the interplay between speaker/leader/singer and his or her audience, often with an added dimension which blended Catholicism with remembered rituals of traditional African ceremonies.

In searching for order and meaning in the new reality, black men and women utilize old forms as far as possible, particularly as they functioned on a social level to teach, to persuade, and to dissent. In the New World, the old underlying patterns mixed with new folk materials, imagery, and symbols to penetrate the complexities of human existence. It remains to be seen what the final outcome of the transition from the oral-aural traditions to a body of written literature will be, what is gained, and what is lost thereby.

We must concern ourselves, therefore, with another stage of black literary development. While folk oral cultures were asserting their own identity in song and story, there were a few black men and women, given the advantage of an education, who could read and write in English, French, or Spanish, and who learned to accommodate their published works to prevailing European literary standards. They were, in effect, colonial writers, not dissimilar from white writers of the time who produced a colonial literature in the Americas. Far fewer in number than their white counterparts, they nevertheless appeared with a moderate degree of consistency in the eighteenth and nineteenth centuries in scattered regions, among them Cuba, Haiti, and the United States. These writers cannot be said to constitute the beginnings of a literary movement, for very good reasons. They were too isolated, hence largely unaware of each other's existence, and their access to writing and publishing was contingent on factors too far beyond their control to allow them to present themselves with any degree of regularity to a reading public. Their works are important, however, because they signal both the dilemmas and the promise of black literature, which, in the twentieth century, writers like Langston Hughes, Jacques Roumain, and Nicolás Guillén, among others, would try to resolve. They also demonstrate the precarious oral-written axis on which black literary art turned before finding its own balance and direction among the emerging New World cultures.

References

Cobb, Martha K. *Harlem, Haiti, and Havana: A Comparative Critical Study of Langston Hughes, Jacques Roumain, and Nicolás Guillén.* Washington, D.C.: Three Continents, 1979.

Henderson, Stephen. *Understanding the New Black Poetry: Black Speech and Black Music as Poetic References.* New York: William Morrow, 1973.

Jahn, Janheinz. *Neo-African Literature, A History of Black Writing.* Translated by Oliver Coburn and Ursula Lehrburger. New York: Grove, 1968.

The Afro-American Griot

William W. Cook
Dartmouth College, Hanover, New Hampshire

> The gospel must be published among all nations. But when they shall lead you, and deliver you up, take no thought beforehand what ye shall speak, neither do ye premeditate; but whatsoever shall be given you in that hour, that speak ye; for it is not ye that speak, but the Holy Ghost.
>
> Mark, 13:10–11

No story can live if it is read from a paper.

James Weldon Johnson's *God's Trombones* was published in 1927. The work contained eight sermon/poems which were based on Johnson's memories of black folk preaching. Johnson did not attempt to reproduce the language of the sermons as he had heard it. He says of a user of that language: "He had the power to sweep his hearers before him; and so himself was often swept away. At such times his language was not prose but poetry" (Johnson 1927, 5). He also comments on the vocal instrument which was the vehicle for this poetry.

> He brought into play the full gamut of his wonderful voice, a voice—what shall I say?—not of an organ or a trumpet, but rather a trombone, the instrument possessing above all others the power to express the wide and varied range of emotions encompassed by the human voice (1927, 7).

The relationship of the sermon to the Biblical text was at its best tenuous. "A text served mainly as a starting point and often had no relation to the development of the sermon" (1927, 4).

Johnson, although he was aware of the music of the preacher's instrument and of the sermon itself, chose to avoid another musical referent: he chose not to reproduce the sermons in the dialect of the speakers. He did this in spite of his realization that "dialect is the exact instrument for voicing *certain traditional phases* of Negro life" (emphasis mine). He concludes that because of this, it is "a quite limited instrument." For Johnson, there were two stops on the dialect organ: pathos and humor. Because it was not "capable of voicing the deepest and highest emotions and aspiration," it prevented the artist from dealing with "the widest range of subject and the widest scope of treatment." Johnson chose not to use this variant of American English in his sermon/poems.

Modern students, having the benefit of the research of language scholars like Dillard, Smitherman, Dalby, Kochman, Labov, and others, and the systematic studies of black folk culture done by researchers like Jackson, Abrahams, Rainwater, Hurston, Dance, Jahn, Dollard, and Dorson (to name only a few), may find Johnson's attitude rather quaint and naive, but would find it difficult to dismiss some of his observations. Johnson's introduction points to a number of those characteristics of the black folk sermon which those researchers who have followed him deal with in more systematic ways. He recognizes in the idiom of the black preacher "some kinship with the innate grandiloquence of their old African tongues." He recognizes in the texts a fondness for "big words" for the sound of eloquence and erudition.

> The old-time preacher loved the sonorous, mouth-filling, ear-filling phrase because it satisfied a highly developed sense of sound and rhythm in himself and in his hearers (Johnson 1927).

This same love for the "sound of sense" (to steal a phrase from Frost) can be found in black artists outside the United States. Sepe in the Thoby-Marcelin brothers' *All Men Are Mad*, a Haitian novel, displays not only a love for grandiloquence but also for extended narrative or narrative sequencing.

> All I can deduce from that sordid and crude, albeit very fragrant, misadventure is that the infernal fire of original concupiscence was lustfully burning in the demented seat of her volcanic sexuality (Thoby-Marcelin 1970, 139).

Verbal decoration and elaboration shape the work of the Caribbean calypsonians and chantwells. Like them, the black folk preacher is the master of the power of Nommo; like them he can trace this propensity to African roots. African griots are interested in the "flourish of words."

> So strong is this tendency to construct and deliver sounds that
> it appears the bard is frequently driven to formulate various words
> that have no traceable meaning but are simply there to give the
> impression of a rich phonological repertoire (Okpewho 1979,
> 224).

Roger Abrahams in a chapter devoted to verbal contest and creativity
describes the sacred and secular function of the man of words. In
both instances, he is connected to power and sexuality.

> His ability with words is as highly valued as physical strength.
> . . . It may seem strange that preaching demands the same type
> of avid control and had the same emotional basis in sexually
> oriented contests as singing, but such is the case. Not only do
> both require the ability to persuade and to construct effective
> imaginative playgrounds (for example, in the use of Bible stor-
> ies); both also involve the overt contest of words (Abrahams
> 1970, 59–60).

The ability to create witty turns of phrase, to play on words is possessed by the best folk poets. "Brothers and sisters, this morning—I
intend to explain the unexplainable—find the undefinable—ponder
over the imponderable—and unscrew the inscrutable" (Johnson 1927,
4–5). The performance does not betray itself by lapsing into the
cadence of everyday speech. Word and gesture are formalized and
heightened. Narrative lines are embroidered, pitch and volume varied
more than in casual speech; and variations in rapidity of narration
are frequent. Once the black folk preacher becomes the vessel of the
word, his performance takes on a chanting tone. Sentence and phrase
units are shortened and produced in recognizable patterns. These are
punctuated by responses from the congregation and are marked by
shouts of encouragement and affirmation. In this they are not unlike
the narrative recitations of the West African griot. African audiences
inject themselves into the griot's narrative, and they do so in response
to specific signals, for "oral performance alerts us—by a recognizable
technical and structural device—to significant moments in the story
. . . when the audience is considerably impressed by a turn of phrase,
a well-represented detail, or even a histrionic movement by the bard.
. . . A member of that audience throws out a phrase instantly in
recognition of the bard's excellence. . . . These phrases of call-and-
response" are the way in which the audience signals "its recognition
and encouragement of the bard's good job" (Okpewho 1979, 212).
Other characteristics of the heightened portion of the narrative are
the dominance of active verbs and of action itself. Single word modifiers and descriptive passages are used as intensifiers of the action.

Musical Elements

Johnson, in his description, notes still other characteristics which mark a successful oral sermon. He comments on the use of musical referents (particularly on the use of the spirituals), the singing and moaning which accompany the most effective sermons, and the importance of kinetic elements—"He strode the pulpit up and down in what was actually a very rhythmic dance"—like gesture, pantomime, and dance. The intoning and chanting described above is more "musical" than casual speech. It "is always a matter of crescendo and diminuendo in the intensity—a rising and falling between plain speaking and wild chanting. And often a startling effect is gained by breaking off suddenly at the highest point of intensity and dropping into the monotone of ordinary speech" (Johnson 1927, 10). The shifting from casual speech to the chant is found in a number of oral narrative traditions, but it is especially important to traditional African performances. In that tradition, the griot uses the chant to signal significant prospects of action. They are "recognized and realized in an instant chant. . . . The climactic chant is also employed at moments when heroic figures deliver a boast" (Okpewho 1979, 215). The chant serves to heighten and dramatize those moments which are not narrative in the strictest sense of the word; they signal dramatic and emotional highpoints and are a "worrying" of the narrative line.

Because the sermons, like spirituals, blues, calypso, ijala, halo, and Ifa recitations are not structured according to syllable count, as is much European poetry, another performance tradition is necessary if the chanted portions are to have the rhythmic effect which they should. Since lines may be and usually are of uneven length, the singer must perform them as equal rhythm units. Melisma, bent tones, and worrying the line are techniques which make possible stretching shorter lines in order that they may be synchronous with longer lines. Longer lines may be made to conform to shorter lines rhythmically paired to them by rapid delivery.

Since chanting is the performance mode which the black folk sermon adopts, a more detailed description of the technique of chanting and its influence on the "shape of things unknown" is in order. John Bennett's observations (1906) are helpful here, for they are mated with an attempt to present formulaic portions of the sermon with musical notation. (Bennett does not use the term "formula," but he did understand the technique.) The chanted sermon/prayer can be found throughout much of nineteenth- and twentieth-century literature. Dunbar's "Antebellum Sermon" catches not only the tone of the sermon, but also its use as a weapon against the enemies of the community; its way of "hitting a straight lick with a crooked stick." J. W. Johnson's versions have already been mentioned. Langston Hughes exploits both the humorous and serious potential of the form in his poems, stories, and tales. His Jesse Semple is a secular and sacred man of words. Zora Neale Hurston records most of the text of "Behold the Rib" in *Mules and Men* (1935), even though she, like most of her Harlem Renaissance colleagues "regularizes" the language.

William Faulkner, even though he could not rid himself of certain received racial stereotypes, does recognize the black folk sermon as a distinct and powerfully moving art form. Rev. Shegog's sermon in *The Sound and the Fury* follows the pattern of chanted sermons recorded by scholars in the field: it begins in a kind of standard dialect but then moves into a chanted black dialect. "They did not mark just when his intonation, his pronunciation became negroid; they just sat swaying a little in their seats as the voice took them into itself." Ellison's Homer Barbee delivers a sermon on one of the most popular themes in the canon: the train journey. The protagonist of *Invisible Man* in his speech before the Brotherhood demonstrates the secular uses of the oral sermon. (No paper this length can do justice to the rich store of folk material which Ellison includes in the novel. That study is yet to be undertaken. The novel is without peer in its accurate rendering of black folk art and in the variety of samples presented.) Baldwin, given the intensity of his love/hate relationship with the black folk church and his early career as a preacher, can be expected to reflect the pulpit styles of that church. He finds his greatest moments of eloquence when he surrenders his text to the cadences of the sermon. Sister Margaret in *The Amen Corner*, and Meridian Henry in *Blues for Mr. Charlie* express themselves through the medium of the sermon. Gordone in *No Place to be Somebody* has his protagonist/narrator Gabriel use the sermon form to launch his attack on the black church and its leaders. His "Whiter Than Snow" sermon, like Baldwin's *Go Tell It on the Mountain* and most black folk sermons, depends for much of its meaning on our knowledge of song. The "March on Washington" sermon exhibits the satiric potential of the form.

Bennett presents the climax of the chanted portions of the sermon in the following transcription:

> "Now I gwine tell you erbout dese hebbenly manniehs. W'en de Chillen of Isrum-mm wuz een de Wildahness-ummm, dey had nuttin' ter eat an' tuh drink-mmm!" His voice now rose to an

ecstatic shout, half a recitative and half a chanting song, in the midst of the words, like some stringed instrument playing, subordinate, through a chant; and at every humming pause, he bent, and kissed the Bible lying on the altar before him: "An' de brooks wuz gone dry-mmm, an' de springs wuz tu'n ter dus-mmmm . . . an' dey shill hongry no mo'-mmmm . . . an' de Lo'd-mmm 'e say tuh ol' Moseh-mmm 'Moseh-mmmm! Mo-seh-mmmm!' 'W'at yo' want, Lo'd? W'at yo' want-mmm?' 'Go, Moseh-mmmmmmmm, go, go; an' smote de rock-mmmm!' . . . an' dey shill thusty no mo-mmmm! An' ol' Moseh-mmm, 'e gone, an' 'e smote-mmmmm de rock-mmmm! . . . and dey shill thusty no mo'-mmmmmmmmmm! An' de hebbenly manniehs fell lak fall de midnight dew-mmmmmm! An' dese manniehs bin erbout de bigness er a w'ite bean, so long, an' so big-mmmm . . . an' de Lo'd say ter de Chillen ob Izrum-mm, 'Go, go; pick 'em up fo' yo' famblies; go, git yo' breakfusses, an' yo' dinnahs, an' yo' suppahs!' An' dey gone, an' dey pick 'em up, an' dey eat dey fill . . . an' dey shill hongry no mo'! An' de angel showed John a bushel medger er dem hebbenly manniehs . . . an' dey shill hongry no mo' . . . no mo'-mmmmmm!"

The Climax

As an illustration, this sample presents many of the characteristics of the sermon climax. Because the purpose of the preacher is less intellectual than emotional, the preacher will climax his sermon in a vision of joy and celebration no matter what his text. He wishes to move, to exhort his listeners, to bring down the spirit. The service of which the sermon is the center piece is more invocation than adoration. The selection above is marked by elaboration of narrative, the use of formulaic words and sounds (the text itself becomes a formula: "They shall hunger no more; neither shall they thirst."), dramatic action (kissing the Bible, pantomiming the size of the manna), dramatic dialogue which as a result of its patterned repetition in the sermon becomes another kind of formula, homely speech, and imagery ("what you want, Lord?" and comparing the manna to a white bean), and the interspersing of musical figures into the text of the sermon.

Henry Mitchell (1970), in describing the climax of the sermon, misses the point when he criticizes it as not resisting the temptation to digress or destroy the logical symmetry of its ideas. He states: "the black climax is not required to teach or deal with concepts or to convey facts," and adds the opinion that at that point in the sermon, the "black preacher has shifted from objective fact to subjective testimony." He gives way to "I." Mitchell concludes that the formulaic climax, which usually deals with heaven, the cross, or the reward of the faithful, leaves something to be desired.

> In the area of creative and relevant climax, the black pulpit needs improvement badly, but it has within its tradition the elements of its own perfecting. Its greatest lack has been at the point of not being aware of the need of such discipline as this (Mitchell 1970, 190).

The formulaic climax which Mitchell deplores has as its purpose the uniting of the preacher with the congregation. He shifts to the subjective in order to offer his personal testimony to the truths which he has expressed and to demonstrate his closeness to his co-worshipers and their everyday experience. The very language illustrates this.

> I said I'm in trouble this evenin'
> I need someone to go all night long
> If you never hear me no more
> Keep your hand, in God's hand
> . . . .
> Don't worry Saint Paul about folk misusing you
> No no don't worry about folk misusing you
> The Christ of the Bible sooner or later,
>   is gonna overtake them
> He's my speed-cop
> See he's my speed-cop
> Amen!
> . . . .
> Those of us who have gotten citations
> You're in a hurry, left late
> Amen and you're overspeedin'
> Oh yes I've gotten them
> Amen
> And the moment you least expect, the Highway Patrol
> You look up in your rearview mirror and you see a
> red light
> Blinking in your face
> He's overtakin' you
> So it is with the Christ of the Bible
> You may mistreat me
> You may talk about me
> But just keep on livin'
> The speed-cop gonna take care of it.
>   (Rosenberg 1970, 193–194)

The metaphor is drawn from the common experience of the people; it is drawn out. The preacher presents his own experience and assurance as token of the assurance all can expect. The testimony is not only framed in the words and actions which the congregation knows, it is also framed musically by songs which are familiar to the entire group. What is important is not the logical relationship of this climax to what has preceded it, but its emotional rightness. Doubt and tribulation must be resolved in ecstasy and assurance; the Holy Spirit must be invoked to the extent that worshipers experience spirit possession. (I choose to call this the logic of the spirit.) For these reasons, whatever the subject of the sermon, the preacher turns in the climax to standard themes: the triumphal entry into heaven, the punishment meted out to the enemies of the tribe, the rewards due the faithful, and the glorious reunion with the saints who have gone on before us. Since the purpose of the service is to invoke the spirit, to have it manifest itself in the worshipers, the sermon has failed if no spirit possession takes place.

> The sermon is the culmination of an ever ascending spiral which satisfies those who need essential information for the maintenance of their lives.

The Text

The text is not all. It is a source and a subject for creation and verbal elaboration. Narrative sequencing, as is obvious from the above example, is something other than telling a story. It is the elaboration of that story, the linking of it to the everyday world of the worshiper.

> The black preacher uses scripture more for the interpretation of recent experiences than for predicting the future or for detailed prophecy. The literal, impersonal use of the scriptures would be foreign to this mind and spirit (Mitchell 1970, 113).

> Modern preaching, even in black, must lend interest to the text rather than assume that widespread interest in it already exists (Mitchell 1970, 118).

For the black preacher, the Bible exists more "as an inexhaustible source of good preaching material than as an inert doctrinal and ethical authority." He depends, therefore, less on logical persuasion and argument and more on probing the depths of the Biblical text, examining it; linking it to the world of his co-worshipers. In doing so he avoids heavy dependence on historical and philosophical theories of ordering. His is a present-centered world.

Formulaic Structure

Like most oral narrative, the black sermon depends heavily on formulaic structures for its success. Milman Parry in *Studies in the Epic Technique of Oral Verse Making* (1930) defines the formula as "a group of words regularly employed under the same metrical conditions to express a given essential idea" (Parry 1930, 30). Rosenberg (1970) alters this definition slightly. For him sermon formula systems are "groups of words, which, when recited, are metrically and semantically consistent, related in form by the repetition and identical placement of at least half of the words in the group." If one accepts the usefulness and rightness of worrying the line, melismatic singing, and metrical and syllabic suppression, Rosenberg's definition can be helpful. It fails, however, to account for call-response formulae which may vary greatly metrically but which are introduced regularly and rhythmically into the body of most black folk sermons. The responses vary in length and in intensity but they are patterned and are a part of the folk knowledge of the people. Our definition of formulas then must include them; must account for formulas which are repeated verbatim, formulas which are metrically consistent though slightly altered *and* formulas which are repeated in varied meters although they may be introduced at regular and predictable intervals.

The call-response pattern is familiar to most students of African and Afro-American art. Okpewho's description of African call-response patterns has been discussed earlier. These same patterns can be found in black sermon recitations.

> If the black preaching tradition is unique, then that uniqueness depends in part upon the uniqueness of the black congregation which talks back to the preacher as a normal part of the pattern of worship (Mitchell 1970, 95).

This talking back will take the form of rhythmic exclamations like, "Yes, Lord!" "My God, my God!" "Oh, Yes!" "Hallelujah!" "Preach the word, brother!" These are rhythmic repetitions of key words uttered by the preacher; or moaning or singing accompaniment to the sermon. The response may not always be verbal. Percussive responses like hand-clapping or foot-stamping, and gestures like hand-waving or jerking are as frequent as verbal responses. These responses may have as their purpose encouragement of the speaker, approval of his ability or of the accuracy of his statements, or they may be reflections of spirit possession. When the latter is the case the responses frequently give way to holy dancing, laughing, o speaking in tongues. The intensity and rapidity of the responses increases as the emotions of the worshipers become so intense that they can no longer be contained. At this point, the congregation and the spirit possessing are in control of the sermon. The good preacher moves with this emotional tide; he does not try to stem or redirect it.

Other formulas include praise names of the divine—"Sweet Mary's baby!," "O Wonderworking Jesus!"—for holy persons—"Po' left lonesome Mary!"—and for sinners. Incremental repetition of stock phrases from the Bible form another kind of formula, for they are repeated in extremely varied sermon situations. These are sometimes, but not always, variations on the text of the sermon. Still another formulaic utterance is the song lyric or title. The congregational response and the sermon itself frequently allude to or quote song titles or lines. These may be picked up and "lined out" during the sermon. They may be led by the preacher, a deacon, church mother, or any member of the congregation. Individual members will have favorite songs which they may hum or moan when the spirit is upon them, and these may not always be sung by other members, but the individual is not deterred from singing his or her religion.

Standard rhetorical devices, in addition to those already mentioned, include dialogues of temptation. These are usually signalled by the introduction into the narrative of an indefinite antagonist—"Somebody said, 'The road is too weary'"; of a divine intercessor (note the conversation between God and Moses quoted earlier in this discussion), or a diabolical enemy. (Olmstead (1970) describes such a moment in his description of a black service.) Frequently these dialogues consist not only of verbal exchanges; they are acted out. Another rhetorical device, the narrative sequencing mentioned earlier, is also signalled in the body of the sermon. Patterned phrases such as "With the eye of faith, I can see you now," "My Bible tells me that he went to island of Patmos," or "Can you see my Jesus sitting there surrounded by his enemies?" serve to signal extended narrative or descriptive moments. Request for divine guidance and for the collaboration of the congregation is formalized: "Help me, Lord, to preach yo' word this evening!" "Help him Lord!" Testimonials to the redemptive power of grace and especially recitations of the moment of salvation are introduced by stock phrases like "I don't know about you, but I have determined to follow Jesus." "I remember the day and hour when the Lord spoke peace to my soul," and "I know I have a building not made with hands" are part of the ritual of testifying. Finally, the preacher invites members of the congregation to open their hearts to the power of the spirit: "Have I got a witness?" "Let the church say amen." "If you been redeemed you can shout and sing." "If you know the Lord in the redeeming of your soul, let me see your hands." "Somebody here knows about the power of the Lord."

The sermon, which becomes a vehicle for comment on the experiences of the congregation, includes political, social, humorous, and even sexual references. It communicates because it is delivered in the language of the congregation; it employs rhetorical devices with which they are familiar.

> To lose one's language is to lose one's identity. To refuse to learn and use the people's language is an affront to the people one presumes to serve (Mitchell 1970, 150).

It is no accident that Ellison's invisible man is a man who does not know his own language. He speaks the language and uses the words of others, and because he does, he must journey back to the lost language and the folk games built around it. He must learn to say "no" to the enticements of those who want to remake him in their image. Only then can he have a voice in his own destiny.

Du Bois devotes the closing chapter of *The Gift of Black Folk* (1961) to religion, and his comments on the African-ness of black American traditional religion are a fitting close to this discussion. There are African survivals in the religion of black America. Although slaves lost their language and many of the traditional social and political structures which had sustained them in their home, they retained an "African" attitude toward art, toward movement, and toward music and language. They also retained much of their original religion.

> The vast power of the priest in the African state still survived; his realm alone—the province of religion and medicine—remained largely unaffected by the plantation system in many important particulars. The Negro priest, therefore, early became an important figure on the plantation and found his function as the interpreter of the supernatural, the comforter of the sorrowing, and as the one who expressed, rudely, but picturesquely, the longing and disappointment of a stolen people (Du Bois 1961, 182–83).

Johnson closed his introduction with the following statement: "The old-time Negro preacher is rapidly passing. I have here tried sincerely to fix something of him" (1927, 14). Johnson's obituary was a bit premature. The black folk preacher has not disappeared. He has led S.C.L.C., has created Operation P.U.S.H., and has sold records. In the process, he has helped shape the direction of American religion and the art of public speech.

References

Abrahams, Roger D. *Deep Down in the Jungle*. Chicago: Aldine Publishing, 1970.

Bennett, John. "A Revival Sermon at Little Saint Johns." *Atlantic Monthly* 98 (August 1906): 256–68.

Dance, Daryl. *Shuckin' and Jivin'*. Bloomington, Ind.: Indiana University Press, 1978.

Du Bois, W. E. B. *The Gift of Black Folk*. Greenwich, Conn.: Fawcett, 1961.

Hurston, Zora Neale. *Mules and Men*. New York: Harper & Row, 1935.

Jackson, Bruce, ed. *The Negro and His Folklore in Nineteenth Century Periodicals*. Austin, Tex.: University of Texas Press, 1967.

Johnson, James Weldon. *God's Trombones*. New York: Viking, 1927.

Keil, Charles. *Urban Blues*. Chicago: University of Chicago Press, 1966.

Kochman, Thomas. *Rappin' and Stylin' Out: Communication in Urban Black America*. Urbana, Ill.: University of Illinois Press, 1972.

Lord, Albert B. *The Singer of Tales*. Cambridge: Harvard University Press, 1960.

Mitchell, Henry H. *Black Preaching*. Philadelphia: J. B. Lippincott, 1970.

Ngal, M. A. M. "Literary Creation in Oral Civilizations." *New Literary History: A Journal of Theory and Interpretation* 8 (Spring 1977), 335–44.

Okpewho, Isidore. *The Epic in Africa*. New York: Columbia University Press, 1979.

Olmstead, Frederick Law. *A Journey in the Black Country*. New York: Schocken, 1970.

Parry, Milman. "Studies in the Epic Technique of Oral Verse-Making." In *Harvard Studies in Classical Philology*, Vol. 41. Cambridge: Harvard University Press, 1930.

Rosenberg, Bruce A. *The Art of the American Folk Preacher*. New York: Oxford University Press, 1970.

Smitherman, Geneva. *Talkin and Testifyin: The Language of Black America*. Boston: Houghton Mifflin, 1977.

Thoby-Marcelin, Philippe, and Pierre Marcelin. *All Men Are Mad*. New York: Farrar, Straus & Giroux, 1970.

Exploring Multi-Ethnic Literature for Children through a Hierarchy of Questioning Skills

Sharon White Williams
Hampton Institute, Virginia

Through the art of memorable words and captivating illustrations, multi-ethnic literature brings delightful, rich experiences to children exposed to it in meaningful and varied ways. It further provides invaluable opportunities for authors and illustrators to interact with children's imagination and critical thinking habits and abilities.

There is need for teachers to continue exposing children to differentiated cognitive processes. Certainly one vehicle to encourage children's thinking processes while effectively guiding their literary experience is for teachers systematically to utilize questioning skills that promote thought patterns on varying levels.

This article presents Benjamin Bloom's six levels of cognitive processes as one method which teachers may use to develop a hierarchy of questions for effective teaching of multi-ethnic literature (Bloom et al. 1956). A description of the six levels is first presented and followed by a hierarchial sampling of questions pertaining to multi-ethnic children's books. Moreover, since the teaching of literature includes aspects in the affective domain, it is essential that some attention be devoted to samples of affective questions.

Bloom's Level of Cognitive Processes

Knowledge—Knowledge questions require the recalling of specific facts or the reciting of directly stated information. Such questions are usually characterized by key words such as "who," "what," "where," and "when."

Comprehension—Questions on the comprehension level call for the explaining of information or the rephrasing of acquired information in one's own words. Such questions generally contain key words such as "compare," "contrast," "explain," "rephrase," or "explain in your own words."

Application—Application questions elicit the application of previously acquired information to determine one correct answer. These questions often contain key words such as "classify," "employ," "apply," or "solve."

Analysis—Questions on the analysis level call for the identification of motives, the drawing of conclusions, or the deriving of evidence. These questions include key terms such as "analyze," "support," or "conclude." They further ask students "why."

Synthesis—Questions on the synthesis level elicit the making of predictions or the solving of problems having varied answers. They include key words such as "develop," "construct," "predict," "design," "produce," and "what happens if." They also stimulate creative thinking.

Evaluation—Evaluation questions are described as representing the highest level of cognition involving making judgments, formulating opinions, providing personal reactions and criticisms. These questions are usually characterized by key terms such as "give your opinion," "judge," "validate," or "argue."

Hierarchical Sampling of Questions Pertaining to Multi-Ethnic Children's Books

   I.   Haley, Gail E. *A Story—A Story* (New York: Atheneum, 1970).
       A. Summary
          A Story—A Story, the 1971 Caldecott winner, shows Ananse, the "spider man," using his cleverness, bravery, and wits to buy the Sky God's stories. As his reward, Ananse takes the stories, now called "Spider Stories," back to earth, where they are scattered to the corners of the world. A truly delightful and tender book, filled with a sparkling dialogue and captivating illustrations.
       B. Sample of Story-Related Questions
         1. *Knowledge*
           a. Who was the main or principle character in *A Story—A Story?*

b. How did Ananse capture Osebo, the leopard-of-the-terrible-teeth; Mnboro, the hornet-who-stings-like-fire; and Mnoatia, the fairy-whom-we-never-see?
c. What did the Sky God want for his stories?
d. Who wanted the Sky God's stories?

2. *Comprehension*
   a. Explain in your own words the main idea of *A Story—A Story*.
   b. Describe how Ananse told the leopard to play the binding game.
   c. Compare and contrast the personalities of Ananse with Osebo, the leopard-of-the-terrible-teeth.
   d. Describe, in your own words, the technique Ananse used to capture the hornets-who-sting-like-fire.

3. *Application*
   a. Would you classify *A Story—A Story* as fantasy or realism? Explain.
   b. After reading *A Story—A Story*, choose at least one positive idea about elderly people you think the author wants the reader to grasp.
   c. Give an example of an illustrator of children's books who utilizes woodcuts as an illustrative technique.

4. *Analysis*
   a. Support or refute the idea that Osebo was an inconsiderate person.
   b. Analyze the language that the author uses to determine what effect it has upon the readers.
   c. Compile evidence to support the following statement: Ananse was clever in capturing his victims.
   d. Analyze the aspects of *A Story—A Story*, which you feel are similar to *Pandora's Box* or *Br'er Rabbit and The Tar Baby*.

5. *Synthesis*
   a. Predict what you feel would have happened if Ananse had failed to obtain the Sky God's stories.
   b. Develop a dance depicting the mood or temperament of Mnoatia, the fairy-whom-we-never-see.
   c. Design an alternate plan for Ananse to capture Mnboro, the hornet-who-stings-like-fire.
   d. Write a position paper in which you communicate how *A Story—A Story* could be used to demonstrate cleverness to children.

6. *Evaluation*
   a. Assess whether or not your friends would enjoy *A Story—A Story*. Substantiate your feelings.
   b. In your opinion, what could Nyame have done with his prisoners? Explain.
   c. Give your reaction as to whether or not Ananse and Nyame made a fair trade. Justify your beliefs.
   d. In your judgment, what implications can be drawn about the illustrations contained in *A Story—A Story* in their relationship to the story's contents.

II. Isadora, Rachel. *Ben's Trumpet* (New York: Greenwillow Books, 1979).

A. Summary

Ben desires, more than anything, to be a trumpeter although he only plays an imaginary instrument. His dream finally comes true when a musician in a neighborhood nightclub discovers his ambition. An endearing story accented with extraordinary and striking illustrations.

B. Sample of Story-Related Questions

1. *Knowledge*
   a. Where does the story, *Ben's Trumpet*, take place?
   b. What are the names of two instruments Ben hears at the Zig Zag Jazz Club?
   c. What is the name of the musical instrument Ben pretends that he plays?
   d. What is the name of the club Ben visits every day on the way home from school?

2. *Comprehension*
   a. Explain how you think Ben felt when the boys laughed at him.
   b. Discuss the reason why Ben had no trumpet at first.
   c. Express Ben's attitude toward music.
   d. Discuss and compare Ben's feelings at the beginning of the story with his feelings at the end of the story.

3. *Application*
   a. Give an example of a time your peers laughed at you for something you did that did not fit the norm.
   b. Demonstrate the way Ben felt when a member of the Zig Zag Jazz Club said, "Come on over to the club, and we'll see what we can do."
   c. Classify Ben's playing the trumpet on his way from school as happy or sad.

        d. Dramatize how Ben's face looked when the other children laughed at him.

   4. *Analysis*

        a. Support your reason(s) for liking or disliking the story, *Ben's Trumpet*. Explain why.

        b. Analyze Ben's reasons for pretending he had a trumpet.

        c. What conclusions can you draw about Ben's interest in the musicians?

        d. Analyze the language structure used in the book, *Ben's Trumpet*, to determine how it helps to achieve the author's general intent.

   5. *Synthesis*

        a. Predict what would have become of Ben if the trumpet player had not come out on a break and seen Ben sitting there. What effect would the consequences have had on Ben's later life experiences?

        b. Write a sequel to *Ben's Trumpet* in which Ben has another childlike experience.

        c. How can parents, teachers and other concerned citizens improve the life-styles of the other "Bens" in America?

   6. *Evaluations*

        a. Assess the potential which *Ben's Trumpet* has for initiating group discussions relating to emotional crises in life. Present personal reactions.

        b. Judge the significance of the story in terms of authenticity of the characters and story plot.

        c. Revise the story and place Ben in a middle-class family which gives him a trumpet at an early age. In your judgment, would Ben's experiences reflect those portrayed in the book? Explain.

        d. Critically analyze the illustrations portrayed in *Ben's Trumpet* in order to determine their relevancy, appeal, and appropriateness.

III. Yarbrough, Camille. *Cornrows*, illustrated by Carole Byard (New York: Coward, McCann & Geoghegan, Inc., 1979).

   A. Summary

   Through the stirring voices of Mama and Great Grammaw, a moving, poetic story unfolds which explains the historical significance of the hairstyle patterns of cornrows and their symbolizing courage and strength for outstanding Afro-Americans. The book contains remarkable illustrations.

B. Sample of Story-Related Questions

1. *Knowledge*
   a. Define what is meant by "cornrows."
   b. What are the names of some of the cornrow styles presented in *Cornrows?*
   c. Identify the main characters in *Cornrows.*
   d. What is meant by the term "suku"?

2. *Comprehension*
   a. Explain the origin of cornrows.
   b. Compare and contrast the cornrow hairstyle to the traditional style Japanese women and children wear.
   c. In your own words, summarize the story *Cornrows.*
   d. Describe in your own way, the story character, Me-too.

3. *Application*
   a. Apply information obtained from reading *Cornrows* to demonstrate how cornrows are made.
   b. How would you classify the book *Cornrows?* As fantasy or realism? Explain.
   c. Give an example of another children's book which contains the same theme as *Cornrows.*
   d. Present an example of how the story, *Cornrows,* contributes to the understanding of important traditions of black Americans.

4. *Analysis*
   a. Analyze the authenticity of the characters portrayed in *Cornrows.*
   b. Appraise the value of the story *Cornrows* in terms of its interest to children of other ethnic groups.
   c. Explain why prominent black leaders were included in *Cornrows.*
   d. Present evidence which indicates whether or not a change in your attitude regarding the "cornrow" hairstyle occurred after you read the book *Cornrows.*

5. *Synthesis*
   a. Produce appropriate music and sound effects which may be used in retelling *Cornrows.*
   b. Design your own cornrow hairstyle. Try it out on a friend. Explain the significance of your design.

   c. Why do you suppose Camille Yarbrough, the author
      of *Cornrows*, used poetic words, captivating illustrations,
      and rhythm to convey the story?
   d. Write a poetic sequel to *Cornrows*.
6. *Evaluation*
   a. What do you feel would have happened to the cornrow
      tradition if the first weavers had not been captured?
      Explain.
   b. Explain why you believe *Cornrows* is or is not a good
      book which positively promotes black awareness and
      pride.
   c. What is your personal reaction to the language content
      of the book? Justify your reaction.
   d. In your opinion, to what age group could you recom-
      mend *Cornrows?*

Just as there is a need for black children to be stimulated by questions which require cognitive responses in understanding multi-ethnic
literature, there must be further exposure to questions in the affective domain which engender emotional responses or reactions.

Following, then, are some sample questions in the affective domain
that relate to the study of the three multi-ethnic children's books
previously presented.

1. After reading *Ben's Trumpet,* how do you think Ben felt when he
   no longer had to play an imaginary instrument when the trumpeter in the Club let him play a real trumpet?

2. As a result of listening to *A Story—A Story,* put yourself in
   Ananse's place when Nyame, the Sky God, revealed the price
   he had to pay in order to buy his stories. Share your emotional
   feelings and thoughts:
   a. Would you have thought the price was too high and tasks
      too difficult for you to accomplish?
   b. Would the tasks have been a challenge to you?
   c. Would you have given up?

3. In the book *Cornrows,* which part of the story inspired you the
   most? Express your feelings in such a way that others can
   share them.

Children need to become increasingly aware of the value and significance of multi-ethnic literature. They must be stimulated by a
variety of questions that are both cognitive and affective. This article

has presented sample questions which teachers can use to promote such an understanding and stimulate children's thinking habits and abilities.

Reference

Bloom, Benjamin, et al. *Taxonomy of Educational Objectives: The Classification of Educational Goals.* London: Longmans, 1956.

Literature and Black Children

Jane Hornburger
Brooklyn College, CUNY

"A first step in the development of effective reading/language arts skills is the interest students have in the materials; young people enjoy books and stories that portray real life situations with which they can identify" (Hornburger 1975, 22). To have appeal, the reading matter not only must be appropriate for students' reading levels, it must also be what *they* consider relevant and meaningful. We know from our own experience and from research (Belloni and Jongsma 1978) that children work better and learn better when dealing with materials they like. Other studies since 1955 have consistently shown that children learn better from materials they enjoy.

If books and stories are to be effective in achieving instructional goals, they must be selected on the basis of attitudes, interests, and aptitudes of the learners. Their interests are strongly influenced by the times in which they live, and, therefore, the benefits of these interests can best be reaped through book content and illustrations that reflect life the way it is—with all of its joys, sorrows, pressures, anxieties, aspirations, and achievements. Since many black students have strong ties with their ethnic group, materials portraying them in ways that build positive images worthy of respect and dignity could prevent the student alienation which often leads to disruptive behavior and low achievement. Teachers will certainly want to use some materials which reflect life and environments different from those of black students, since it is good practice to use works by and about *all* ethnic groups. Honest, sensitively written books and stories whatever the setting avoid characterizing blacks as weak, ignorant, subservient beings but instead accurately reflect the perspectives and feelings of this group through character behavior, content, and illustrations. (See also Rosenberg 1973.)

Increasing Achievement through Literature

Black youngsters easily relate to books such as *The Soul Brothers and Sister Lou* (K. Hunter); *Canalboat to Freedom* (T. Fall); *I, Charlotte Forten: Black and Free* (P. Longsworth); *Malcolm X: Black and Proud* (F. M. White); and *The Story of Stevie Wonder* (J. Haskins). They enjoy reading about today's life and times, people they know, such as Stevie Wonder— who, in spite of his handicap, has excelled as a composer, singer, and recorder, and has won ten Grammy Awards and recorded seventeen gold records. They also enjoy reading about the past if the character images bolster their egos and engender pride in their race as do characters such as Lou *(The Soul Brothers and Sister Lou)*, Lundius *(Canalboat to Freedom)*, Charlotte *(I, Charlotte Forten: Black and Free)*, Benjamin *(Benjamin Banneker: Genius of Early Black American Scientists)*, and Malcolm X *(Malcolm X: Black and Proud)*. Such characters understandably arouse pride in black readers and lead to increased satisfaction and achievement. In his eulogy of Malcolm X, Ossie Davis said, "Malcolm was our manhood, our living black manhood! And in honoring him, we honor the best of ourselves" (Colquit 1978, 193). Black citizens/ characters—past or present—who exemplify characteristics which some youngsters admire, overtly or covertly, "turn them on" to reading. Our heroes are not always *their* heroes.

In *The Essentials of Education*, NCTE advocates teaching/learning activities that enable children to: utilize a combination of skills, feelings, and knowledge to assist them in coming to terms with their world; realize the interdependence of skills and content; and gain an appreciation of other languages and cultures. Literature can be of great value in achieving these goals. Many children learn best through the active classroom participation that literature offers in abundance. One of the greatest advantages of using literary activities is their adaptability and flexibility; most of them can be used with many achievement levels. Activities such as the following are appropriate to several achievement levels and help to develop a variety of language arts skills.

Teachers can help black children understand, accept, and respect people with dialects and ways of life different from their own by using well-known books such as *Huckleberry Finn* by Mark Twain, *Strawberry Girl* by Lois Lenski (New York: Dell, 1975), and Newbery winner *Bridge to Terabithia* by Kathryn Patterson (New York: Thomas Y. Crowell, 1977). Students may choose to read about one of the black Americans listed below and share information with classmates in oral or written form, explaining how the nation has benefited from that American's invention and telling why they chose that person for a report.

> Dr. Charles Drew—invented a method for preserving blood plasma, The Blood Bank
>
> Dr. Daniel Hale Williams—performed the first successful open heart surgery on a human being
>
> Jan Matzeliger—invented the shoe-lacing machine
>
> Garrett A. Morgan—invented the three-way traffic light
>
> Frederick McKinley Jones—pioneered refrigeration engineering, invented portable air coolers for transfer trucks
>
> Robert Rillieux—revolutionized the sugar industry with his invention of the Multiple Evaporation process

(The persons above and their patent numbers are included in Robert C. Hayden's *Eight Black American Inventors* and in his *Seven Black American Scientists*.)

Oral expression can be enhanced and special interest categories determined by letting students choose a person from the following list; organize and hold a debate involving some issue or cause involving that person:

> Frederick Douglass
>
> Marian Anderson
>
> Crispus Attucks
>
> Benjamin Banneker
>
> Jane Addams
>
> Willie Mays
>
> Harriet Tubman
>
> John F. Kennedy
>
> Ossie Davis
>
> Ralph Bunche
>
> Althea Gibson
>
> Wilma Rudolph
>
> Martin L. King, Jr.

Thurgood Marshall

Benjamin O. Davis

(Most of the foregoing are included in Brown and Brown 1968.)

Critical and creative reading requires children to judge, reason about cause and effect, make inferences, compare, and synthesize. To read critically means to "read between the lines," a skill that is often necessary for a full understanding of an author's message. Critical reading involves not only the two lower skill levels—the literal and the interpretative—but also a much deeper level of engagement. It requires the reader to evaluate, to give reasons why one answer is better than another, to pass judgment on the value and truthfulness of what is read, to compare it with personal experiences and known standards, and to create concepts applicable to situations different from those in the text. Creative thinking and creative reading require that the student judge what is read, bring new insights to it by seeing the same information from a different point of view, extend what has been read or create something different.

Jane Porter has described the benefits of children's discussion of literature. "Discussion can be encouraged and inquiry, judgment, and interpretation of literature strengthened when provocative questions are used as stimulants to student involvement and interaction" (1973, 191). Lively discussions usually grow out of well-formed questions which discourage one-word or factual responses and motivate thinking and talking. Large- or small-group discussions based on literature provide the stimulus for meaningful group interaction. A wonderful source of help for this purpose is *The Web* (a quarterly journal of the Center for Language, Literature, and Reading, Ohio State University). *The Web* reviews children's books and offers suggestions for their use.

After a book has been read by an entire class or a group of children—or read by the teacher to the class or group—many creative activities may follow. Literature-based questions that aid in the development of critical/creative reading skills might include some similar to the following:

Why do you think the author wrote this book?

Do you think the author is thoroughly familiar with the topic?

Is she or he likely to be biased? Why do you say so?

Has the author implied things not stated directly? How can you tell?

Do the dialect and dialogue sound realistic? Why? Why not?

Within the story setting, are the characters believable? Why?

How do you feel about (character's) behavior? Would you have acted the same way? Differently? Why?

Does the story ending seem reasonable? Why do you think so?

Why do you think Stevie (*The Story of Stevie Wonder*) objects when people attempt to "label" him?

Genny's father has moved out of the house (*Talk about a Family*, E. Greenfield, 1978). Who do you think will become family leader now?

What do you think might have been some of the reasons why (title) was named winner of the (award)?

Summary

Bringing children and books together through active involvement can provide great benefits, among which are sustained reading interests and achievements in all the language arts. Since most literary activities require students to use many skills, experiences, and feelings, they learn to do problem solving by dealing critically with situations presented in the books. The interdependence of skills and content becomes evident as students learn the skills necessary to reading, writing, listening, and speaking in connection with book activities.

References

Allen, Roach Van. "Bring Your Own: An Invitation to All Children to Bring Their Personal Language to School." *Claremont Reading Conference Yearbook* 30 (1966): 25–32.

Belloni, L., and E. Jongsma. "The Effects of Interest on Reading and Comprehension of Low-Achieving Students." *Journal of Reading* (1978): 106–9.

Brown, Vashti, and Jack Brown. *Proudly We Hail*. Boston: Houghton Mifflin, 1968.

Bruch, C. *A Proposed Rationale for the Identification and Development of the Gifted Disadvantaged*. Athens, Ga.: Department of Educational Psychology, University of Georgia, 1969.

Colquit, Jessie L. "The Teacher's Dilemma in Facilitating the Black Experience." *Journal of Negro Education* 47 (1978): 192–204.

Essentials of Education, The. Urbana, Ill.: National Council of Teachers of English, 1978.

Greenfield, Eloise. *Talk about a Family.* Philadelphia: J. B. Lippincott, 1978.

Haskins, James. *The Story of Stevie Wonder.* New York: Lothrop, Lee & Shepard, 1976.

Hayden, Robert C. *Seven Black American Scientists.* Reading, Mass.: Addison-Wesley, 1972.

————. *Eight Black American Inventors.* Reading, Mass.: Addison-Wesley, 1972.

Hornburger, Jane M. "Bringing Their Own: Language Development in the Middle Grades." *Childhood Education* 46 (1969): 155–57.

————. "Teaching Reading by Way of Literature." In *Innovations in Education,* edited by L. Golubchick and B. Persky. Dubuque, Iowa: Kendall/Hunt, 1975.

Porter, Jane. "Reflections of Life Through Books." *Elementary English* 50 (1973): 189–94.

Reissman, Frank. "Digging the Man's Language." *Saturday Review* 49 (1966): 97–98.

Rosenberg, Max. "Criteria for Evaluating the Treatment of Minority Groups in Textbooks and Other Curriculum Materials." *Audiovisual Instruction* (1973): 21–22.

Torrence, E. Paul. *Discovery and Nurturance of Giftedness in the Culturally Different.* Reston, Vir.: The Council for Exceptional Children, 1977.

The Black Teenager in Young Adult Novels by Award-Winning Authors

Rosalie Black Kiah
Norfolk State University, Virginia

In a pluralistic society where racial, cultural, and social diversities abound, each group eventually develops traditions and special interests. Within each group are exhibited mutually shared experiences that are unique to and characteristic of people of the relatively same background. It is the sharing of these experiences that provides a cohesiveness, or feeling of togetherness to a particular group. These experiences become crucial and salient to the members of the group as they strive to maintain and preserve that which gives them a sense of worth and self-identification.

Identity and self-esteem of black children has been the subject of a number of studies. Ward and Braun (1972) conducted a study on self-esteem and racial preference in black children. This team of researchers used an adaptation of the Clark and Clark doll test, using puppets instead of dolls (one black and one white) to test sixty black girls and boys between the ages of seven and eight. The group was equally divided between suburban and inner-city school children. The results in no way paralleled that of the Clarks'. Instead, Ward and Braun found that black children growing up since 1963 rejected the white models in preference for the black models. This led the researchers to conclude that various social changes, as well as social and political movements (i.e., "black awareness movement") have been effective in causing these children (who are now sixteen and seventeen years old) to identify and adopt their own group as acceptable.

Capitalizing on this study and similar ones, the 1960s and 1970s saw an outpouring of black-oriented books for children. More and more writers of fiction and poetry offered the black child alternative reading fare; black biographies and information books were also well represented. As a result, the market was flooded with "made-to-order" books about blacks that generated a great deal of controversy, particularly among segments of the black community. The controversy dealt with the false image drawn from "collective experiences" of black people.

What, then, are these "collective experiences?" They are what the writer chooses to call the "salient shared experiences." By definition, they are those dominant beliefs, values, cultural and institutional arrangements, that are shared by the majority of the black population. These institutional arrangements fall into three categories: the *family,* the *social world,* and the *world of work.*

An examination of sociological research reports reflecting the salient shared experiences of black people in the United States reveals that the study of black *family life* has received extensive attention from social scientists, which accounts for the volumes of work done in this area. The *social world* of black people, examined somewhat less has been found to be divided into two subgroups: Interim Institutional Arrangements (formal groups) and Leisure-Time Activities (informal groups).

The formal arrangement group includes the black church, the second most important institution in the black community. Leisure-Time Activities, which are informal arrangements, consist of "the Street," or "the Block" (which is a social institution frequented by people of all ages), and group socialization.

Probably the activity that blacks participate in most readily is work, because work is a major indication of one's well being, status, and future outlook, and constitutes those activities people engage in to make a living. Hence the third in the category of institutional arrangements is the *world of work.*

Using these categories, the writer carefully extracted statements and phrases from sociologial studies that revealed salient shared experiences of black people in the *family setting* and the *social world* (to include the *world of work*) and placed them in "direction" categories (favorable, unfavorable, and neutral). The purpose was to analyze the effects these experiences had on the protagonist as reflected in the fictional accounts.

The books for analysis had to meet the following criteria:

1. They were limited to those that were classified as contemporary, realistic fiction written for young people of approximately twelve to sixteen years of age.

2. Consideration was limited to fiction published between 1964 and 1979. The beginning date was considered important in the his-

tory of black people because of the passage of the 1964 Civil Rights Act, for example. No poetry, drama, historical fiction, fantasy, biographies, or factual books were used in the study.

3. The protagonist had to be black, and the main action of the story had to focus on black people.

4. Only those books that had received significant literary awards or were written by authors who had received such awards in the years before 1964 for books about black people were considered.

5. The action in these stories had to have taken place in contemporary times. This action should have paralleled the publication date, but not have preceded the last twenty-five years.

6. Texts of the stories were used to gather the data. Illustrations were not considered as a means of gathering data.

Over eighty titles met the first five criteria with only thirty-five receiving significant literary awards or having been written by award-winning authors who had previously written books about black people in the United States. The annotations that follow are representative of how the black teenager is depicted in young adult novels by award-winning authors.

Bonham, Frank. *Durango Street.* New York: E. P. Dutton & Co., 1965.

Rufus Henry has only been released from the forestry camp two days when he finds himself in trouble with the Gassers, an organized fighting gang. He has been warned by his parole officer to stay out of trouble and away from gangs, but Rufus knows that the only way to survive in the Durango Housing Project is to join a gang. He moves on to become headman of the Moors. Fighting gangs are the central focus of this story.

————. *Mystery of the Fat Cat.* New York: E. P. Dutton & Co., 1968.

When fire destroys the Dogtown Boys Club, Buddy Williams and three of his friends look toward the inheritance that will come to the Boys Club as a resource for rebuilding the club. This inheritance can only be collected after the death of a rich, fat cat. They begin to put together evidence that will prove that the fat cat is dead and has been replaced by another cat. Adventures abound. Many references to family unity are made as well as references to leisure-time activities for youth.

_____. *The Nitty Gritty.* New York: E. P. Dutton & Co., 1968.

The hopes and dreams of Charlie Matthews go unnoticed by his mother and father, but not by his teacher, Mr. Toia. Frequent visits by his Uncle Baron are always well received by Charlie who plans to travel with his uncle the next time he comes to visit the family. Family and kinship bonds are highlighted in this story.

_____. *Cool Cat.* New York: E. P. Dutton & Co., 1971.

The teenager and the world of work are the focus of this story as Buddy Williams and his friends initiate a hauling service to earn extra money. Organized gang behavior is highlighted in this story, but not toward violence.

_____. *Hey, Big Spender!* New York: E. P. Dutton & Co., 1972.

Cool Hankins is selected by Breathing Man to distribute a half-million dollars to the needy in the community. One adventure leads to another as Cool goes about his appointed task. Reference made to family life and the world of work in this story.

_____. *The Golden Bees of Tulami.* New York: E. P. Dutton & Co., 1974.

Cool Hankins, a high school senior and city boxing champion is being pressured by Turk Ransom, the leader of nine Dogtown gangs to join up. Cool is against joining gangs as well as fearful of the powerful Turks. A handsome African on a mysterious mission with a hive of golden bees steps in just when all seems lost. Aside from organized gang behavior, kinship bonds are evidenced in this story.

Graham, Lorenz. *North Town.* New York: Thomas Y. Crowell Co., 1965.

David Williams and his family move to North Town from the South after several unpleasant experiences with prejudice and violence. They find that the differences are not that great in the North. This is a very moving story of family life and the world of work as David becomes head of the house during the prolonged illness of his father.

_____. *Whose Town?* New York: Thomas Y. Crowell Co., 1969.

Racial tension is the theme of this story as David Williams and his friends are attacked by a group of young white boys at a carry-out restaurant. Family strength and unity are highlighted in the story.

_____. *Return to South Town*. New York: Thomas Y. Crowell Co., 1976.

This novel rounds out the two above and the earlier one, *South Town* (Follett, 1958). It is the powerful story of David Williams and his return to the community that he left as a teenager.

Greenfield, Eloise. *Sister*. New York: Thomas Y. Crowell Co., 1974.

This novel embraces many aspects of the human experience—life, death, love, laughter, and sadness. All of these are carefully documented by thirteen-year-old Doretha (or "Sister" as she is known to the family) in a book she calls her "Doretha Book" as she observes her older sister withdraw from the family following the death of the father. Family strength and kinship bonds are present in this story.

Guy, Rosa. *The Friends*. New York: Holt, Rinehart & Winston, 1973.

Fourteen-year-old Phyllisia Cathy has just moved to Harlem from the West Indies. Her adjustment to school is slow, coupled with the problems of coping with her strict father. She is befriended at school by Edith Jackson, a very sloven and unkempt girl. At first Phyl refuses Edith's friendship, but eventually she comes to rely on it. Family problems are highlighted in this story. The later sequel to this book, *Edith Jackson* (New York: Viking, 1978), is a moving story of a black teenager who tried to keep her family together after the death of their parents.

Hamilton, Virginia. *M. C. Higgins, the Great*. New York: Macmillan, 1974.

Family life is the theme of this story as an Ohio hill boy tries to come to a decision about the future of his family and their home. Family unity is stressed throughout the story with an unusual relationship existing between father and son.

_____. *The House of Dies Drear*. New York: Macmillan, 1968.

Thomas Small's father has a college teaching position in a town in Ohio and has bought an old house that once served as an Underground Railroad Station. Set in contemporary times, this is a suspenseful story of the Small family and their experiences in Dies Drear's old house. The black church receives attention in the story together with emphasis on the strong family ties.

_____. *The Planet of Junior Brown*. New York: Macmillan, 1971.

The major theme of this story is survival. Buddy, a "street child," befriends obese Junior Brown. After several traumatic experiences with his mother and his piano teacher, Junior collapses. It is at this point that Buddy takes him to one of his "planets," an underground hideout for homeless children. The message is friendship and brotherhood, and although the boys are black, the author does not give the story a racial overtone. The "street" is highlighted in this story as unwanted and misunderstood children band together to help each other.

_____. *Zeely*. New York: Macmillan, 1967.

Elizabeth "Geeder" Perry and her brother spend the summer on their uncle's farm. It is when Geeder finds a photograph of a Watusi queen in an old magazine that she is absolutely sure that Zeely Tayber, the girl on the next farm, is a direct descendant of this queen. This is the story of how Geeder is brought face-to-face with her African heritage.

Hunter, Kristin. *Guests in the Promised Land*. New York: Charles Scribner's Sons, 1973.

A collection of eleven short stories that tell of the experiences of black teenagers and the way they cope with their environment. The stories run the gamut from domineering mothers to rival street gangs.

_____. *The Soul Brothers and Sister Lou*. New York: Charles Scribner's Sons, 1968.

Louretta Hawkins is torn between militancy and moderation in this story of black life in the ghetto and the effect it has on the youth. Pride in heritage, gang behavior, family life, and the church are highlighted in this story.

Jordan, June. *His Own Where*. New York: Thomas Y. Crowell Co., 1971.

The focus of this story is on the universal experience of being in love. Buddy, sixteen, and Angela, fourteen, are in love. They turn their backs on society and begin to live their lives together in an abandoned house in the cemetery. A few references are made about kin sharing responsibility for child-rearing as Buddy finds himself on his own with his mother gone and his father hospitalized.

Lipsyte, Robert. *The Contender*. New York: Harper & Row, 1967.

Alfred Brooks is a high school drop-out who has to make a decision between going straight or joining a gang. He lives with his aunt and his cousins in a Harlem apartment and works in a grocery store. This is a story of identity and survival and of how nonconjugal members aided Alfred in making his decision. Visiting kin frequently are stressed in this story as Alfred, his cousins, and his aunt visit an aunt in Queens on a regular basis.

Mathis, Sharon Bell. *Listen for the Fig Tree*. New York: Viking, 1974.

This is a family story that centers around Marvina Johnson, a black sixteen-year-old blind girl, and her widowed mother. The story takes place during the Christmas holiday which marks the year-old murder of Marvina's father. Her mother turns to drinking in her grief and Marvina is torn between remaining home with her mother or attending her first Kwanza, an African harvest celebration. Nonconjugal members are also highlighted in this story.

————. *Teacup Full of Roses*. New York: Viking, 1972.

This is a family story about three brothers: Joe, Davey, and Paul. Joe, the middle son, is emotionally the strongest. He dropped out of school to help Davey, the youngest son, get through high school and on to college. Davey is smart and good at basketball. Paul, the oldest of the three boys, has just been released from the hospital after nearly dying from an overdose of drugs. Of the three boys, Paul is the mother's favorite. She makes no pretense about it as the events of the story unfold. An elderly aunt and an invalid father complete the composition of the household.

Myers, Walter Dean. *Fast Sam, Cool Clyde and Stuff*. New York: Viking, 1974.

Francis "Stuff" Williams, who is now eighteen, tells about the time when his family first moved to 116th Street. In this story, he recalls the friendships he made, the adolescent joys and grief, the "hanging around" on the steps or at the club, and his coming of age during the five years he lived in Harlem. The story tells of the teenage life-styles of these Harlem youngsters as well as the families.

_____. *Mojo and the Russians.* New York: Viking, 1977.

Dean accidentally knocks down Drusilla, a Mojo lady, while having a bicycle race with Kitty. Drusilla vows to get the person responsible. Convinced that he has a voodoo spell on him, the gang devises a plan to "unfix" Dean from the spell placed on him by Drusilla. A humorous story that brings together teenagers bent on helping each other.

_____. *The Young Landlords.* New York: Viking, 1979.

This lighthearted story features the same teenagers from the other Myers books. The new addition to the gang is Paul. The story is based on the acquisition of a slum building by the gang and their efforts at restoring it. An excellent example of nonviolent gang behavior.

Rodman, Bella. *Lions in the Way.* Chicago: Follet, 1966.

Eight black students enroll in previously all white Fayette High School. The story is about the week-long events that changed the entire composition of the community. Although the main focus is on segregation in education, references are made to the families of the black students as well as the black church.

The implications of the findings and conclusions of this study indicate that writers of children's contemporary realistic fiction about black people in the United States, for the most part, are serving as "reporters" on the aspects of the salient shared experiences of black people as they "see" them. Basically, the authors are saying that all people, regardless of their race, national origin, or ethnic affiliation, are similar in their experiences. The black experience is not as simplistic as that. The black experience expands the world of experiences which in many ways influences our experiences in the United States. Black people have a whole normative world and as such should be represented this way in the literature about black people. The values and protective attitudes toward kin and others who are not blood-related is an example of this. Moreover, there is considerable flexibility in the roles assumed, and the emphasis is on the importance of the role rather than upon who performs it. These examples of salient shared experiences and others should be portrayed in such a way that the reader will recognize them as a source of cultural diversity that accounts for the greatness of our society.

Many of the authors of the stories tend to focus totally on the familial aspects of the salient shared experience of black people. The black family is a very important institution in the black community, but black people do not exist solely in the family.

Another important finding is that many of the writers are consistently writing about the deplorable ugliness of ghetto life. What is implied here is that more writers need to present both sides of the issue, thereby presenting the "big picture," which would not result in "blaming the victim." Writer Frank Bonham, who had the largest number of titles represented in the study, does not present a way of life in which the black child can see himself and his people presented in a positive way. The Bonham books abound with stories on organized gang behavior and fighting gangs, phenomena that are not representative of the total black community.

Perhaps the children that Bonham patterns his protagonists after are those that he observed in his work at halfway houses in the Los Angeles-Watts area. Further, he wages an all-out war on the black male in most, if not all, of his stories. They are portrayed as absent fathers, hustlers, or uncles, who are not to be trusted, and fathers who show no interest in their children. These stories do not provide good male role models for the black child. There is little doubt that the popularity of the Bonham books has caused the black child to read them in search of literature with characters and bad situations that purport to be like him only to find that this is not the case. These novels are examples of sources of some of the many misrepresentations found in stories about black people and black life-styles.

Many writers of stories about black adolescents introduce social problems in their stories, but they do not develop the problems well enough for the child to be able to gain from the experience. This is evidenced in *A Hero Ain't Nothing But a Sandwich*, an impressionistic novel by Alice Childress. Benji, the protagonist, experiments with drugs and experiences all the complications that accompany drug addiction. However, the story ends without a resolution. In exploring the issue, perhaps Childress is showing that there are no easy solutions to this most difficult problem. She is no doubt exercising an iconoclastic approach to the writing of fiction for teenage readers, by presenting this open-ended story and thereby forcing the readers to come to grips with their own set of values.

One book in the study that provides a good model for teenage boys because of its duality of purpose is *The Contender* by Robert Lipsyte. The book seeks to provide a source of identity for adolescent boys, while at the same time addressing itself to the specific problems of being black and adolescent in a society where things and people are defined in limiting ways.

Finally, to say that the stories highlighted here all fail to authentically portray those aspects of the salient shared experiences of black people would be a grave injustice. The major categories referred to earlier in the discussion (i.e., the *family,* the *social world,* and the *world of work*) were presented to some degree in most of the stories. Over half of the stories are more detailed in their portrayals of the salient shared experiences. These stories show such aspects as:

> Families that are nuclear, extended, and augmented where children are "absorbed" or informally adopted.
>
> Kin share responsibility for child-care and child-rearing practices exhibited by uncles and aunts (maternal and paternal).
>
> Nonconjugal members (relatives or friends) are available to retain and insure the survival of the family through financial and/or emotional support.
>
> High achievement orientation for children exists as typical attitudes of parents and/or significant others.
>
> Teenagers participate habitually in loose, fluid, shifting bands, lacking regular leaders, well-defined membership, and clear-cut organization.
>
> The world of work is restricted to the black adult community, where the black youth is usually unemployed or underemployed.
>
> Involvement in the world of work replaces other social and recreational activities for black adults and subsequently the youth.

The aspects above are representative of what the sociological research reports have found to be experiences that are salient and shared by most black people. Absent proportionately from these stories are those that highlight the prominent role of the church in the black community together with mutual aid and fraternal organizations. The latter, also known as "lodges," are not as popular as they once were, but still play a prominent role in some rural and urban communities. Hence there are noticeable gaps in the stories as the major focus centers on the protagonists existing exclusively in the family with only fleeting attention given to other areas of black life.

Non-black children will receive information that will enable them to empathize with people whose culture and heritage are different

from their own, while at the same time developing a better understanding of and appreciation for the uniqueness of black people that
manifests itself both culturally and historically.

Reference

Ward, Susan H., and John Braun. "Self Esteem and Racial Preference in
  Black Children." *American Journal of Orthopsychiatry* 42 (July 1972): 644–47.

Black Experience, Black Literature, Black Students, and the English Classroom

Darwin T. Turner
University of Iowa, Iowa City

A geneiation ago, Frank Marshall Davis, black poet, phrased the dilemma of a black writer:

> You asked what happened to Roosevelt Smith
> Well . . .
> Conscience and the critics got him
> Roosevelt Smith was the only dusky child born and bred in the
> village of Pine City, Nebraska
> At college they worshipped the novelty of a black poet and pre·
> dicted fame
> At twenty-three he published his first book . . . the critics said he
> imitated Carl Sandburg, Edgar Lee Masters and Vachel Lindsay
> . . . they raved about a wealth of racial material and the charm
> of darky dialect
> So for two years Roosevelt worked and observed in Dixie
> At twenty-five a second book . . . Negroes complained about
> plantation scenes and said he dragged Aframerica's good name
> in the mire for gold . . . "Europe," they said, "honors Dunbar
> for his 'Ships that Pass in the Night' and not for his dialect
> which they don't understand"
> For another two years Roosevelt strove for a different medium
> of expression
> At twenty-seven a third book . . . The critics said the density of
> Gertrude Stein or T. S. Eliot hardly fitted the simple material
> to which a Negro had access
> For another two years Roosevelt worked
> At twenty-nine his fourth book . . . the critics said a Negro had
> no business imitating the classic forms of Keats, Browning
> and Shakespeare . . . "Roosevelt Smith," they announced, "has
> nothing original and is merely a blackface white. His African
> heritage is a rich source should he use it"
> So for another two years Roosevelt went into the interior of
> Africa
> At thirty-one his fifth book . . interesting enough, the critics
> said, but since it followed nothing done by any white poet it
> was probably just a new kind of prose

> Day after the review came out Roosevelt traded conscience and
> critics for the leather pouch and bunions of a mail carrier and
> read the papers until his death; how little the American Negro
> had contributed to his nation's literature (Davis 1971).

Mr. Davis' personal experience attests the validity of his complaint.
Although he published his books of poetry in the 1930s and 1940s, he
was not discovered and anthologized until the 1960s when publishers
and editors—responding to demands from students and educators—
began to darken anthologies by including black writers.

A black who belabors this point is sometimes accused of demanding
advantages for black writers. Herman Melville, the critics say, disappeared for almost sixty years before he was rediscovered. The fate
of one or two writers, however, is not the issue. The issue, instead,
is that, for the first sixty years of this century, editors and anthologies,
trainers of English teachers, and, consequently, teachers themselves
ignored all black writers except one or two. Paul Laurence Dunbar and
Countee Cullen occasionally appeared, but scarcely another.

The reasoning sounds good but is false. The fact is that during the
years of neglect of black writers, the black experience and black characters were quite popular as long as they were seen through the eyes
of such whites as Mark Twain, Joel Chandler Harris, Thomas Nelson
Page, Eugene O'Neill, Sherwood Anderson, DuBose Heyward, William
Faulkner, and other whites who sympathetically or hostilely delineated
black people from their own perspectives—for their own purposes.

In this paper, I do not intend to belabor the question of relevance.
Even since the term gained ascendancy in educational circles during
the 1960s, I have suspected that "relevance" is not determined solely
by the material itself but also by the manner in which the material is
presented. For example, the enthusiasm which has caused some
teachers to realize that black students will be interested in black subjects has caused others to imply that blacks are interested only in
black subjects. Therefore, they insist, many of the materials affec-
tionately taught in English classrooms are irrelevant to black students.
Certainly, it is absurd for any teacher to present "Sir Patrick Spens"
or *A Tale of Two Cities*—two works from my own high school days—as
examples of the "human" experience while the same teacher never
discusses any work in which blacks represent the human experience.
Nevertheless, I insist that an imaginative teacher can create relevance. Who says that a play about two young Italian lovers is
irrelevant to black students? Let the black student—and the white—
imagine that Juliet is a young daughter of Archie Bunker, Romeo is a
teenage black who lives in the same neighborhood, and the Prince is

a white policeman who has threatened to jail the families—the black males at least—if any further disturbance troubles the neighborhood. Now that's a story which could emerge from South side Chicago, Detroit, or a number of other cities. Black authors themselves have worked with the theme of social pressures which tragically interfere with, separate, and destroy lovers from antagonistic cultures. (Bryant Rollins, a black novelist from Roxbury, Massachusetts, modified the theme and called his work *Danger Song*. Ernest Gaines, a black novelist from Louisiana, varied the theme and called it *Of Love and Dust*.)

Since "relevance" is a relative term, I do not wish to have inferences drawn that I believe black students respond only to black materials. Nor am I suggesting that black materials be used only for the spiritual, moral education of white students. Instead, I wish to discuss a few problems related to the inclusion of the materials and to the teaching of black students.

Problems

First, the black experience. Despite my own use of the phrase, there is no single entity which can be identified as *the* black experience. One does not speak of *the* white experience. Why should blacks be presumed to be less capable of variation? Certainly, all blacks in America have shared a common experience in the sense that all have been made aware psychologically that restrictions imposed solely because of racial identity would prevent their ability to select homes, hold jobs, and discover opportunities equal to their talents. Aware that only one black is the president of a large university; that only one is a senator; that before 1945, no blacks competed on teams in the "major leagues" of organized professional sports—aware that the careful development of talent may lead not to the riches promised by the American dream but to a barred door, many blacks share a psychology of failure. Furthermore, many share a common awareness that their fortunes and lives have been subject—outside legal redress—to the whims of members of a different, frequently hostile race.

Despite such a commonness of experience, however, there are many individual variations upon that common theme. Let me illustrate by referring to two works which should be known by any English teacher who professes to be knowledgeable about American literature: *Native Son* by Richard Wright and *A Raisin in the Sun* by Lorraine Hansberry. Both writers set their stories in the South Side of Chicago. Both wrote about male protagonists from working-class families which had migrated north from the South. Both protagonists are chauffeurs for wealthy whites. Both protagonists recognize society's restrictions and repressions. Yet the experiences and the psychologies of the Thomases in *Native Son* differ significantly from those of the Youngers in *A Raisin in the Sun*. Paule Marshall's story of the maturing of a young black girl in Brooklyn is not identical in theme or content with Louise Merriwether's story of another black girl in a Northern city. Ronald Fair's delineation of the psychological problems for a black youth seeking manhood in Chicago *(Hog Butcher)* is different from Ernest Gaines's treatment of the maturing of a black child in Louisiana ("The Sky is Gray"). I have never heard any teacher contend that the American experience described by Edith Wharton is identical with the American experience described by Mark Twain. To focus on one or the other would cause omission of significant portions of "the American experience." Why then should a teacher presume that a single work by Richard Wright or Ralph Ellison or James Baldwin will reveal all that needs to be known about the experiences of black people?

Since I am revealing one of my biases, let me explain further. Regardless of the sentiment expressed by many teachers on all levels of academe, I do not believe that the *primary* function of a literature class is to help students learn about various nations and races. (Does anyone read *Huckleberry Finn* primarily to find out what Missouri youth are like?) I judge that attitude to be partly a defensive gesture by English teachers who, awed by the God of Practicality, seek to prove that the study of literature has as much utilitarian value as a study of chemistry or physics. Nevertheless, whatever purpose is made paramount for teaching literature, literature, by the very nature of its subject matter, will inform readers about human beings, about the emotions, needs, aspirations, psychology, and ambitions of people. Restricting the subject matter of a general literature class to one particular group of people or one particular race implies dangerously that all humanity can be defined by the behavior of that group. Is hunger not hunger if the starving are black? Is love not love if the lovers are black?

To discover such humanity in literature about the black experience, however, a teacher must expel the notion that "universality" is defined by the action of white characters of European ancestry. Black characters must not be viewed as a different species, but as people reacting to their individual circumstances. I cannot understand how any rational being can profess to find universality in Tennessee Williams's illusion-demented Southern belles or Faulkner's frustrated Mississippians, yet fail to find it in LeRoi Jones's dramas about black youths tormented and destroyed by the magnetism of European middle-class value systems. Can one find universality in Hemingway's story of revolutionaries in Spain but not in Black Arts writers' stories about black revolutionaries in America?

The teacher, therefore, must avoid selection which enforces a distorted concept of the black experience. Although many blacks today live in inner cities in the North, not all do. Therefore, it is misleading to the white students in the class if the teacher chooses only literary materials which portray the black experience in inner cities in the North.

I must re-emphasize that I am not urging that the responsibility of a literature class is to present a total picture of the black experience. Since that total picture cannot be presented, the teacher must emphasize that the work is art which reflects a black and a human reaction.

How does the teacher know that the presentation of black life is representative if the teacher is as unfamiliar with black people as the students are? I could argue that it is the teacher's responsibility to study history and sociology and psychology to sufficient depth that the teacher acquires a knowledge of the black experience. I could argue this, but I will not. I will say instead that this limitation of the teacher's knowledge is even greater reason for selecting works about blacks because the works represent American literature with black subject rather than selecting works merely as sociological representations of black experience.

Even the selection of works as literature, however, poses problems for the teacher whose knowledge of black people is restricted to what has been read in the newspapers or heard over television. Rather than merely repeating ideas I have already published, let me suggest that you examine *Theory and Practice in the Teaching of Literature by Afro-Americans*, which I co-authored with Barbara Stanford and published through NCTE.

Principles of Selection

A few ideas about selecting and evaluating material, however, deserve emphasis and repetition. Black literary works should not be restricted to autobiographies of current celebrities. Willie Mays, Sammy Davis, Jr., Hank Aaron, and Pearl Bailey are very talented individuals in their respective fields, but, as writers, they must be compared with Joe Namath and Joe DiMaggio, not with Henry James and William Faulkner. A teacher can motivate uninterested readers by providing access to such materials, but those works should not necessarily be the basis of classroom analysis. Furthermore, this kind of autobiography—even if written by Claude Brown—may be deleterious rather than beneficial. It reflects the popular rags-to-riches theme which, unfortunately, typifies neither the white nor the black experience in reality.

Second, as I have said before, one is not observing black humanity if one sees it only through the eyes of white authors. William Styron's *Confessions of Nat Turner* is a notable example. The work tells quite a bit about the psychological delusions of a white author but very little about black people.

Third, and most important, one must approach the question of evaluation of black literature as carefully as one would approach a wrinkled green man sitting on a cigar-shaped object hovering several feet off the ground. What seems to be the familiar and normal may suddenly become the unknown.

It is patronizing to assume that black talent is so limited or so equal that a poem by a teenaged black is necessarily as significant a literary achievement as a poem by a black who has been practicing his craft for two decades. On the other hand, black writers should be permitted to benefit from the generosity of criticism applied to whites.

Think of the apologias used to protect non-black authors. If Thomas Hardy seems aesthetically weak because he overuses coincidence, he must be respected for having a philosophy of life which presumed the inevitability of coincidence. If Charles Dickens seems melodramatic, he is praised for humor and for serious social commentary. (Is this not the same as the protest for which black writers are castigated?) If Henry James seems to say nothing significant about life, he is, nonetheless, venerated for the artistry with which he says nothing.

Use the same measure of approval for blacks—praise them for their virtues rather than focusing solely on their weaknesses. But do not give that approval condescendingly.

Let me re-emphasize my point. I am not suggesting that patronizing excuses be made for black writers—that they be praised merely because they have written a book; that is condescending. What I am suggesting instead is a faithful adherence to the practices employed in the study of non-black writers. Despite their weaknesses, the Shakespeares, Miltons, Jameses, Eliots, and Faulkners are praised for their strengths. Each is worshipped even though he can be judged deficient morally, aesthetically, intellectually, or sociologically. Why then should a black writer be condemned if he is not superior according to all four of these criteria?

Similarly, if a writer develops a theme which reveals black people's despair because of oppression by white America, is the theme to be judged weak because this thought runs contrary to the optimism, presumed to be an inherent and essential trait of American character? Or is the writer to be praised for realistically reflecting the psychological patterns of many black Americans? One would assume this to be almost a rhetorical question were it not for the fact that a white critic such as David Littlejohn criticizes black writers for giving major attention to oppression by whites—even though few would deny that oppression by whites is a major and continuing concern of most blacks. Phrasing the problem slightly differently, is the black writer to be demeaned because his black characters do not think as middle-class white Americans do? Is the work less reflective of life because the antagonist is not the force of Nature but the force of white society?

Black writers who have denounced the treatment of blacks in America are frequently identified as propagandists. The label identifies them as individuals who wish to persuade others to accept conclusions which are not supported by reason. But if a black American is judged unreasonable when he performs in ways considered reasonable for white Europeans (such as rebelling against oppression), can black writers ever hope to persuade white judges that black literary conclusions are based upon reason?

All of this seems to support the contention of Nick Ford, a black critic, that the major distinction between propaganda and art is the question of whether you agree or disagree with what is written. When all possible has been said about style, characterization, structure, and so forth, the fact still remains that Milton's Paradise poems and Hawthorne's *The Scarlet Letter*, for example, are propaganda pieces in the sense that they were contrived to manipulate readers emotionally to adopt a particular philosophical or social view. How many ministers in New England engaged in adultery with members of their congregation? How many cuckolds are spiritually destroyed by desires for vengeance? Who knows? It's not important. Hawthorne told his story, and the literate continue to praise the credibility of the work. But, when one discusses Richard Wright's "Long Black Song," a story in which a white salesman seduces/rapes a black housewife, a segment of a class in literature is almost certain to object: "But that's sentimenal and melodramatic. Most black housewives have not been raped or seduced by traveling salesman." Propaganda need not be art (whatever that is), and art need not be propaganda; but propaganda and art may be interrelated in a literary work, which should not be rejected merely because it is written to express the views of the members of a minority group.

Let me raise other problems involved in evaluating the thought of black writers. One question is, "How representative is the thought?" The logical response should be, "Who cares?" but many students refuse to accept that answer. I was asked recently whether *Invisible Man* was autobiographical. As a teacher, the questioner felt that she could not introduce the work to her students as a valid presentation of black life and black thought unless Ellison had experienced the incidents he recounted. Conventionally, I might have talked about the ability of a writer to project himself into a situation through imagination and about the fact that the question itself reflected the fallacious assumption that the only value derived from Afro-American literature is autobiographical commentary on society. My response was simpler. The mere fact that American society identifies Ellison as a Negro means that *Invisible Man* represents the attitude with which at least one Negro is willing to be identified publicly. How in the name of academe can white Americans presume that William Styron, a white Virginian, faithfully recreates the feelings of a black rebel who died a century before that white many was born, yet question the validity of a contemporary black man's presentation of the feelings of some contemporary black Americans?

There is too often a tendency to judge the work of black writers according to the respectability of their morality. Let me cite an example of the problem. A white college professor who has proposed an anthology of poetry by contemporary blacks says that he will select entries according to the moral quality of the work. Does that mean that he will automatically reject black Revolutionary writers whose morality insists upon the destruction of the white establishment? Or does it mean that he will reject blacks who do not insist upon destruction? Does it mean that he will include only poems which approve the publicly professed morality of the middle-class American (Anglo-European)? Or will he include only poems which honor the morality of the lower-class rural or ghetto dweller? For the high school teacher, the problem is intensified by the fact that many contemporary black writers treat social and moral issues unthinkable for those adults who refuse to admit that school children know about drugs, sexual intercourse, homosexuality, and crime. Furthermore, many black writers use language which school boards deny that school children know or can hear on the most respectable streets or in middle-class homes.

Such pressures, of course, can censor the desire of any teacher. Nevertheless, one can find usable materials in the poetry of Gwendolyn Brooks, Robert Hayden, and Mari Evans, or in the fiction of Ernest Gaines, James MacPherson, Eugenia Collier, Kristin Hunter, and Ronald Fair—to name only a few of the many good black contemporary writers.

The Black Aesthetic

Finally, teachers need to give attention to the question of a black aesthetic—that is, a basis for the judgment derived from African American culture rather than from European-American culture.

Until recently, few individuals questioned the validity of European-American literary standards as a basis for judging the quality of works by black writers. Critics and teachers assumed that all, or certainly most, Afro-American writers imitated the forms respected in Euro-American literature. However, since contemporary Black Arts writers are consciously modeling their work upon styles derived from Afro-American culture, a conscientious teacher must consider the need to examine Afro-American culture to understand the bases of some styles and language patterns. It is absurd to denounce a black poet as non-rhythmic because he fails to use iambic pentameter if he, like Langston Hughes, is following a jazz rhythm, or if he, like Haki R. Madhubuti (Don L. Lee), is imitating the melodies of John Coltrane. Of what value is the judgment that a novelist's language lacks the elegance of a Henry James or the complex syntax of a Faulkner if the black writer is imitating the terse retorts of the dozens, or the repetitiveness of the call-response chants of black churches, or the image laden rhetoric of the sermon of a black minister?

Beauty—or an aesthetic—surely may have more than one form. Consider that African art was judged crude until Picasso improved European art by using African styles. Rather than judging a black writer as necessarily inferior because he does not use a European model, the teacher must acquire sufficient cultural breadth to be able to judge whether the black has created beauty according to a non-European model. (Note that beauty does not result merely from the use of a non-European model. A black may write inferior poetry in black style just as easily as a white can write nonartistic poetry in traditional European style.)

Today, the use of a black aesthetic as a criterion for evaluating style is especially important, as many Black Arts poets are not only imitating rhythms familiar to black culture but are also emphasizing intonation, gesture, pantomime, and other devices which have been traditionally significant in singing and story-telling by black Americans, who developed their literature from oral traditions. In contrast, such devices seldom have been respected fully by teachers who favor poetry derived from traditions which stress written words. Literary work cannot be evaluated outside its own tradition. Certainly, one does not condemn an apple for not being a good orange.

Conclusions

What I have stated should not discourage a teacher from introducing black literature. Instead, my comments should emphasize that a teacher must study black literature as carefully as one would examine a work written by Will Shakespeare or Herman Melville.

In concluding, I wish to underscore some things about black students. As I have stated previously, one black is not all blacks; but all blacks are human. One black student is not all black students, but all black students are human beings with human sensitivities. It is as reprehensible to presume that black students should be restricted to reading literature about blacks as it is to deny them the opportunity to study that literature. Some black students will be annoyed when an excess of black literature is presented—particularly if it is assumed that they are incapable of understanding nonblack literature, or if the subject is a contemporary black who has committed an act judged to be criminal and the black student is expected to be a defense attorney for a white-student jury. Let me explain this with a digression. A few years ago, I knew that if I talked with a white group, sooner or later someone would ask what I thought about the Panthers or Rap Brown and Angela Davis—whether I did not think that they were creating unfavorable images for black people. I do not believe that my questioners would have even understood what I was talking about if I had asked them whether they though Richard Nixon and Spiro Agnew were making matters difficult for whites—whether Agnew was a discredit to Greek people. My unconsciously racist questioners would not even have considered the possibilities that groups other than whites could or should be judging human behavior. They would have known that their own behavior and character could not be adduced from the behavior and character of a Nixon, an Agnew, a Raskolnikov, a Sister Carrie. Yet such false inferences are drawn daily about blacks and black students.

My favorite example comes from Ann Arbor, Michigan, where a black librarian was studying for a Ph.D. while on leave from the college where she worked. Because her husband was studying for a medical degree, he remained in the Southern town where they had their home while she took the children with her. During the first year of her study, her oldest son brought home a report card on which the teacher had written that the child was having difficulty with schoolwork because he came from a "broken home." When the mother told me the story, her anger had subsided into the ironic amusement blacks can manifest towards the asininities of supposedly intelligent white folks. Neither one of us needed to ponder the teacher's faulty syllogism: black boy; therefore, slow student. Black boy from the South; therefore, even slower student. No father in the home (so the teacher learned from the boy, who did not bother to explain the history of his family); therefore, a broken home. So, in the same state where a teacher told Malcolm that blacks could not become lawyers; in the same state where a white high school counsellor had tried to dissuade a black student from accepting a scholarship at the University of Michigan on grounds that blacks could not meet the standards of that university; in that state of Michigan, a white teacher in 1970 clucked her tongue sympathetically and dismissed as disadvantaged and unteachable a black child from a family whose level of education and standard of living probably exceeded those of the teacher.

Teachers must regard black students as individuals with individual needs and abilities. Some students will need preparation for college; some will not. Some will like literature; some will not. It is sinful for the teacher to assess judgment according to skin color, then abdicate responsibilities for teaching. Black students, like white students, can be lazy. In fact, many may seem lazier, since often nothing in their experience suggests a correspondence between energy exerted in school and the promise of a good life. Northern blacks frequently have less motivation to perform well in school than even the average Southern black, who is still taught by parents that education represents a means to a better life. If the black student lacks motivation, the good teacher must assume responsibility for generating motivation rather than assume that the student's indifference is evidence of his or her racial inferiority.

References

Brooks, Gwendolyn. *Selected Poems.* New York: Harper & Row, 1963.

Davis, Frank M. "Roosevelt Smith." In *Black Insights,* edited by Nick A. Ford. Waltham, Mass.: Ginn & Co., 1971.

McKay, Claude. *Harlem Shadows.* New York: Harcourt, Brace & Co., 1922.

Walker, Margaret (Alexander). *For My People.* New Haven, Conn.: Yale University Press, 1942.

Putting Africa into the Curriculum through African Literature

Mildred A. Hill-Lubin
University of Florida, Gainesville

African literature may be used by the teacher of history, sociology, anthropology, humanities, art, social studies, and perhaps other disciplines; but teachers of English and language arts can enjoy a special privilege, for they have many opportunities for placing it in the curriculum. Although the suggestions given in this paper have been used primarily in classes in English, they can be used by instructors in all disciplines because they are designed to acquaint students with Africa and to improve the language arts skills of students, an area in which, from all accounts of the poor reading and writing habits of many students, the services of all teachers are needed.

I have used African literature in composition classes, introduction to literature courses, and special topic courses such as "Parallels in African and African-American Literature," "Search for the African Aesthetic," and a "Comparative Study of Black and European Writers and Africa." A course entitled "African Literature in English" can present many possibilities. It may concentrate only on Black African Anglophone writers in Africa, Black African English-speaking writers throughout the diaspora, or African writers of English, writing about Africa. In addition, in any African-American or Afro-American Literature course, we can always include a few selections of African oral literature since much African-American literature has its roots in African-American folklore which traces its roots to African folklore. Certainly, the English teacher in high school or college is also able to offer the various genre courses such as African Fiction, the African Novel, African Poetry, and African Folklore. There also is the chance to offer thematic courses such as the theme of Education in West African Literature, Women in West African Literature, The City, Work, Politics, The Village, The West African Family, African Ritual, Religion, and the theme of "Africa" itself.

The bigger hurdles, however, for getting Africa into the curriculum in every school situation are first, convincing school and curriculum supervisors that such courses are needed, and secondly and perhaps the greater hurdle, gaining an audience and putting the audience at ease.

My advice is to work on the second hurdle before dealing with the first because it is quite important that students be prepared for African Literature. "Prepared," here does not mean a thorough knowledge of African culture, perhaps not even a superficial knowledge. This feat can be accomplished, at least partly, once the courses begin, but a ready reception from most students should not be expected. First, most of them have little information about Africa, and what they may know consists of myths which frequently are derogatory. It is true that efforts have been made since the 1960s to change the image of Africa, and perhaps many concepts have been modified. Some of these modified concepts—that Africa is more than a country, that it is a continent; that there are countries such as Nigeria and Uganda which are potentially wealthy because they either have oil or coffee which the world needs; that there are places like South Africa, Zimbabwe, and Zaire because they have been in the news lately—contribute to a new image of Africa.

But basically many of the stereotyped ideas linger because of biased news coverage. The media still continue to project the notion of African people as savages and inhuman. "Idi Amin of Uganda kills people and expels nice people." "People of Zaire kill missionaries, and the same may be said of the people of Rhodesia. They kill innocent airplane crash victims." "The African guerillas in South Africa and Zimbabwe do not want peace." With images like these floating in their minds, most students will respond negatively to the word *Africa*. Secondly, once past the bothersome African connotations and the presentation of an African novel or short story, the next greatest complaint is that they cannot pronounce the names of characters or places. As a result, many poor readers begin to lose interest in the novel or short story.

To help eliminate some of these problems, I begin to include materials about Africa in regular English classes such as my composition or introduction to literature classes. With such a beginning, I create an audience and also prepare my argument to the administration that I will have ample students to fill a class or that such a course is significant for our curriculum.

Composition Classes

In the composition classes, I may include a poem as a motivation to write on a particular theme. For example, if I am teaching students the comparison/contrast paper, I give the class a translation of "Black Woman," a poem by Leopold Senghor, as a comparison piece to Langston Hughes's "Mother to Son." The class and I spend time discussing both the poems with the idea of arriving at a thesis sentence for writing a comparison/contrast paper. In the discussion, of course, I mention that Leopold Senghor is from Senegal, and I may even acquaint the class with the term "Negritude" and include in my discussion a few more references to African writers or African life and culture.

Another suggestion to employ in a composition class to stimulate imagination or creativity is the use of folktales. For example, give students copies of one of the "why" folktales such as "How the animals got their color," "How it came about that some people are good looking and others are not," or "How the turtle got its shell." After having students read these particular tales, request that students create their own "why" tales on the same topics. Tales also can be used to allow students to write different endings or resolutions than the ones which appear.

In writing classes, to teach diction and effective word usage or proper choice of words of rhythm, one can teach the proverb. The instructor can select them out of one of the African novels (another good way to acquaint the class with an African novelist) or get them from any number of collections. Students are then encouraged to write their own proverbs patterned after the African proverbs.

To teach unity or coherence, use an African fable emphasizing to students that fables usually provide a moral. Ask the students to begin with the moral in mind and then move from the moral statement as a thesis to writing a tale to illustrate the moral.

Because my approach to writing instruction is a language-arts one, I use African literature to show the interrelationship of the language arts—reading, writing, speaking, and listening. African literature is quite useful in teaching these activities, since much of the creative literature has its roots in the oral folk tradition. Beginning with storytelling, either with selected stories from anthologies or selections extracted from the works of Chinua Achebe, Amos Tutuola, Exekiel Mphahlele or other authors, students may be encouraged to read the story, to perform it for the remainder of the class, and then write a new version. The instructor may also ask the students to respond to the performance or to the story itself, or the student may select a theme from the story and write about it.

Introduction to Literature or Reading Classes

A similar approach is useful in introduction to literature classes or in reading programs. To help students with comprehension of the plot and understanding of characters, include African folktales and literature in class reading assignments. Permit students to dramatize or role-play the characters. Such a technique aids the teacher in knowing whether the student has perceived the character well, understood the work, and, if the piece was read aloud, listened well. The dramatization also can be useful in improving the student's speaking skills and his or her self-confidence before an audience.

The elements of the fable can be taught through the use of African fables. When teaching folk literature, permit students to collect and record their own folk legends. These collections may then be compiled and transformed into class readers. In compiling the anthology, students may be given exercises which involve them in proofreading and correcting each other's spelling, punctuation, and grammar.

Since the objectives of introduction to literature courses are usually to acquaint students with the fundamentals of reading various literary genres and assisting them to appreciate literature, teachers are always looking for approaches which will stimulate students. By using meaningful pictures of African scenes or African music, students can be encouraged to respond to this African stimuli by writing their own poems or essays to the music or pictures. Thus African art can be used as another medium to provoke a written response. Teachers may follow up such sessions with the inclusion of poems, stories, and other works by African authors.

The above ideas may be used on any level—elementary, high school, or college—as a means of introducing Africa into the curriculum and getting an audience for courses or mini-courses on African literature. The activities to follow are designed for mature students or for elementary and secondary teachers who wish to increase the amount of African information in the curriculum.

Other Literature Courses or African Studies Courses

Most of these ideas can be included in courses in African-American literature or classes in literature which may involve literature in

English, African literature or in introductory courses in African
Studies.

Since most persons respond to the familiar, a good way of acquainting students with Africa is to make it clear that blacks or
African-Americans are the descendants of African people. Again,
teachers should be warned that such an approach may cause problems, but it offers many possibilities for eliminating myths about
Africa and creating a sense of pride and self-worth among black
students in the class. Teachers should be aware, however, that many
black Americans still do not identify with Africa. They have been
victims of what Melville Herskovitz calls "The Myth of the Negro
Past," and despite the *Roots* phenomena, many black students have
negative or ambivalent feelings about Africa. Secondly, the myths
are continuing because many scholars and lay persons seem to enjoy
pointing out the differences between black Americans and continental
Africans and perpetuating the idea that black Americans do not like
Africans or that Africans on the Continent do not respect or wish
to be identified with black Americans. Thirdly, writers seem to experience a degree of nervousness when the concept of Pan-Africanism
is introduced. Africa may be discussed in its international context
without arousing too much antagonism with an interracial class or
group, but when the kinship thread is addressed, a certain tension
develops.

One of the best ways to introduce students to Africa and to show
the black American-African connection is to use the theme of Africa,
a major motif in African-American literature. One of my favorite
exercises is to use two poems—"Heritage" by Countee Cullen, a black
American poet of the Harlem Renaissance and "The Meaning of
Africa" by Abioseh Nicol, a poet from Sierra Leone. Using the lines
"What is Africa to Me" from Cullen's poem and "Africa, you were
once just a name to me" from Nicol's work, without too much discussion, I ask students to write a paragraph or a poem on either one
of these statements. I then pick up the students' papers and distribute
the complete poems by the two writers. Then the class moves into a
discussion of the two writers' poems about Africa, both of which are
excellent because they emphasize ambivalence about Africa and focus
on feelings of exile and alienation. In a later class, I return the papers
of the students and have them read their responses. After having
explicated the poems by the authors and noted their lack of complete
identity or confused feelings about Africa, students are more willing
to read their works as well as to express their myths about Africa.

This exercise can serve as a pre- and post-evaluative measure of the students' knowledge of the growth in understanding Africa, for the teacher can have students at the end of the course respond to the same two lines. Here too, the best responses can be compiled for a reader or a class anthology. Teachers can allow the students to select which entry they wish to include in the anthology. I have found it to be a popular and meaningful exercise for every level of audience and for any type of audience—integrated, black American, or African. In addition to opening the class for a healthy discussion on Africa, the teacher is now able to ascertain the direction he or she must take in order to dispel myths, build on ideas already expressed, and exploit new themes suggested by students' responses.

This exercise may also be used in a composition class for a comparison/contrast paper or in a writing or literature class developing the theme of Africa.

As I have indicated earlier, the theme of Africa is a major one in black American literature. In addition to Countee Cullen, other black American writers such as Phyllis Wheatley, Oluadah Equiano, Carter G. Woodson, W. E. B. Du Bois, Alexander Crummel, Langston Hughes, Nikki Giovanni, Haki R. Madhubuti (Don L. Lee), and Alex Haley have written on the subject. These works can be included in literature courses to acquaint students with Africa through black American writers and to point out that black Americans have always been interested in Africa.

Search for the African Aesthetic

I have used another method which I am continuing to research. I have found it to be an excellent way to get students involved in a course with the aim to search for the African Aesthetic. The course would include African-Anglophone writers and African-Francophone writers in Africa and the Caribbean. The assumption is that there are themes and styles common to African poeple though they may be expressing themselves through conventional western patterns or frames using the discovery method. The idea is to locate these common patterns, themes, and stylistic features in the literature and then to write about the findings. Since few studies like this are available, the method permits students and teachers to be researchers, scholars, and critics. In addition, this approach improves reading and writing skills as the student learns about the African heritage, literature, life, and aesthetics.

It has permitted many black Americans such as Alex Haley, W. E. B. Du Bois, Carter G. Woodson, and Joel A. Rodgers to be productive and to make significant contributions to African history and thought.

There are many other ways that literature can be used. In language courses students can collect African-English words, idioms, and phrases from African novels or short stories to show the African borrowings which are found in the English language. In humanities, social studies, or African studies classes, literature can be used to show the interrelatedness of African literature, art, music, and religion. The suggestions in this article attempt to help the interested teacher, particularly the English or language arts instructor, to introduce Africa into the curriculum, acquaint students with African life, culture and writers, and convince students and supervisors of the need for including courses in African Literature in the curriculum. Once administrators discover the success of these approaches, the instructor may introduce the African Novel, African Poetry or the "survey course" in African Literature.

Afro-American Drama in Education: An Instructional Strategy

Edward A. Robinson
Northeastern Illinois University

There is a significant need for all students in American education to understand the inherent worth and the intrinsic value of Afro-American drama. During the 1950s and 1960s there was a tremendous output of drama, such as *A Medal for Willie* and *Take a Giant Step*, which were acclaimed and presented on the Broadway stage. However, after a brief run before predominantly white audiences, these dramas were tucked away and placed on an isolated shelf seldom to be seen again. They were abandoned as though they were totally insignificant.

These dramas did not appear in the textbooks of the 1950s and 1960s. One need only a cursory examination of the curricula of our schools and colleges to discover the omission of works by Afro-American dramatists. Our students are taught the dramatic achievements of Tennessee Williams and Arthur Miller; however, the plays of William Branch and Ted Ward are not included in school anthologies. The plays of Clarence Day and Sidney Howard are being read and studied in English classes, but the works of Louis Peterson and Owen Dodson are not on the agenda. Students in American drama classes are taught the significance of Edwin Booth but not the cultural impact of Ira Aldridge.

In play production classes black representation is even more limited. In many instances blacks have only been allowed to make substantial contributions as members of the production staff. Blacks in predominantly white settings are rarely given the opportunity to study or perform plays written by Afro-American playwrights.

To exclude Afro-American playwrights from curricula leads to the erroneous conclusion that blacks have contributed little to the development of the American theater. In order for Afro-American drama to be fully appreciated, it must be performed. Afro-American drama must be presented as literature, as a viable teaching strategy, as a motivator for the improvement of self-concept, as a tool for oral interpretation and as a medium for attaining information and education about the Afro-American experience.

315

The plays written during the 1950s by Afro-American dramatists offer a wide range of possibilities for developing curricular programs in Afro-American theater. One of these plays is *A Medal for Willie* by William Branch. This is a relatively short play, but is far-reaching in power. The prologue opens with the school custodians cleaning the stage in preparation for a school assembly program. They busy themselves in placing the lectern in an appropriate spot on the stage and arranging the American flag in a conspicuous location. Briefly, the senior custodian seeks approval as to whether the flag is hung evenly. Unsatisfied with the advice from his assistant, he seeks the opinion of Mr. Taylor, who is a teacher at the Booker T. Washington High School. After the custodians leave, Mr. Taylor addresses the audience informing them that the program is being held as memorial service for the late Willie Jackson, a former student at Booker T. Washington High School. Taylor informs the audience that the War Department is awarding Willie a posthumous medal for bravery and the Pentagon in Washington is sending a general to present the medal to Willie's mother. The whole town is excited about the forthcoming occasion. Taylor indicates that the platform is all set for the general, the mayor, the superintendent of schools, Willie's family, and the principal of the high school. Before the assembly gets started, Taylor encourages members of the audience to tour the town of Midway. He claims that the people of Midway are just like the folks that everybody knows.

The prologue serves as an effective instrument for providing the necessary exposition about the kinds of characters who will become involved in a gripping episode of prejudice, injustice, and man's inhumanity to man. It is ironic that Taylor, who serves as the narrator, would say that the town folks are people everyone would like to meet. The antithesis of this assertion is revealed as the drama unfolds.

The play is brought to a dramatic close when Mrs. Jackson refuses to read a speech prepared by the Negro principal. The platform speakers are shocked and demand an explanation. In a closing speech, full of melodrama and powerful histrionics, Mrs. Jackson elaborates on the hypocrisy of the assembly program and the tragedy of her son's death.

Instructional Strategies

There is a case for advocating that *A Medal for Willie* be taught as dramatic literature. Some teachers will experience enormous success in dissecting the strategic components that establish the basic continuity of the play. Many of the speeches are well written and should be examined for their effectiveness. The speeches of the Mayor, the General, and Mrs. Jackson are excellent examples of vivid character portrayal. The teacher who utilizes this play must certainly be concerned with the specific stylistics devices that Branch uses in achieving the totality of effect.

The following approaches can be successfully utilized in teaching *A Medal for Willie:*

1. Read and discuss the play as dramatic literature.
2. Read and discuss these excerpts from the play:
   a. The opening scene between Mrs. Jackson and daughter Lucy.
   b. The airport scene with the Mayor and the General.
   c. The barber shop scene.
   d. The entire final scene.
3. Explain the role of oral interpretation in understanding drama.
4. Use composition activities that can grow out of individual reactions to the play and the writing of character sketches.
5. Prepare the play for performance before a live audience and conduct a discussion on the quality of the play.

Plays written by Afro-American playwrights lend themselves well to oral performance. The use of voice and body are the techniques that help convey mood, tone, personality, and character delineation.

Teachers often avoid the use of innovative strategies for teaching because they assume that these strategies will require enormous preparation and expensive equipment. It is relatively simple to present a reader's theatre presentation of a drama like *A Medal for Willie.* The participants can include volunteers interested in reading a specific role. Those students with well-modulated voices would be excellent choices, but the success of a reader's theatre presentation is not based on the quality of a student's voice alone. The ability to project enthusiasm and a credible interpretation of character is far more important.

The use of video and audio recorders is an excellent resource that can improve the quality of an individual presentation. The playback of performances enables the viewer or listener to identify those areas that require additional practice. Listening to other readers, the student can become a critical observer and offer helpful constructive suggestions.

An equally exciting play by William Branch for classroom use or stage presentation is *In Splendid Error.* In this play Branch leaves the contemporary scene and explores a facet of the life of Frederick Douglass. Darwin Turner's compact description of the play, in William Brasmer and Dominick Consolo's *Black Drama: An Anthology*, focuses on the structure of action that reveals Douglass's fervent wish to work toward the eradication of slavery. After escaping from slavery, Douglass realizes more than ever the agony and injustice of the system. For a short time Douglass was a supporter of John Brown's endeavors to help slaves fight for their freedom by attacking southern planters. A dispute between Brown and Douglass occurred when Brown decided to attack the federal arsenal at Harper's Ferry. Disagreeing with Brown's approach to the problem, Douglass was forced to choose between unpleasant alternatives: to follow the course advocated by Brown by assisting in the destruction of Harper's Ferry, thus facing certain death; or to refuse to help Brown, thus risking charges of cowardice.

Classroom Methodologies

This play should not be restricted for use in English classes alone. The broad historical references meet the requirements of the social sciences as well as the humanities curricula. The play contains some of Branch's finest writing. The speeches of Douglass, the protagonist, are excellent for oral performance. Panel discussions and symposiums can grow out of an interchange of ideas on the philosophies of John Brown and Frederick Douglass. Students also can be encouraged to explore the historical accuracy of the play and write short papers and reports on their findings. The creation by students of another version of the play, one in which Douglass joins Brown at Harper's Ferry, also could be a challenging project.

In utilizing Afro-American drama for the improvement of reading skills in literature classes, teachers should expose students to dramas with a variety of themes. This approach will enable students to examine critically the modes of expression used by various authors. In *A Medal for Willie*, Branch focuses on the racial attitudes of a southern community and how blacks are affected by those attitudes. However, in the play *In Splendid Error*, he concentrates on the significance of making choices. The themes of the plays are significantly different.

The quest for identity has been a favorite theme in American drama. In Afro-American drama Louis Peterson utilizes this theme in his highly successful *Take a Giant Step*. In *Black Portraiture in American Fiction*, Catherine Juanita Starks views Spencer Scott as a sensitive black youth who gains insight into grappling with the black man's perennial dilemma of adjusting to racial exclusivity in a society that is predominantly white.

A Teaching Design

Take a Giant Step is a fine play that has received little exposure in contemporary classrooms. Although written during the 1950s, its theme is timeless. Spencer Scott's quest for personal identity is a familiar crisis, one that many urban youths have experienced. In teaching the play as dramatic literature, it is significant to note that Spencer's identity dilemma can be likened to John Grimes's struggle for manhood and self-actualization in James Baldwin's *Go Tell It On The Mountain*. Each protagonist is a victim of insensitive parents who are incapable of understanding the emotional needs of growing young men. For its full impact, *Take a Giant Step* should be performed on stage. The role of Spencer Scott should be performed by a youth with the ability to project emotional sensitivity. The play can also be utilized as an activity for role-playing and improvisational theater. For example, after the play has been read, students may be asked to summarize the play in their own words. A new ending may be added, the middle may be changed entirely, and the characterizations altered. The class can discuss the various versions of the play they have created in terms of their strengths and weaknesses. For added variety, selected members of the class can present dramatic portrayals of individual characters. Their dialogue can be improvised and presented as short dramatizations.

Another approach that can be effectively utilized is the "mock trial technique" in which the class is transformed into an imaginary courtroom. Volunteers are asked to perform the roles of prosecuting and defense attorneys, and other characters in the play. A jury is selected by the class. Each character in *Take a Giant Step* is called to the witness stand by the defense and the prosecution to answer questions concerning the role he played in the alienation of Spencer Scott. After each character has been questioned, the class can evaluate the effectiveness of utilizing this technique as a teaching strategy.

Some advocates of the teaching of Afro-American drama suggest that these courses should be taught in predominantly black schools.

While it is my view that black students should be exposed to the works of Afro-American dramatists, I am convinced that students attending predominantly white schools should be introduced to the works of Afro-American dramatists. While students must learn that Afro-American drama did not begin or end with *A Raisin in the Sun*, it is essential that they become acquainted with the wide range of philosophies advocated by traditional as well as contemporary black playwrights. They must recognize that there are Afro-American playwrights who mirror the literary style and structures of their white counterparts, but it is imperative that teachers develop curricula that focus on contemporary black drama. They should teach their students that just as Pinter, Genet, and Albee broke with tradition and embraced an iconoclastic view of the theater, Afro-American dramatists like Baraka, Bullins, and Milner are the practitioners of a new literary aesthetic that is as functional as it is liberating.

Two questions that were of enormous significance during the late 1960s in the teaching of Afro-American drama are still posing problems for some teachers today: (1) Who should teach the course? and (2) Should the course be taught separately or integrated into existing courses? George Kent offers a valid response to the former issue when he indicates in *Basic Issues in the Teaching of Black American Literature* that those individuals who achieve a high degree of success in teach ing Afro-American drama are individuals who can enter empatheti cally and patiently into the broad contours of the drama and into itb history and the unique area of its culture. Many students, both black and white, are apprehensive that those dimensions in the drama that reflect the black experience will be avoided by white teachers and that there is a possibility that these plays, especially the cultural nationalist drama, may place the white teacher in an ambiguous position, since the plays, at times, assault whites and whiteness. In responding to the latter query concerning a separate or integrated course, I agree with Kent that a teacher is more likely to do an excellent job of teaching an integrated drama course if he or she has experience in teaching the separate course. The "multi-ethnic" drama course alone, however, is not enough.

Theater arts teachers must utilize traditional as well as contemporary Afro-American drama as a resource for play production. Only a few black plays have been presented as dramatic production in our academic institutions. In selecting a play for production, the drama teacher can no longer rely on old favorites but must develop a broad familiarity with the total range of American theater. Students in urban schools are certainly willing to perform old standards. However, they are also adamant about their desire to participate in the drama of "our" time. The responsible theater department can no longer get by with just a quick reading of a few plays by Afro-American playwrights. Schools must provide students with a total theatrical exposure.

Black students are often hesitant to participate in theatre. It is their opinion that there are no plays written for them and consequently, no reason to volunteer for try-outs. Sensitive and knowledgeable teachers must counter this belief by making Afro-American theatre available to all students. The drama teacher must discover and rediscover black plays and make them an integral part of classroom curricula.

The textbook industry has recently made progress in cataloging black literary achievements. I would now insist that they devote greater attention to Afro-American drama—the neglected literary genre—through a continuous publication of drama by Afro-American playwrights. Thus, the classroom teacher will not only recognize the legitimacy of the drama, but will also make a greater effort to include the drama in classroom curricula.

Considerable work remains to be done in the area of Afro-American drama, particularly as it relates to the development of teaching methodologies. Teacher training institutions must develop methods courses that focus on teaching Afro-American drama in the secondary school. In order for prospective teachers to gain an understanding of the new curricula, they must receive a wide exposure to a variety of teaching techniques that will not only give them confidence in teaching Afro-American drama but will provide them with a broader view of American drama.

References

Abramson, Doris E. *Negro Playwrights in the American Theatre: 1925–1959*. New York: Columbia University Press, 1969.

Archer, Leonard C. *Black Images in the American Theatre: NAACP Protest Campaigns*. Nashville, Tenn.: Pageant, 1973.

Banks, James A., and Jean Dresden Grambs, eds. *Black Self-Concept*. New York: McGraw-Hill, 1972.

Beardsley, Monroe C. *Aesthetics from Classical Greece to the Present*. New York: Macmillan, 1966.

Bentley, Eric Russell. *The Playwright as Thinker: A Study of Drama in Modern Times*. New York: Meridian Books, 1955.

————. *The Theatre of Commitment, and Other Esasys on Drama in Our Society*. New York: Atheneum, 1967.

Bogle, Donald. *Toms, Coons, Mulattoes, Mammies, and Bucks: An Interpretive History of Blacks in American Films*. New York: Viking, 1973.

Brown, Sterling A. *Negro Poetry and Drama, and the Negro in American Fiction*. New York: Atheneum, 1969.

Bullins, Ed. *New Plays from the Black Theatre*. New York: Bantam, 1969.

Couch, William, Jr. *New Black Playwrights*. Baton Rouge, La.: Louisiana State University Press, 1968.

Dent, Thomas C., Gilbert Moses, and Richard Schechner. *The Free Southern Theater*. Indianapolis: Bobbs-Merrill, 1969.

Edwards, Randolph. *Six Plays for a Negro Theatre*. Boston: Walter H. Barker, 1934.

Hansberry, Lorraine. *"Les Blancs" and the Last Plays of Lorraine Hansberry*. New York: Random House, 1972.

Harrison, Paul Carter. *The Drama of Nommo*. New York: Grove, 1972.

Hatch, James Vernon, and Ted Shine. *Black Theatre, U.S.A.: Forty-Five Plays by Black Americans*. New York: Free Press, 1974.

Jones, LeRoi. *Four Black Revolutionary Plays*. Indianapolis: Bobbs-Merrill, 1969.

King, Woodie, and Ron Milner, eds. *Black Drama Anthology*. New York: American Library Publishing, 1972.

Locke, Alain, and Montgomery Gregory. *Plays of Negro Life: A Source-Book of Native American Drama*. New York: Harper & Row, 1927.

Oliver, Clinton F., and Stephanie Sills, eds. *Contemporary Black Drama: From "A Raisin in the Sun" to "No Place to Be Somebody."* New York: Scribner's, 1971.

Patterson, Lindsay. *Black Theatre*. New York: Dodd, Mead & Co., 1971.

————. *Anthology of the American Negro in the Theatre*. International Library of Negro Life and History. Washington, D.C.: Associated Publishers, 1967.

Reardon, William R., and Thomas D. Pawley, eds. *The Black Teacher and the Dramatic Arts*. Westport, Conn.: Negro Universities Press, 1970.

Turner, Darwin T. *Black Drama in America: An Anthology*. Greenwich, Conn.. Fawcett, 1971.

For in the Beginning Was the Word: Integrating Vocabulary Study into the Literature Courses for the Entering College Student

Marie H. Buncombe
Brooklyn College, CUNY

Undergraduate students entering freshman-sophomore introductory courses in literature are usually tongue-tied when asked to explain, summarize, or react to a literary work. Every sentence is punctuated with "you know," "I mean," "I know what I want to say, but I don't know the word I want," or finally in despair and defeat, "I don't know" (meaning, "I just can't express it"). We literature teachers quite often very quickly exclaim, "You ought to read more!" And so we pile on the reading, actually only compounding the injury.

Then we demand an essay from the students which explains or analyzes the readings; we soon find out what we already suspected—that they cannot say what they mean on paper not only because they have misread the material, but also because they are confused by the vocabulary the writer uses as well as by the syntax, grammar, and rhetoric of the work. When told to consult a dictionary or handbook on composition, the students discover that they are just as confused by the words that explain what they are looking for. Thus the injury is further compounded. So why not start with the word—a word-study in the literature course? "For in the beginning was the Word!"

Most vocabulary studies I have encountered have formal and sometimes elaborate systems for teaching how to build an extensive vocabulary. In addition to lists of words every literate person is supposed to know, one spends an inordinate amount of time memorizing exhaustive lists of Greek and Latin roots, prefixes, and suffixes; doing endless exercises in dissecting words into their components; and then recombining the various parts to form new words. While this kind of study can be useful and even fun, it can also prove to be a rather sterile exercise since one has no immediate use of many of the words, indeed, may never encounter them in either written or oral communication. Moreover, most freshmen do not elect vocabulary-building courses, and most freshman literature instructors are hard-pressed for time to do all of the things that one feels must be included— literary analysis, writing, grammar, and rhetoric—all usually in one term.

Only when a vocabulary study enables the student to communicate effectively in speaking, reading, or writing, without the sense of self-consciousness and hesitancy that often accompanies the use of new words, is the program beneficial. The purpose, therefore, of such a study in a course on freshman literature and composition should be to create a desire in students to experiment with the search for the precise word which expresses their ideas rather than to rely on their meager stock of repetitive, vague, bland generalities. For a period of three weeks, I introduced an intensive unit on word study and found the following procedure quite successful in integrating the teaching of a working, non-technical vocabulary to a predominantly black class, meeting three times a week for a semester, into the regular instruction in literature and composition, along with grammar and syntax that continued at its usual pace.

From a list to be studied in connection with an assigned selection in the text—an anthology of essays, poetry, drama, and fiction—I chose ten words for every class meeting as the ones most frequently encountered by college undergraduates. I wrote each on the board and asked the class what associations they made with the word, thereby getting them to draw immediately upon their own experiences and incorporate them in their study of language and literature. Often a student was able to recall how a word was used in a particular context though unable to give a precise synonym for the word. After several attempts by members of the class at trying to define the word, I then gave two or three of the most common meanings for the word before we consulted the dictionary.

For instance, while studying Keats's "On First Looking into Chapman's Homer," as we read the following lines:

> Much have I travell'd in the realms of gold,
>> And many goodly states and kingdoms seen;
>> Round many western islands have I been
> Which bards in fealty to Apollo hold.
> Oft of one wide expanse had I been told
>> That deep-brow'd Homer ruled as his demesne;
>> Yet did I never breathe its pure serene
> Till I heard Chapman speak out loud and bold:

we noticed the word *realms*, which a few of the students recognized, and the word *demesne*, which was unfamiliar to just about all of them. Upon consulting *The American Heritage Dictionary of the English Language*, we noted that *demesne* has two pronunciations listed: dĭ·mān' and dĭ·mēn'. The first one, with the long *a* sound, reminded the students of a more familiar world, *domain*, which indeed is given along with *realm* as a synonym for the unfamiliar *demesne* used by the poet. At the same time they discovered that the rhyme scheme in the sonnet makes the second pronunciation, with the long *e* sound, preferable in order that it may rhyme with *seen*, *been*, and *serene* at the end of lines 2, 3, and 6, respectively. Upon noting further that *domain* originally came from the Latin *dominus* (meaning lord, master, or ruler) and *dominum* (meaning rights of ownership, property, realm), the students very quickly and naturally thought of *dominate* and its derivatives: *dominant*, *dominance*, and *dominion*. The class became aware of the ripple effect that each new word created by adding many other words to their vocabularies. We then discussed why Keats selected *demesne* and *realm* rather than other synonyms for his sonnet, emphasizing the fitness of certain words within a particular setting.

Great pains were taken to differentiate the shades of meaning expressed by various synonyms and to illustrate their uses in several sentences, thereby showing that completely interchangeable synonyms are rarely found. Using *allude* and *refer* as examples of synonyms that require precise usage, I informed the class that one might say that Keats *alludes* to Homer among other poets in line 4 of his poem when he speaks of the "bards," but he *refers* to Homer in line 6 when he speaks of the Greek epics he had read prior to George Chapman's superior translation.

In addition, the class was taught to look for contextual clues to the meaning of words found in the literature assigned since the author often would use the synonym of a word in the same passage or use a familiar word in an unfamiliar way. Take, for instance, Countee Cullen's sonnet, "Yet Do I Marvel" :

> I doubt not God is good, well-meaning, kind,
> And did He stoop to quibble could tell why
> The little buried mole continues blind,
> Why flesh that mirrors Him must someday die,
> Make plain the reason tortured Tantalus
> Is baited by the fickle fruit, declare
> If merely brute caprice dooms Sisyphus
> To struggle up a never-ending stair.
> Inscrutable His ways are, and immune

> To catechism by a mind too strewn
> With petty cares to slightly understand
> What awful brain compels His awful hand.
> Yet do I marvel at this curious thing:
> To make a poet black, and bid him sing!

After determining that to *quibble* is to make insignificant distinctions or objections about unimportant matters, the class discussed why the poet used the term *quibble* in connection with such profound mysteries as the inexplicable defects of nature, the mortality of human beings patterned after an immortal Being, and the inconstancy of human fate. The answer was provided in the second sentence of the poem: these questions are the irrelevant preoccupations of a human brain incapable of comprehending the grand designs of an omniscient, omnipotent, though benevolent God, who should not be expected to be concerned with such trivial matters. Thus the synonym for *quibble* in line 2 is "petty cares" in line 11. The allusion to Tantalus provided the opportunity to discover the mythological source for the more familiar term *tantalize*. Beginning to get the hang of things, students then pointed out that *bait* is a synonym for *tantalize*, thus explaining Cullen's reason for stating that Tantalus "Is baited by the fickle fruit" (l. 6). Furthermore, since *capricious* is given by the dictionary as a synonym for *fickle*, the meaning and impact of Sisyphus' doom by "brute caprice" (l. 7), the same fickleness afflicting Tantalus, became more apparent to the students. They also observed that the words *mirrors* in line 4 and *brute* in line 7, most often thought of as nouns, are used here as a singular verb and an adjective, respectively; while *tortured*, though at first glance is taken for the past tense of a transitive verb, actually is a past participle describing Tantalus. Hence, word study coupled with the analysis of literature satisfied three major objectives simultaneously: (1) to expand the vocabularies of the students by providing a context for new words and old ones used in new ways, (2) to review principles of grammar and syntax and see them applied in a literary work, and (3) to heighten significantly the enjoyment of the work by illuminating the meaning and technique of the author in creating a desired effect on the reader.

It is now apparent that along with vocabulary study went a study of the dictionary itself. Instruction and exercises in the use of the phonetic key, syllabication, and variants in spelling, pronunciations, dialects, and usage were given when needed. Both the class and I found the discussion of origins and usage quite informative, for the presence of many West Indian and African students threw a different light on current usage in other English-speaking countries. Jamaicans, for instance, informed us that they called a person who gave references for someone's character or competency a *referee*; and most of the American students were unaware that the British counterpart of an *elevator* is a *lift* or the *hood* of a car is a *bonnet*. These differences were also apparent, of course, in the literature read in the course from Britain, America, Africa, and the Caribbean.

To help students overcome the fear of pronouncing an unfamiliar word, using an opaque projector, I flashed the phonetic key on the screen and carefully analyzed and articulated the sound for each phonetic symbol. The students practiced by reproducing the sound and by pronouncing and correctly spelling several common familiar words that I wrote phonetically on the board. The students then tried pronouncing long, technical, unfamiliar words spelled both conventionally and phonetically. The study of roots, prefixes, and suffixes was undertaken only at the point when an unfamiliar word was introduced rather than have the class learn a list of Greek and Latin terms. Students soon began to overcome their fears about pronouncing or using newly-learned words.

As a final exercise in the word study, the students composed a short narrative or poem using any ten words previously studied. The attempt to use the recently acquired stable of new words was the source of much unintentional comedy. Misled by the word *cupid* in *cupidity* (meaning inordinate desire, hence greed or avarice, one conscientious young man wrote, "The actor showed great cupidity for the leading lady." Another, using *venal* (meaning obtaining for a price rather than merit), said, "All the cars on the lot are venal." Finally, while trying to use *venereal* to mean lovable or social since a *venereal* disease is a social disease transmitted through lovemaking, one student declared passionately, "Students flock to Professor B's classes because of his venereal personality." To combat this common fault, students were taught to provide contextual clues to the meanings of the words by using the literary works as examples.

Students read their exercises aloud, after which the class commented on the efforts in terms of concreteness of images, precision, and appropriateness of usage. This exercise offered a wonderful opportunity for finding the apt word chosen both for its connotative and denotative meanings in order to create the mood and tone the writer tried to convey. Reading aloud not only offered the obvious advantage of practice in saying the words correctly, but also provided the chance to hear and feel the rhythm of the right word used in the right place. Students then realized that words must "look right," "sound right," and "feel right." Furthermore, they began to discover and appreciate, like the poet of the Old Testament, "How forcible are right words!"

Since the students were instructed to keep card files for new words encountered both in and out of class, they soon had their own personal portable dictionaries with appropriate illustrations, which they consulted often because their regular weekly readings and themes continued to be assigned during this entire period of intensive, focused word study, thereby creating for the students an immediate need for the new vocabulary in their own writing. They began to realize that a single precise word frequently would say what they used to say before in three or four sentences. No quizzes were given, since the aim of the study was not to test how many verbatim definitions and illustrative sentences could be memorized. A surprisingly large number, studies have shown, are soon forgotten after such tests.

As a unit in a freshman language and literature class, in this particular instance composed mostly of black students, heirs of a very rich oral tradition, the vocabulary study served the very useful purpose of making them aware of the incalculable power and resources of the written word, a relatively new experience for most of them. As one student put it to me at the end of the term, for the first time he was studying vocabulary without a high score as an indication of his ultimate achievement, and he was not afraid any longer to use the words he had learned. Such a response was what I had hoped for.

Tips: The Battle for Books

Jacqueline Brice Finch
College of the Virgin Islands, Christiansted, St. Croix

Fresh from a college education replete with Chaucer, Shakespeare, Whitman, and Frost, with a major/minor concentration of Afro-American literature, perhaps, the secondary school English teacher arrives at the assigned school ready to teach students "good" literature. However, a book shortage can drastically inhibit one's good intentions about the teaching of literature. Without ESAA, ESEA, or other federally funded reading programs to provide money for recent, relevant, class sets of texts, the teacher may wish fervently to curtail the literature component of the curriculum. However, strong arms, fast talking, and innovative teaching methods can result in a rewarding literary experience. Students will be forthright in their interest in literature, and the teacher will be pleased with their progress. The process involves two phases.

Research

1. Find a copy of the book inventory, noting the number of copies for each text for your class.
2. Order sample copies of texts, instructor's manuals, student workbooks, teaching tests useful for your class; since books must be mailed to your school, state clearly that you want only free copies. You now have your own resource library.
3. Peruse all textbooks available to you in the department for material relevant to your class.
4. Make note of disused and odd lots of books for possible use.
5. Talk to fellow teachers to find out when their students are not using their literature books; clearly identify borrowed books
6. Obtain approval to substitute selections by the same author, and so on.

Preparation

1. Acquaint students with your idea of how not to let the book shortage hamper the literature program; instead of fewer books, they will probably have more books for shorter periods of time.

2. Demonstrate your willingness to cart books from storeroom to classroom and from classroom to classroom to ensure student assistance, both female and male.

3. Match book selections with published teaching tests, instructional guides, etc. to assist in lesson planning and evaluation; allow students to select their own assignments from your previewed and assembled reading collection.

4. Establish a classroom library of books donated by students, family, and friends, which are suitable for the students and which can be borrowed for home reading.

Most students will positively reevaluate their interests in literature after observing your keenness and persistent efforts to win the battle for books.